HOW TO

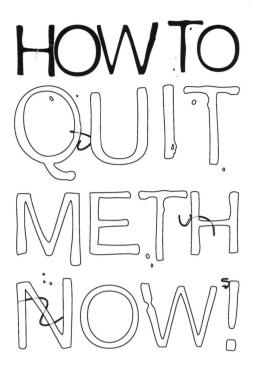

QUIT METH NOW!

A Self-Help Guide to Kicking Your Addiction to Methamphetamines or Cocaine

By Jay P. Hotrum

Welcome to the world's first and only absolutely anonymous drug treatment program. You don't have to show up, you don't sign in, and nobody will ever know you were on a program unless you tell them yourself.

Welcome to the show. This book is the most important work, in a series of literary information on how drug production and distribution has shaped the history of the world. With the goal of informing the masses globally and providing solutions to individuals who have already fallen into the patterns of drug use and abuse, this process intends to provide an honest movement to change the scope of history by offering systems and methods which will have the actual power to reverse these trends for now and in decades to come. This book was written for the drug addict, and no one else. (This is a SECOND EDITION).

CHANGE THE ADDICT, SAVE THE WORLD
GlobalAddictionSolutions.org

SAVE THE ADDICT, CHANGE THE WORLD
GlobalAddictionSolutions.org

This book is dedicated to;

Nichole and Charlie

Had they not come into my world, this book would simply not exist.

And to

Ron Roos

And

Mike Teal

And

Randy Hotrum

For being there from the beginning, helping to mold every aspect of this project. From design to personal opinion and advice, I will always be indebted to these three individuals.

Second Edition Supplement

It is with great honor that I am reaching out with a second edition of this book, which has created miracles out of thousands of meth addicts around the globe. True to its original intention, this program is not flawed by the normal principles of other drug treatment programs, and true to its promise, not a single person has ever said that this program did not work for them. Contrary to what we're supposed to believe, thousands of addicts have kicked their personal addictions with this program, and you can see with your own eyes that the reviews on the Amazon pages are stunning to read. The following are actual reviews you can find for yourself on the Amazon pages for this very book, but it was the hundreds of people who have reached out to me directly that coerced my decision to expand on the original program. Besides the fact that I know I am a better writer now and can relay my points more efficiently, I have also learned so much new information that would expand on the original program, making it a better deal for the reader. I am also 'educated' now from a major university, which gives me better insight on what I am trying to achieve here. The following are reviews of this book, from people I don't even know and have never met;

Tiffiny

5.0 out of 5 stars **Life Changing**

When I found this book I was desperately looking for a way out of my addiction. I can honestly say that I'm not the same person I was when I first picked this book up. I am so grateful to have found this book and the program within it gave me hope and freedom from an addiction I've been struggling with for 8 years. This book does everything it promised and I would definitely recommend this to anyone struggling with a meth addiction who is looking for a way out. I haven't touched the stuff nor had any real desire to since completing the program. Honestly I could go on and on so I'll bring this to a close with this... Jay Hotrum, you are such an inspirational man and to put it simply you saved my life. So with all my heart, thank you. There were times I really felt like you wrote this just for me.

Shelby

5.0 out of 5 stars **If your serious this book works!!**

This book literally saved my life .. which is kinda funny to write but it honestly really did . If you are serious about quitting then read this book and don't jump ahead! I was using every day for over 4 years and I am now 7 weeks clean! It was the Best purchase I could have ever done !

Dee B.

5.0 out of 5 stars **Gratitude for this process!!!**

Reviewed in the United States on March 20, 2021

I must say this book was a BLESSING to discover and has the most practical, down to earth process for combating the devastating disorder of substance use. Its the first step before the first step and ABSOLUTLEY RECOMMEND for personal use as well as for any facility, sponsorships, and/or educational curriculums. THANK YOU !!!!!

Nadadas

4.0 out of 5 stars **Sort of Quaint...**

Reviewed in the United States on July 14, 2021

It was heartening to see someone have the courage and conviction to stand up to many of the myths regarding the effectiveness of counseling, rehab, the medical "profession", pharmaceutical companies, interventions, etc. It was even more heartening to read some of the other reviewers and find that even in this current climate of whiny cry babies that accept zero accountability, they were many who resonated with and were successful with his basic tenets that 1) it's not a disease (cancer is a disease), so you are responsible 2) you are on your own and no one can or will do it for you, particularly doctors and drug counselors who are making bank on exorbitant priced rehab and stay in business as long as people relapse and the doctors hide their true motivations 3) While a 12 Step program has certainly helped some people, it is not necessary since it's personal responsibility and accountability you rely on and not a Higher Power. I also appreciated the graphic art at the beginning of each chapter.

Shon

5.0 out of 5 stars **AMAZINGLY GOOD KNOWLEDGE TO AIDE IN QUITTING CHEMICAL ADDICTION!**

Reviewed in the United States on December 22, 2020

This book has amazing knowledge to aide in the quitting of chemical addiction!

David W.

5.0 out of 5 stars **IT WORKS!**

The folks I've given this to says this writer knows exactly what he's talking about -and it helped them kick Meth!

Jena

5.0 out of 5 stars   **You saved my life! ❤**

Not sure if you remember me I emailed you 14 years ago on the brink of suicide begging for help with meth addiction. You were bluntly honest not sugar coating anything. I'm happy to say I'm 14 years clean. I did enter a 30 day program but relapsed once before turning back to your response. It changed me & I'm forever grateful. Today my son is 19 & going to college for medical/psychology. My life isn't perfect but at least it's an honest one. I just happened to be cleaning out my nightstand when I came across my old poems/drawings with our email letters printed. Congratulations on your book & hope anyone struggling with an addiction has the power to quit & live a productive normal life. Thank you ❤

MJS

5.0 out of 5 stars   **If you're ready — this works !**

Reviewed in the United States on July 31, 2021

I quit meth on my own and actually came across this book after I was already clean for 6 months — I wish I had found it before as it would have made the process so much easier. Follow it to the letter and do everything the author suggests — he is really on to something here.

I walked a friend struggling with meth through the entire book —even read him the chapters out loud every day (he hates to read) and it worked for him. When you're well and truly done with all the misery meth brings into your life come back here and buy the book — it will change your life.

And new reviews from the UK and Canada as well…

Daniel C.

5.0 out of 5 stars **AMAZING BEST RECOVERY BOOK EVER. Period !**

Reviewed in the United Kingdom on 16 November 2021

I really can not stress how much this book makes sense and made my recovery possible. I have been trying ca and aa for the past year only to fail but this book is something else. I really got lost in the amazing way it is written and so to the point and i really feel it explains it perfect as well as giving a solution to my problem i have never found in other recovery methods. I just love it best read ever. THANK YOU SO MUCH YOU SAVED MY LIFE ❤

Thomas Baxter

5.0 out of 5 stars **Rational recovery but better**

Reviewed in the United Kingdom on 2 January 2022

I got this on Kindle first because I saw next to no reviews. I'm telling u now, if you're struggling with cocaine. GET THIS BOOK. It's nothing groundbreaking if you've read RR but it's a much better interpretation of the tools used in that book. The writer identifies with the reader (as an ex addict) and doesn't beat about the bush in telling us that he basically can't stand addicts. He basically tells you to stop thinking you know anything about recovery. Sit down. You're the student. Just follow the instructions. It feels refreshing but not patronising in any way. Why would it be patronising? the writer got clean. He knows how to do it. The way the writer gets u to visualise the "list of pain" from RR is extremely powerful and his list of supplements that will help in the crash period is helpful. I got this free on kindle but i defo need a real copy now. Shocking how few reviews there are of this so mine hopefully makes u want to check it out. Put it this way......TRUST ME. GET IT.

Marc

5.0 out of 5 stars **Very helpful and informative**
Reviewed in Canada on May 20, 2021
Very good book. It helped me a lot and I believe it would help a lot of other people as well.

Always remember that there has never been a single negative word about this program, only thousands of people saying that this book you are reading right now…changed or saved their lives. This is the alternative drug treatment program that you were looking for, and the information you are about to obtain will give you the tools you need to change your life as well. It contains all of the answers you are looking for, including a 14-day self-detox you can do in your own home, after you decide when you want to quit.

Besides all of that, on January 1st, this year, I actually met someone who recognized me from a video I made a long, long time ago who told me that I saved his life 16 years ago. This was a very powerful moment for me and it indeed changed my life, knowing that my work has been valid this entire time. Though I am driven by the need to get this program out to other meth addicts who are still struggling, I've never had or needed the validation that my work was actually helping people, despite all of the positive reviews. I don't take any of this to heart, because I believe this is my job now, to do what nobody else has done; to offer an actual cure for meth addiction that is valid and actually works. Honestly, I never wanted this job, I just wanted to move on and have fun, like everyone else.

Anyway, I was singing in a band called RoadWork for a few days because their singer had other plans for the New Year. I thought it was a great opportunity because I had followed that band since I was a kid. Destiny realized, I got to sing with them on New Year's Eve and another party on New Year's Day in the most awesome place; an outdoor venue called The Bunker Bar in Lake Havasu Arizona (about a 4 hour drive from my house), hidden deep in the hills with a 3 mile dirt road cut into a hill, with access for off-road vehicles only. It was very cool as there must have been at least 200 off-road vehicles there and hundreds of people who stop in this location to hear live music and drink beer. Good times!

After our third set I seen a guy coming towards me pretty fast, with about 8-10 people following him. I didn't know what it was about but it didn't look too friendly at the moment. He cuts me off and says "Hey, I wanna ask you a really weird question"…I said "okay, anything, go"…He asked me "did you make a video a while back where you were talking to people?"…I said "no, I've made music video's" and he says "no, it wasn't a music video, you were talking about meth addiction"…I had totally forgotten that I did make a video long before I ever thought about writing this book.

When I told him that I did but forgot about it, he wrapped his arms around me and picked me up and yelled in my ear "YOU SAVED MY LIFE!"…he said it over and over after that. Funny that it was New Year's Day and I had just said on stage that "nothing changes on New Year's Day" like the song. I think this moment changed my forever. His name was Ron and he said he had been slamming meth daily for years. He bought the old program online (for $300 before it was a book) and watched the video twice and never did meth again. Just like that. And that was 16 years earlier, and I never knew it. Then his wife asked if she could give me a hug and his friends all lined up and hugged me as well. When his wife hugged me she whispered in my ear "You really did save his life"…

This was a profound moment in my life. Imagine that for 16 years the universe kept this from me because…you tell me. Maybe I would have let it go to my head or strayed off of the course. Either way, I am still on the path. I don't know for sure that the original program helped everyone that got it, but I do know that Ron was grateful for my efforts. People always say "if you can just help one person" but I've never been after any personal gratification for my work. I'm not here to help one person; I'm here to fix this problem for everyone, one person at a time. People also say (way too often) that "there is no cure for drug addiction" which couldn't be further from the truth.

If you are a drug addict and you follow a program that helps you kick your drug addiction for the rest of your life; that is a cure! If you follow a program while you are using drugs, and you complete the program and are drug free, you are cured, correct? That is the goal here. You should let go of the myths which have kept you addicted to this point and start following alternative processes that lead you to the Promised Land. This book is the cure to your drug addiction. All you have to do is read every word and follow the simple instructions provided for you herein. It really is that simple. Just ask the thousands of people who have already proven this to be a fact…and try to find one single negative comment that says this program does not work. Work the cure and stay on the path. You are exactly where you belong now. You have my heart…

Jay P. Hotrum

Table of Contents

Chapter 1

An introduction

If you don't already believe in destiny then I strongly urge you to reconsider. In your life there are certain discernible chains of events which cannot be discounted as mere coincidence. For the sake of argument there are two distinctive forms of destiny; that which you make happen, and that which happens to you. It's easy to speculate in hindsight and determine that given your own personal set of circumstances, you were destined to become a drug addict. It happened to you. Notwithstanding the fact that had you known you would end up an addict, you may have considered altering your path in the early steps of drug experimentation, but it still happened. Now it's time for you to decide if you are destined to become an ex-drug addict. This is the kind of destiny that you can make happen, however true destiny lies at the intersection of both what you make happen and what happens to you.

When I was young, a local rock radio station (KMET in Los Angeles), was hosting an 'April Fools' morning party at the Hollywood Palace, which is directly across the street from the famous Capital Records building in Hollywood California. I showed up at the building as one of 300 or so contestants in a "fools contest" because the grand prize was a VIP package that included meeting rock hero Sammy Hagar just before he took the stage at the Forum supporting his Three Lock Box tour. I showed up with this great idea of wearing a T-shirt that said 'ET, The Extra Testicle' and had pink balloons protruding from my shorts. To make a long story short, I won the contest and met Cheech Marin (of Cheech and Chong) backstage after my little comedy routine. He told me it was hilarious and he took pictures with me to hang-up, back at the radio station. Later that year, Cheech and Chong stole my bit and put it in their next movie called *Still Smokin'*. Cheech had the same design on his shirt and proclaimed "*ET, The Extra Testicle!*" just like I had done. Maybe you've seen it. Anyways, that *ET, extra testicle* 'thing' that I wrote and performed, went on to become a famous icon of the times. The film made over $15 million and I didn't make a dime from it, and I never got credit for writing the joke. But I did, and such is life. We take our punches and move on.

At the time I had always dreamed of being a rock singer and the thought of meeting one of my two favorites (still haven't met Ted Nugent) had easily made this one of the best days of my life to that point. The Palace was a huge venue and I had just 'performed' for well over 2000 people and emerged victorious as the crowd favorite. Remember it was a 'fools' contest.

As the four-hour party was nearing the end, my friends and I were heading towards the front door and I stopped and turned around because I felt an intensely overpowering urge to look at the stage one last time. At that point I knew destiny was going to play a part in my life, whether I liked it or not. One of my friends yelled out at me because I was holding them up. "Jay, what the hell are you doing?" he said. I remember my answer as if it were yesterday. "I'm looking at the stage one last time" I yelled. "I just got a strong feeling that the next time I see it, I'll be on that stage singing with a band." Two of my friends snapped in unison "you don't even have a band," they laughed.

Well, over the years I had told that story to a bunch of people and as time worked against me the Palace was eventually closed down and boarded up. I did put together a couple of bands and eventually I helped form a band called **Kill Era** (everywhere on social media) that held together for almost five years and had started to make a pretty good impact in the hard-to-crack LA music scene. We were making a name for ourselves by opening for major bands as they toured the club scenes across the nation and ended up in the Los Angeles or Orange County areas. We had worked our way up to the prime-time position with the headliners going on after we finished around midnight. We had opened for so many national acts including Armored Saint, Pantera, Corrosion of Conformity, Wrathchild

America, Nuclear Assault, Flotsam & Jetsam, Excel, Death Angel, Lizzy Borden, and Exodus to name a few.

Without our knowledge, somebody had bought up the old Palace and completely remodeled it. We had just played a show with Pantera opening for them on their *'Cowboy's from Hell'* tour three months before I got the call, and I couldn't believe it. We were opening for Pantera again at the grand re-opening of the newly renovated Hollywood Palace.

It was a sold out show and everywhere you looked there was somebody you knew from the pages of who's-who in the music or movie industry. Pantera treated us like VIP's, hung out with us after the show, and even paid our bar tab for the night. Our show was at its peak and the audience treated us as if we were the headliners. Destiny realized!

Some nine years later my vision had become a reality. I know that had I not formed a band and positioned myself for the call, it wouldn't have happened, but divine intervention linked together all of the 'ifs, ands, or buts'. If it were a mere coincidence, why was I forewarned years before the event? Would-of, could-of and should-of didn't have a chance.

To this day, opening for Pantera at the Hollywood Palace was the best day of my life. It was also the last show I ever did without methamphetamines in my system. The downward spiral was hastened by my bass player Marc getting fronted two ounces a week and within a year the band had broken up completely. We played our last show at the Hop in Anaheim, CA with Flotsam and Jetsam and after Marc showed up 20 minutes after our starting time, the promoter was so mad he made us set up on the floor in front of the stage.

Drug abuse had infested the band members and had eventually made it impossible for us to function as a unit. Naturally, it wasn't too long before drugs made it impossible for me to function as an individual as well. I lost everything, just like people had said I would. My house, my car, my wife, my dignity, my pride and self-respect…somebody stop me!

You can finish the story yourself from here. At this point we all went through the same things exactly. When people say different people react differently, don't you believe it. We all act the same on this drug, and we all do the same things. Only genetic personality traits sometimes make it appear that we act differently but it's all the same, believe me. We're all screwed.

Drug addiction is a death wish, straight up. When casual use evolves to a chemical dependency, the daily torture of self-medication comes with a somber will to reach an end sooner than later. One day you realize the only thing that can save your life is quitting altogether. So you think about the big question; "do I really have anything to live for?" Because you already know that without clear motivation, attempting to quit will never become anything more than an attempt. You have to define your motivation because you have to know 'why' you want to quit.

When I was ready to quit, I looked everywhere for help. With the exception of programs I couldn't afford, there really was no help. There was little or no help at my local library and the Internet was so crammed with unreliable nonsense that it was at best, humorous. I remember the first time I turned to a computer for help and I typed in the word 'methamphetamine' and I got something like 120,000 hits with the number one position entitled "How meth is made and how to manufacture methamphetamine." It was a dead end. The only thing other than that were several sites offering the horror stories of meth addiction, which I was already familiar with from my own personal experiences.

I couldn't believe it. With all of the progressions of our country and the world, nobody was offering a solution for drug addiction. Then I heard that voice in my head again. I decided that somebody had to make available a drug dependency solution for the general public, and that somebody was going to be me. I would do it. I would clean up and spend all of my time researching existing drug treatment methods and talking with drug addicts who had already kicked the habit on their own, and we would develop our own methods.

I've always believed that one man can make a difference. I know I can and I know that you can too. With the help of my friends, I've developed the perfect drug treatment program. I designed the web sites and I wrote every word of its content. Now, it's time to write the book. This will be a self-help manual that guides the addict through a step-by-step process that leads to a 14-day detox, and offers real and usable techniques for staying sober. Shamefully, I am the best man for the job and lucky for you, it is my destiny.

At this point we can skip the blame-game and move on to fixing the problem at hand. If you're reading these words, you are most likely addicted to meth and you have come to the realization that you have to either quit soon, or you'll be taking it to the grave with you. Lucky for you, this book is the answer to all of the questions that have passed through your head about when to quit, and how you were going to pull that off. I know you wouldn't be reading this if you didn't feel that you were addicted, and I also know that you're looking for an efficient path to redemption; a life free of the chains which now hold you down. The intention of this book is right there in the title, to teach you the "how to"…and you've already started reading, so we're both on the same page, sharing this very moment. Kicking this addiction is now a part of your destiny, and all you have to do is keep reading, that's it.

The pathetic path of drug addiction has become a societal norm, but for those of us who find ourselves addicted, the horrible choices we've made in the past have become something far more personal. We understand that drug addiction was never going to provide us with the keys to the promise land, but something far more sinister has invaded our lives and we've come to the conclusion that we no longer wish to be pawns in the aspirations of drug cartels around the world. It's not only methamphetamines that rule our world, but the fact that all narcotics are addictive and flow freely around the globe with little or no government intervention. We have to ask ourselves at some point "are we doing this to ourselves, or are they doing this to us?" Whatever the cause, you now find yourself addicted to meth, and the pathway to a drug-free lifestyle has now become your journey to find a way out of this exercise in personal failure. In your quest to end this downward spiral, it's important you understand the addiction processes of everyone else, so that you can focus on how you can kick your personal addiction as well. Rest assured you're in the right place, here and now, to kick this addiction once and for all. And if you keep reading and trust in the path I have chosen for you, you will be drug free by the time you finish this book.

The very depth of these words should shock you, as nobody has ever said this to you before (and meant it). All you have to do now is follow the bouncing ball, all the way down the path, and walk out at the end, without the crutches. It's that simple, that's it. But first, it's important for you to understand the totality of the problem, before we focus on approaching how you will kick your personal addiction. So, let's talk about the other elephant in the room; opioid addiction. (Your actual program will start in chapter 2, so just stay on the path). I believe it's important that we talk about all drugs before we focus on your current meth addiction, because you need a better understanding of the big picture, so you can become an expert on drug addiction as a whole. This is the journey you are on now, so the levels of enlightenment include many factors which may not cross your mind in this moment, but will all make sense to you down the road, when you have finally kicked your meth addiction. Trust in my words, and stay on the path. Kicking your addiction is a process, and this is where it begins.

As far as opioids are concerned, it is shameful that the recent deaths of so many high-profile artists has caused major government actors to stand-up and take notice of the current opioid epidemic, when this has been a huge problem in societies around the globe for decades. Opioid addiction has always been regarded as a societal sin whose tangled underbelly is self-corrected by attrition. The taboo of heroin addiction has now taken a backseat to new delivery methods, which once chased the rational users away. By changing the name of heroin into several different reclassifications, drug manufacturers have provided the appearance of caution, by taking the assumed risks aside and allowing these new delivery methods to be referred to as pain relievers, prescribed by doctors. This has aided the events which led to addiction as seeming more acceptable, as society has always believed that those in the medical industries had nothing to gain but for the notoriety of being good at their profession. Street vendors' aside, legitimacy has been added to the sale of heroin, by simply changing the name of the drug and getting a seemingly professional stamp of approval for using the drugs 'properly' by following the instructions on the side of the bottle. If only that were the case, as users often raise their doses after determining that the instructions are only recommendations, written to cover liability issues, and that their personal pain was much worse than their doctor understood.

We call this an opioid epidemic because these drugs have spread into so many outlets that it's impossible to narrow it down to one type of drug or even one manufacturer. But do not be fooled, my friend. When you hear the word 'opioid', you are hearing a term the pharmaceutical giants would like you to refer to, in their monopoly on all terms created for the drug. But always remember, we are simply talking about heroin. Old school, worst drug you can ever get addicted to; heroin. Heroin is made from the poppy plant, which is illegal to grow almost anywhere, and poppies are processed to make heroin and synthetic drugs that often break down the active ingredients, which allows pharmaceutical companies to invent and produce so many different synthetic drugs that it can get confusing at certain points, to certain people...and this is intentional, which is the goal when you're selling drugs for a living. You give the people what they want, and eventually you are selling them what they need. You can change the name, change the dose, change the application, convince the user it's only needed until the pain goes away, but you still have to detox the user (who becomes addicted to the drug) or that user's life will tailspin out of control, while certain death is always on the table.

Common opioids invented as pain relievers are now being sold with refabricated names including hydrocodone (Vicodin, Norco), oxycodone (Oxycontin), fentanyl, codeine, morphine, and so many others. But they should all be considered as heroin, because that's what you are actually taking. I don't care what they want me to say, and I'm not interested in politically correcting ideologies planted in society by the drug manufacturers who profit from this horrible world they've created, they're selling us heroin, with a pink bow on the bottle. It's as horrible as the picture of a junkie on the streets looking for a fix, and its killing good people, just as it always has. But now the people are revolting and they want answers. And the answers are the same as they've always been: if someone becomes addicted to such a drug, you can cure them of the addiction or you can watch them die slowly…or as is the case with the newer, higher potency knock-offs, we can watch them die every single day, without notice.

So why would anybody take a drug which they already understand is highly addictive? That, my friend, is the million dollar question. A perfect example of this trend is the former artist known as Prince. Besides the assumed fact that everyone knows the addictive qualities of opioids, Prince, at 57 years of age, had previous knowledge that this drug was killing him. Only 6 days prior to his death by an assumed accidental overdose of the opioid fentanyl, Prince had overdosed on his jet, on April 15th 2016. He was unconscious upon arrival (some reports say dead) at the airport, and was brought back to life with an injection of Narcan, a new remedy for opioid patients that reverses the effects of opioids on the spot.

Prince was well aware that he had literally died that night, but even death was not enough to persuade him to seek immediate treatment for his addiction. 6 days later, on April 21, he was found unresponsive in an elevator at his Paisley Park compound in Chanhassen, Minnesota and was pronounced dead on site. Prince had lived to die another day, and with this knowledge he reassumed the risk, still not able to get a grip on his personal addiction.

Fentanyl abuse is a death-wish, straight up. It is 50-times more addictive than heroin and it can be up to 100-times more powerful than morphine. An average human adult can be killed with only 3 milligrams, a dose you would hardly notice on the tip of your finger. This drug is mainly produced in China and illegally exported around the globe. The Chinese government could care less about who dies while using this drug, as their only real concern is profitability and the price dealers are willing to pay. This brutal regime absolutely has the power to curb the dissemination of the drug but choses to turn a blind eye to the trade.

The death of rock icon Tom Petty is extremely troubling as well. Not even a year and a half after Prince's death, Tom Petty must have had a clear understanding of the dangers of opioid use, yet he continued to convince himself and his family members' that his pain was unique to him, and that his abuse of these same types of drugs were somehow essential to his being. His life ended peacefully on October 2nd, 2017 and the media again reported his death as an 'accidental' drug overdose, when we don't know as a fact that this was the case. His family members were quick to point out that Petty had no suicidal tendencies. So it must have been an accident…and I'm not saying that it wasn't. I'm only pointing out that there is an alarming number of deaths among opioid users and a high percentage of those are by suicide. When Kurt Cobain (of the rock group Nirvana) took his own life on April 5, 1994 it was hard for the news media to say it wasn't a suicide, since he put a shotgun in his mouth and pulled the trigger with his toe. But they still gave it a shot, saying that there may have been some lame conspiracy involved in making his death appear as a suicide despite his heroin addiction, the hand-written note, his long past of suicidal talk, his diagnosed depression and bipolar disorder, and the facts. By the way, all of these are side effects of a heroin addiction.

I believe it should be noted that there is something in the downward spiral of opioid addiction that involves extreme mental instability and the actual death wish (meth addiction has these same risk factors as well). We like to believe that our stars and heroes are supermen with super-human strength, but they're just human beings, like the rest of us. You do heroin and at some point, you wish you were dead. It's a huge part of the addiction process and it is real, despite what those closest to our heroes would like us to believe. We know that heroin kills people, and we don't need some big college study to prove this as fact. All you have to do is read the newspaper or turn on your television (reported deaths by meth overdose are far fewer, yet way under-reported).

The liberal media always reports such deaths as accidental overdoses, which gives respect to the fallen but does nothing to spotlight the actual events. This is counterproductive for those who are still stuck in the downward spiral of heroin addiction and again, just paints a pretty pink bow on the end of the story…'oh, what a great man and what a tragic accidental death'. Societies are easily calmed by inaccurate stories of tragedy because it's so much easier than confronting the truths about drug addiction, and it would just take too much time and energy to address such issues. People would rather walk a marathon for breast cancer (one of the most highly funded causes in history) than to address problems such as suicide by heroin and other drugs. The media lacks compassion and understanding for the addict who lives on. To pretend to enter the thought processes of the dead addict by reporting his death as an accidental overdose, presents a false conclusion with a predetermined narrative, which does no real service to society. It almost seems as if the pharmaceutical companies responsible for the deaths had a hands-on dialog with the liberal media outlets on how they should approach such stories. Let's not forget that these cases usually involve legally prescribed pharmaceuticals, as well as illegally obtained drugs, bought on our streets.

The history of death-by-heroin is well documented in wars past, as morphine was available on most battlefields since it was invented. Those still alive after their bodies were blown to bits, usually self-administered the lethal doses which eventually took their lives, allowing them the decisions involving their personal death with a pain-free resolution. Philosopher Sigmund Freud is one of hundreds of great examples of intelligent individuals who took their own lives by using opioids to ease the pain of living. Freud had developed mouth cancer and requested a prescription of morphine from his personal physician, which he eventually used to take his own life. In my personal opinion, death by heroin would be the most peaceful and pain-free remedy to a horrible existence, and because of this fact I have always questioned the 'accidental overdose' as a possible suicide scenario, despite what the media and the family members of the dead would like me to believe.

The list of famous deaths by 'accidental overdose' is a long trip to nowhere. Singer Janis Joplin died of a heroin overdose. Comedian John Belushi died from slamming heroin mixed with cocaine. Elvis Presley had a heart attack but was found to have a large cocktail of pharmaceuticals in his bloodstream, including codeine. Comedian Chris Farley mixed morphine and cocaine, which took his life. Actor Philip Seymour Hoffman died by mixing cocaine and heroin. Actor Heath Ledger mixed opioids (heroin) with Xanax and valium which caused his death (and they gave him an Oscar for it). Actor River Phoenix mixed morphine with cocaine which caused his death. Slipknot bassist Paul Gray also mixed morphine and fentanyl, and died.

The writing is on the wall here, and it couldn't be more clear. These were all major stars at the times of their deaths, but many of them have already been forgotten *(some that you recognize, some that you've hardly even heard of)*. I have purposely skipped many other examples here because of my personal distain for their actions which caused their deaths. I do not like dead drug addicts, especially when their lives were elevated by fame and fortune. It angers me to no end. At what point do we realize that there is something in the human condition which causes us to want to end our lives at some point after becoming addicted to these drugs? Their collective gifts to society will always come with a blind asterisk next to their name that says 'drug addict' without the mention of the drug. Death-by-heroin, accidental or otherwise…their gifts are tainted.

It may seem harsh to the non-addict that I could care less about these dead icons, but this is where I am now. When their music or movies cross my daily routine, I change the channel. This is my tribute to those still living, addicted to exactly the same chemicals, with a much harder daily routine. As for the rich and famous, I don't really care what their contributions to society were; they're just dead drug addicts to me…those who will be remembered for their worth are only equal to those hundreds of thousands who died the same way but will be forgotten, as if they were never here. Their actions are even more atrocious, being they had every warning sign, and every opportunity afforded the rich for changing their paths. Please do not shed a tear for those who have failed at what you are trying your hardest to do now. They do not deserve your empathy, and pity is only for those who know not…what it is to walk a day in your shoes. I have nothing to offer the memories of such artists who let these drugs rule their very being, and I can only use them as examples of failed missions of hope. The media likes to paint a picture of a fallen hero, as societal leaders offer memorials and posthumous death awards to keep their memories alive, as if they were somehow bigger than life…but we know who they were…they were people just like us, but they failed at life. In the end they were not heroes at all. Just dead drug addicts who's heroes are among the living…because living is harder than dying.

I am not here to cry for the dead anymore. I'm here to offer you options, in case you don't want to meet the same demise. You have some big-boy life decisions to make …and they start now.

Drug addicts have always had the real choice of quitting their drug or going through the motions of kicking, often without actually trying to get the job done. Many treatment centers offer every alternative and half-assed technique for quitting, without the ability of actually making it happen. This is the same game-plan the pharmaceutical giants followed with the invention of Methadone. It was an easy course to persuade the heroin addict that any alternative to heroin was a trade for the better. Just as the meth addict who was trying to kick his addiction to speed, any substitute for meth will always be considered as better for the addict than the meth itself. If you can kick the addiction that enslaves you, you can kick any substitute as well, somewhere down the road, after the fact. With the belief that kicking your current addiction is priority one (and it is) any trade-off substitute would give the impression that it was better for you than the drug you are currently addicted to. Methadone was invented as a cure for heroin addiction, straight up. It was mass produced and disseminated around the globe for kicking heroin addiction, and it actually worked like a charm. Heroin addicts would line up at methadone clinics to get their daily dose of the savior drug methadone, which would allow the addict to detox from heroin without feeling any of the normal side effects associated with kicking a chemical dependency cold turkey.

But methadone turned out to be just another leach on society. Heroin addicts soon realized they were addicted to the cure. Methadone addictions skyrocketed and demand for methadone soon outpaced any new demand for heroin. The only upside was that addicts could now get the drug they were addicted to from the legal pharmaceutical companies, in specialized clinics and pseudo-kiosks worldwide, instead of purchasing unknown quality of drugs from local street vendors. The trend of addiction was still alive and well, only the profiteers had changed the origins. Methadone is a synthetic version of morphine and is still just another opioid. It has extremely addictive qualities and the only thing that has really changed is the name of the drug and the purity. Methadone patients (because now they need a prescription) more often than not, prefer methadone to heroin anyway. And people are dying to take this drug as well, literally.

Methadone clinics around the globe make their users jump through hoops to obtain their daily dose. In most cases, a new user has to show up every day to prove they are really trying to kick heroin. They have to report at certain hours of the day that are not usually the waking hours of addicts, and they have to test clean for heroin in order to get their methadone. This is understandable since a dose of each may cause the user to overdose. Once a user has proven to be worthy, he can pick up multiple doses on a single day in building a link-of-trust between the clinic and himself. The problem is that the common drug addict is not very good with instructions and time schedules, especially if he is going through some sort of personal detoxification, despite the alternative medicines. The common occurrence is that the methadone user misses his appointment at the clinic, and reverts back to the streets for a dose of heroin. Upon returning to the methadone clinic, the user tests positive for heroin and is therefore denied his dose of methadone.

Now the addict is forced into a conundrum. Stay with the horrors of a heroin addiction, which caused him to seek help at the methadone clinic in the first place, or find the strength to clear the heroin out of his bloodstream (about 3 days) and start back on the methadone, with a new game plan that will allow him to avoid these horrible withdrawal symptoms in the future. This is the full cycle of drug addiction, my friend. Now the methadone user is bullied by the methadone clinic to replace the need for heroin with the need for methadone. This scenario is exactly what got them addicted to drugs in the first place. Want becomes need, and the addict needs a supplier who is trustworthy and there, always there, when needed. Eventually, the methadone addict becomes even more addicted (if you can believe that is a thing) then he was to heroin. But really, he's still addicted to the same drug; he just has a new dealer.

The pharmaceutical companies which produced methadone had an unchallenged authority since they had the appearance of providing a cure for heroin addiction, a monumental accomplishment at face value. Through marketing strategies they soon figured out how to repurpose the drug into other cures and soon convinced the drug-prescribing entities of the world how wonderful this miracle drug would be for so many other markets. Without skipping a beat, methadone was being prescribed for all sorts of pain and depression, and used as 'replacement therapies' for all sorts of mental health issues. This is probably the most wrongly prescribed medicine in the history of the world, and only adds to the long list of addictive drugs that have ruined so many lives in the name of pharmaceutical profitability. It remains almost unchecked by mainstream society, which has swept under-the-rug their personal needs to care about people who have found themselves addicted to drugs.

The pharmaceutical companies have only widened their plan to profit from the miseries of others, and methadone was the goose that laid the golden egg. I could write a complete novel on the horrors of methadone and the systematic abuse these companies have displayed to our current societies, but there would be no point as the goal here is to teach and not preach. Methadone is bad, um-kay...The opioid cartels of the world will continue to profit off of the miseries of others and the stronger they become, the harder it will be to put the brakes on the system that is rotting our society's underbelly. This is now personal to the user, and education is the key which opens the door to freedom.

The current epidemic is a cause-and-effect problem where our leaders are just not leading...and it's not their fault. In most cases our leaders are not now, nor have ever been drug addicts, so they have to rely on experts to relay information to them on what's happening and how to fix the problems. The problem with this picture is that those who tag themselves as experts are also the profiteers of the drug treatment industry. Now we rely on treatment programs which are recommended by the very people who profit from these tragedies. They have a moral investment in solving these problems but a financial investment for prolonging the treatment. Just like the pharmaceutical companies which can't be trusted, neither can any drug treatment program which profits from such an addiction. They have a financial incentive to teach patients that relapse is a real part of kicking such an addiction, but this couldn't be further from the truth. Quitting is quitting for life; one process, one time only. It's not a stage where you constantly fail and start the process over again and again. Kicking a drug addiction is not a temporary fix to get you to keep coming back.

So, how do you get a grip on your current addiction, when all of the cards seem to be stacked against you? And how can you tell if the information you require to kick this addiction is reliable? Is it really possible to kick a drug addiction without entering an expensive drug treatment program which locks you inside a room until you naturally detox from the drug you're addicted to? And isn't that just like being in jail anyway?

Well, actually, yes it is. Lock-down drug treatment programs mirror the effects of our jail systems, which lock you up with no access to the drug, while your body naturally detoxes. And this is good because the first step in kicking a drug addiction is to go through some sort of detox which removes the drug you're addicted to from your system. This allows you to survive while facing the personal horrors of incredible withdrawal symptoms, while you try to adapt to a new life without drugs (and without the people in your life, who are still using daily). So, why do so many people relapse after being clean for long periods of time?

The truth is that people relapse simply because they don't have the tools to know how to stay clean, and they don't believe they possess the talent to pull it off. *The easiest thing a drug addict can do is drugs*…because everything else in life is harder. Addicts just don't have the information which is required for the human mind to accept the fact that addiction is reversible because again, their leaders just aren't leading. So, how do you find hope in a world that offers such deception? You just keep looking, until you see the light. Just as you are doing at this very moment, you keep searching for answers until you find the truth. You keep on trusting people until you find someone who is trustworthy. And when you feel comfortable, you follow a path. And if that path is true, it leads you to the promise land. Right now, you are on a new path, and I will tell you now, if you stay on this path, and stay true to the program, you will finally see the light at the end of the tunnel.

I consider myself to be the world's leading expert on drug addiction and treatment. I really don't care what actual credentials others claim as valid for such a title. I am an expert because I have been a drug addict for many years and I have walked in your shoes exactly. I have felt your pain, and I have lived your life, and I have figured out how to detox my body from the drug, and to walk away (from the drug) forever. And I have documented these actions and personally designed a drug treatment program which has helped countless thousands of people regain their lives, when it appeared they had no more life to live. This very book *How to Quit Meth Now,* has been disseminated around the globe, in multiple languages. It has helped thousands of addicts kick their addictions by offering a self-help guide to teach the addict how to kick their addiction on their time, in the privacy of their own home. The goal has always been to get the information out there, and anyone who copies it pays a tribute to my efforts, with my blessings. That said, I am not funded by any government, by anybody, or by any organization at all. I am motivated by duty and nothing else.

So now the focus changes to the current meth epidemic. Unlike opioids, which bring the user down, cocaine and methamphetamines have similar affects to the human body and mind, and can be treated in similar ways. I know that these are entirely different animals but the techniques for treatment are so similar that I can guarantee you will kick this addiction if you stay on the path. This prediction is absolutely based on the incredible results we've already seen since the Quit Meth program was put into effect. Everyone who reads the book from cover to cover and follows all of the instructions within will be drug free by the time they finish the book. That's just how it works, for everyone. This is hope in the form of literature (something that's never been done before). So again, stay on the path and keep reading.

In picking a drug treatment program that meets your needs, you should understand that most drug treatment programs are for-profit institutions. Most have zero personal experience in what you are actually going through, or the chains-of-events in your life which have led you to this point. You need to be instructed by someone who has walked in your shoes exactly, not by someone who thinks they can feel your pain from what they have learned in a class room setting. These are people who actually profit from your pain and pretend to know what it is that you are going through. They purport to feel sorry for you but there is a huge difference between sympathy and empathy. If the person helping you has not been addicted to narcotics, they do not know what you are going through. If they say they understand because they used to be alcoholics, they are only fooling themselves. You cannot get empathy from a former alcoholic because they do not understand the depths of your drug addiction, as alcoholism pales by comparison. They can only offer you sympathy, like everyone else in your life at this time.

To kick your meth addiction, you will have to trust the information in this book and honor the processes provided to you in the literature. The key to successfully kicking your addiction is the acquisition of knowledge that you do not have at this point, or you wouldn't still be addicted. Agreed? If you already knew how to kick you wouldn't be reading this book, you would be enjoying your life, like everyone else in society who aren't slaves to their past choices.

The cure to drug addiction lies within the understanding of how the body and mind are simultaneously influenced by a chemical dependency problem (Read that again, and let that sink in). At this point, you just need to know why you are addicted and what forces are inside your mind, body, and soul which will not allow you to quit. It is only after you gain this knowledge that you can move-on from this horrible existence, and re-enter society as the respectable human being that hides inside you at this moment.

Believe it or not, there is hope for you, and you do have a future as an ex-addict if you choose to stay on this path. But you need to take a good look inside yourself and decide if you've had enough of this, determine who you are and who you want to be…and start taking the steps required to turn your life around. This is a long book, drawn out to cover every aspect of your addiction for the sake of a full recovery. In the very least, you will have to commit yourself to reading every word of this book, and taking all of this to heart. I understand that's a huge commitment for a drug addict, but if your personal goal is to quit then this is a real part of the process. The world turns with or without you, and there is no one left who really cares if you live or die anymore, just you. You are all alone now and what happens with your life is in your hands, your decision.

This process for kicking a meth addiction is a long journey into all aspects of your addiction, where you will learn everything, from jump-street to walking away entirely. You will be taught simple mind-techniques for getting a grip on your addiction, where information is the key to a successful exit from the drug world. You will learn how your mind has tricked you into your current addiction (like a spoiled child who always gets what he wants), and how you can reverse the process by regaining control of your mind. You will be taught different methods for starting and completing a 14-day self-detox, where several different methods will be offered for you to choose from, as no single pill holds the cure to such an addiction. You will also be provided with several over-the-counter remedies which will help to mimic the effects of your current addiction (while minimizing the horrible effects of withdrawal), while you detox from the drug and remove it completely from your system. All of these techniques are as simple as they are effective.

.

Chapter 2

Genesis

Okay, here we go now…this is where the program starts, so it's important that you start taking every word to heart. Your need to disagree with portions of these writings are a natural occurrence in the mind of a drug addict, everyone does it. The doubt you have in this program at this point is shared by just about every addict wanting to kick, but you must fight the urge internally, as you are not here to question the methods of this program. You are here to learn things that you don't already know, and to create a new belief system around these techniques, so you can move forward to a belief system that has you drug-free for the rest of your life. You have to avoid your mind's idea that it already knows everything there is to know about addiction, and clear that useless knowledge from your brain. You are following now, not leading, and any preconceptions about what will follow here need to be tossed to the wind. You are starting over now, and you are the student, not the expert. You can claim to be an expert after you kick your addiction, when you're able to help others with the techniques you will learn here, while soaking up the information in this literature.

This is your life and you've decided to take control of your addiction by beginning the steps needed to leave your drug days behind you. You're addicted to methamphetamines, however you see it, and that is not up for debate at this time. For your information, the treatment methods for kicking a meth addiction are the same as they would be for kicking a cocaine addiction. They are both stimulants that affect the mind and body in similar ways, though they are quite different animals, and treating them for the purpose of detox and removing the urges to relapse are virtually identical. A cocaine addict could therefore kick on this meth program by following the same steps you are taking now. This is for the record, if it ever comes up, or if you have a friend who is addicted to cocaine who is looking for a way out, they can use this program as well.

The main differences between the severities of a meth addiction are the delivery methods. When you slam any drug directly into your bloodstream via the needle, it will always have a more direct and therefore quicker and stronger reaction then someone who takes their medication orally. Inhaling these drugs, be it snorting or smoking, delivers the drug into your lungs, which contain open blood vessels linking directly to you bloodstream. People who have graduated to the needle are injecting the drug directly into the bloodstream, for an instant effect. Though these would all seem to be different techniques with different effects, they are all roads to the exact same chemical dependency. All meth addicts are therefore addicted to the same chemical. The 'big lie' is only affected by personal choice. You have chosen how you prefer your meth delivered into your body. It's still methamphetamine nonetheless, correct? We are all in the same boat now and the river only flows one way. You have failed the basic life lessons taught in grade school because at some point, you believed the rules of life did not apply to you. You forgot to 'look both ways before you crossed the street' because here you are, on the other side now. If you'd been paying attention to the warning signs, you wouldn't be here, but here you are. Now there's "no use crying over spilled milk" as our efforts have to be shifted to the clean-up process. So, let's fix this mess…

Welcome to the show. You're here today because your quest to kick a drug addiction has led you to this book. You've said the magic words that often lead to a drug free lifestyle "I need help." The three words every drug addict uses after realizing their casual use has now blossomed into a chemical dependency problem. The question is…are you ready to quit? Is kicking your drug addiction the single most important issue in your life right now? If the answer is no, close the book now and come back to it when you're ready. It's no big deal, right?

This is where we weed out the weaklings. *Being a drug addict is the easiest thing that anybody can ever do. It requires no effort at all and supplies you with all of the necessary excuses to be a failure.*

As I've mentioned, this is the beginning of a very long and drawn out drug treatment program, which will take you on a journey through every aspect of your addiction. It will help you understand how and why you became an addict, and eventually supply you with everything you need to know to take away all of the excuses you require to stay addicted. With this program, you'll learn how to detox your body from your drug, and together we'll identify and address all of the triggers in your mind that are keeping you addicted. If you've decided you want to be drug free, you'll have to read every word of this book. That's a huge commitment for an addict, and you'll need to understand there are several different levels of 'want' in "I want to quit." You have to want to quit more then you've ever wanted anything before in your entire life.

Like I said, I'm not funded by any organization or government grant or by any person at all. Unlike other drug treatment programs, I will not lie to you. If I thought that cutting off your arm would help you quit using, I would tell you so. As you may already know, things are going to get a lot worse before they get any better. Kicking a drug addiction is hard work and you have to be strong. It's understood that most people who experiment with drugs are not interested in a drug treatment program and in fact assume they're not even addicted. You can understand this as you've felt this way yourself in the past. It's a common belief that drugs are for recreational use only, and can lead to addiction if you don't monitor yourself wisely. I guess you failed that test because you're now suffering from a chemical dependency.

The main difference between drug use and a chemical dependency is addiction. Addiction occurs over a period of time when the initial effects of the drug are diminished by the human body's own ability to build up a tolerance for such things as drugs and alcohol. As the body's tolerance level climbs, it requires a larger dose of the drug to reach your intended high. As you raise the quantity of drug consumption, you begin to put toxic levels of the drug into your bloodstream, which eventually changes your body's own chemistry. After continued and uninterrupted use, your body adapts to the chemical as if it were intended to operate with it in your system.

The problem is when you attempt to take the chemical away, your body can no longer function without it. It's now 'dependent' on that chemical to function normally, or in a normal state. ***It's this chemical dependency that's keeping you addicted.*** The cycle is clear; If you try to take the drug away while you're chemically dependent, you'll suffer from withdrawal symptoms. This is your body now trying to function without the drug. The shock to your central nervous system is just as drastic as when you first introduced your body to the drug. Everything you think and feel is completely different from feeling normal. That's what withdrawal means. You are withdrawing a chemical that your body now needs to function normally. Most likely you've felt these withdrawal symptoms yourself in the past, as this is the biggest part of addiction. Quitting becomes a horrible experience with an easy solution: *take your medicine and the pain will go away.*

So what now? Now, you need a program to help you clean up and get a grip on your chemical dependency. There's nothing to be ashamed of as everybody who kicks a drug addiction followed a program. Even someone who quits on their own has put themselves on some kind of program; decisions were made and steps were taken to quit, once and for all.

There are really only three ways you can kick a drug addiction. One is in jail or prison, where large doses of the drug are not readily available, another is in an expensive drug treatment facility, where all they're really doing is locking you in a room (just like jail), and the third is to quit on your own. Quitting on your own is the most common of the three and it's also the hardest because you know where you can easily get your drug. Quitting in a lockdown treatment center or jail is easy because you have no choice. That's where the statement "you wanted to get caught" comes from. When you're living in an altered state of consciousness, sometimes your subconscious has to take control of your life. The vicious drug cycle was killing your body off slowly but surely, and your subconscious mind had to do something drastic or your body would deteriorate to the point where it might not be able to help the brain with its drug-quest for much longer.

If your body couldn't supply your brain with any more drugs, your brain would also be suffering the consequences. So your mind took over the process and set you up with this simple strategy; do something stupid that will get you caught and locked up, be forced to rehab, rejuvenate your body and get healthy. Then, get out of jail and start the vicious cycle again. Call it a relapse if you want to, but your brain never intended to let you quit anyway. This program will teach you to get a grip on how your mind is manipulating you into being a drug addict so that you can use this information to quit altogether. So, where do we start?

As I've said before, and let these words sink in; *the cure for drug addiction lies within the understanding of how the body and mind are simultaneously influenced by a chemical dependency.* Only after gaining this understanding can you put an end to this dependency altogether. In order to solve the puzzle of your own personal drug addiction, you must first take a few steps backwards and try to understand exactly who and what you are.

As a human being, *you're a consumer.* Your body works in conjunction with your brain to achieve its primary goal of being content. Therefore the body's actions must satisfy the brain. As you know, we eat food and drink liquids to supply our body with the necessary supplements to maintain a healthy lifestyle so we can live a long life. In this process, our mind and body work as a team and tend to trust each other's instincts unequivocally. When the body is tired, the brain sends us signals and we begin the process of shutting down and getting the necessary rest required to function for the next waking period. When the body is lacking a necessary supplement, the brain figures out what's needed and uses the body to acquire that element. For instance, if your body was lacking a proper supply of vitamin C, the brain might send the body to the store to get an orange (or at least that's how it's supposed to work). Unfortunately, we've entered an age where the orange example has become obsolete. Now, if your body required vitamin C, your brain can simply send you to the kitchen cupboard to take a multi-vitamin. If the brain is not feeling up to par, it doesn't have to figure out what combination of foods and liquids would relieve the problem. It would just instruct you to take a pill. An aspirin or a cold pill could be a chemical quick fix to a biological problem. Can you see where I'm going with this?

With the introduction of chemicals into our bodies in pill form, we have not only figured out how to relieve our illnesses faster and more efficiently, but we've also built up a higher level of trust between our body and our mind. It's this degree of trust that's made it so easy for your brain to trick you into your current addiction. The big problem is this; **your brain cannot be trusted**. Your brain has become the equivalent of an easily spoiled and selfish little kid who knows how to manipulate every aspect of your life and uses its powers to satisfy its own urges, without regard to the ramifications of its actions. If given the opportunity, your brain would screw your whole life up if it could reach its primary goal of being content for today. In fact, that's exactly what's going on here. Your own brain is manipulating you into your meth addiction because meth now eases your mind. *Think about that for a minute*. You do your drug and for a moment, you feel better. Your mind is content and your body is also at ease because it has another dose of one of the major chemicals it needs to function normally. Your own brain is telling you that *all is good*. You're in the heat of addiction, right where your body and mind are telling you to be. The problem is that you cannot sustain your life with this vicious cycle.

I remember the old cartoon character Wimpy from the Popeye cartoons. He always walked around telling people "I would gladly pay you Tuesday for a hamburger today." Anyway, your brain works on the same principals of 'what have you done for me lately?' In the drug world, Wimpy would simply be asking for a front. "I would gladly pay you later for something to fix me right now" he'd say. His statement was nothing short of the brain trying to figure out how to spend money he didn't even have yet, to get what he needed right now. As we all learned, it's a lot easier to picture having money tomorrow then it is to actually acquire it after the fact. But these types of brain manipulations happen to us all of the time. Our mind will convince us that anything is possible as long as we supply the chemicals it needs to feel normal. Your mind recalls every single trigger that has worked in acquiring meth in the past, and it uses these memories as triggers that rule your current addiction. It's always easy for your mind to gauge your current feelings, and use triggers that have worked in the past with these same emotions. Your mind has all of the memories from your complete history of drug abuse. It knows everything you've ever thought and felt, because it helped to create the data. *Think about that for a minute.* Your mind provided the emotions which made you feel indifferent, and then it provided you with the solution to ease the pain it made you think you felt. And meth was always the solution it convinced you to seek out. Later in this course, you'll learn how to gain control of your mind by breaking this link of trust and once again start making decisions that are productive for your entire well-being.

Drug addiction is not a disease. It doesn't matter how scientists have determined these terms and sold them to modern societies as facts, drug addiction is not a disease. If you have already bought into this myth, your actual treatment begins the day you realize that you are not a victim of an incurable disease, but rather a willing participant in your own demise. If you really believe your addiction is a disease, just ask anyone who has ever tried to kick lung cancer. As an addict you have options that simply are not available to someone suffering from a serious illness. You can quit. You can keep on believing you're a slave to your drug addiction, that there is no hope and you'll always be a failure or...you can quit. It is a fact that millions of people just like you have already done that. People who believe that drug addiction is a disease are simply at the end of their rope trying to understand why they or someone they know is still suffering from a drug addiction…when all means of understanding and treatment have been exhausted, and the only valid explanation remaining is that the user is just another victim of a serious illness that's out of their hands. Believe me, the last thing you need is yet another excuse to be addicted, such as you having a disease. Like I said before, *If you've already bought into this myth, then your treatment will start the day you realize you're not a victim of a drug addiction but yet another willing participant.* If nothing else, you should be thankful that you don't have an incurable disease. Also, you should always be skeptical when you hear ridiculous statements that simply don't make sense.

There's a lot of government funding out there, targeted for any study or program that has anything to do with the general public figuring out what's going wrong in the drug treatment industry. People who have never been addicted to drugs don't understand how addiction works and rightfully blame the rise in crime and violence on the drug problem. When the public cries out, government programs are funded and a different type of crime begins. I'm referring to what I like to call *'educated welfare'* where people who have six and eight year college degrees spend their time creating studies to collect government funding, instead of finding real jobs that would actually benefit society. Because they call themselves 'scientists', their conclusions are seldom questioned and their credibility is enhanced just enough to make them eligible for yet another government grant.

That's where the statement "*drug addiction is a disease*" came from. Scientific rhetoric wasn't paying the bills anymore so a conclusion had to be made. Basically, they take photo scans of the brains of people who are on drugs and compare them with photo scans of the brains of non-addicts and make outrageous conclusions based on what they see, not what they know. The conclusions seem legitimate and purport to solve a puzzle, so it all sounds believable, and it may actually have some degree of truth intertwined with the speculation. The true answer of *'we have no idea why someone gets addicted to drugs'* doesn't pay the bills, when your job is to solve the puzzle of drug addiction. Stating that drug addicts must 'have a disease' just bounces the ball further down the road and again, does nothing for those seeking relief from their addictions. Lucky for you, we've figured out why you're addicted and I'll explain it to you so you can understand it and kick your addiction once and for all.

This program is designed as a self-help drug treatment program for people who are currently fighting a meth addiction. There are significant differences between methamphetamine and opioids, so the treatment methods necessary for kicking these addictions are completely different. Unlike opioids, cocaine and meth are both from the stimulant family and have similar effects on the body and the mind. Heroin and other opioids are different animals altogether, and like I already stated, they already have a detox program for heroin, and it's called methadone. Ironically, people who've become addicted to methadone are still just trying to kick an opioid addiction. They're just trying to kick the cure now, and a new cycle of addiction. For this reason, it's important that you not trade methamphetamine for another form of addiction, like cocaine. It's still the same thing you're suffering from right now; it just has a shiny new title.

In this program, we'll attempt to utilize the methadone game plan (without the actual methadone) by mimicking the effects of your drug, while using several over-the-counter pharmaceuticals, vitamins, and herbs to try to relieve the cravings you have during withdrawal, while at the same time detoxing your body and mind from your chemical dependency. This, along with the attempt to minimize all withdrawal symptoms, will make this the perfect program for anyone who's seriously seeking an effective self-detox program. This is a 2 phase, 3-step program that starts in the heat of addiction, while you're still using. It guides the current user up to and through a 14-day self-detox period while employing simple psychological techniques for helping the addict to stay clean forever, by learning how to understand the triggers in the mind that often cause a clean addict to relapse.

Trigger is the word we use to describe the action which takes place in your mind that causes you to use or 'relapse' after you've been clean for any period of time. It's the realization that certain triggers exist in your mind that's caused you to figure out that you're addicted to this drug in the first place. What I mean by this is that while there was a time when you believed you could take it or leave it, you've since learned about the forces inside your mind which are working against you. At some point you wanted to quit but were unable to because every time you tried, something in your head would take control of you and make you want the drug so bad, you would do anything to get it. The longer you waited after deciding you were going to get more meth, the harder it became to wait patiently. That's when you said to yourself 'I guess I am a drug addict' for the first time (a trigger). After that it became easier for your brain to control you because you had already thrown-in-the-towel and decided you could handle the label 'drug addict.' After that, every time you tried to quit, your brain played on your addiction and used one of several different techniques to 'trigger' you back into getting the drug again.

There are many different triggers in your brain that you'll have to identify before you can beat your drug addiction altogether, and I'll teach you how to spot them and gain control over them. *Understanding how the triggers in your mind are manipulating you softens the attempt, and eventually teaches you how to overcome the temptation altogether.* As we progress through this program, I'll teach you how to use some simple mind techniques for overcoming your addiction. These will address the triggers in your mind that keep tricking you into staying on this endless path of addiction.

Chapter 3

The program

A good drug treatment program requires the implementation of several predetermined systems and methods. *Just as your drug use has now taken the form of a daily ritual, your exit from the drug world must also be somewhat ritualistic.* To achieve your ultimate goal of living a drug-free lifestyle, you must follow a system of using several different step-by-step procedures simultaneously. That's why we call it a program; to link all of our actions to a term which best describes our course of action. The goal then will be to find the right program for you; a program that works. The problem with most drug treatment programs is that they're either completely ineffective or they cater to the rich and are out of reach for most addicts. The trick then involves how you not only find a program which works but also one you can afford.

Welcome to the world's first and only anonymous drug treatment program! You don't have to show up, sign in, or talk to anybody about your addiction, and nobody will ever know you followed a program unless you decide at some point that you want them to know. It's absolutely anonymous and controlled by you alone. This is the most effective drug treatment program you'll ever find and if you're reading this right now, you've already figured out the cost.

As I've mentioned, I am an expert on drug addiction and treatment because 1) I know exactly what it feels like to be addicted 2) I know how to kick the addiction and 3) I know how to help you kick your addiction. I firmly believe that you cannot teach an addict how to kick an addiction if you've never experienced a drug addiction yourself, first hand. How can you be counseled through your addiction by someone who doesn't even understand what it is that you actually think and feel? The main problem with most existing drug treatment programs is that they use counselors who've never been addicted to the drug you're trying to quit. You can't be cured, lectured, or even counseled by someone who doesn't completely understand what it is that you're going through. I do know how you feel right now, because I've been there. I've walked in your shoes exactly, thought the way you now think, and I've felt the pain and agony that you feel. I was addicted to the same drug you are addicted to at this very moment, and I know exactly how you feel, inside and out. And I know what it takes to reverse the process and kick this addiction forever. And…I'll explain all of it to you as we progress through the program, but you have to stay with me all the way through. Let nothing in your mind convince you to stop reading. You need all of this information, every word, in order.

This book is written as a self-help guide for kicking a methamphetamine addiction. There are many different words used to describe this drug but all of them are referring to a meth addiction, correct? You need to start thinking and believing that this program was designed specifically for you, because it was. Whatever works for the individual is what's important. We are no longer splitting the hairs of the words we were taught to use for the drugs we're addicted to. I'm just going to call this what it is; a drug treatment program for meth addicts. Now and again, we'll move forward together. Do not let any of your feelings get in the way of your ambitions here. Stay on the path and keep reading.

So we are clear, I am your host and guide, and you are exactly where you need to be right now. I honestly believe that anyone who makes it through this entire program and becomes a recovered addict will also be able to qualify someday as a meth addiction and treatment specialist. Currently you're just another addict seeking a cure but lucky for you, you've come to the right place.

The program you're using is called the Quit Meth program. It was originally developed for the website QuitMeth.com and at one time it sold for $300 on that website. The original program was a multimedia program that included a 50-minute video, an 8-CD audio program, literature on several different topics, and many other items that I will talk about later, when the time is right. The original program included over the counter drugs, vitamins, herbs, and other products, which will be outlined in coming chapters. The program was sold in almost every state in the U.S. as well as several units shipped to users in other countries. I believed wholeheartedly that one of the reasons the program was so successful was because the user had to want to quit bad enough to pay for it. I figured that the price tag would eliminate those who really didn't want to quit, and I think it did, with a 100% effective rate on those who completed the surveys. The trick then was to figure out how to make the program successful for those who couldn't afford the high price tag in the first place (because I don't think the same way anymore). The big problem in putting together this literature was to figure out how to bridge this gap. How would I be able to convince a drug addict that this is the best program for them, if I seriously believed one of the main reasons the program was so effective was because it involved the user buying the program for $300? If getting the addict to spend their own money on the cure was a successful component, how can I get the same results by putting this program into the form of a book?

To bridge this gap, the secret would have to be hidden in the content. The content has to be thorough and current, and has to address all of the concerns of the addict who is still a daily user of the drug. The content would also have to cover every unanswered question the addict has yet to ask himself. Therefore, this book is written in a way to make it so that any meth addict who reads the entire content cover-to-cover and follows the steps provided, will be unable to continue to convince themselves that they're still addicted, because the power to quit was something which they did not possess. I now believe that you can no longer be addicted to this drug if you know you *can quit*, and if you know *how to quit.* If you know *how to quit,* and you know a great program that has worked for thousands of other people just like you, you can no longer blame addiction (or the possibility that you have a disease), as the reason you need your meth. If you know how to quit and you choose not to, you're not really interested in quitting, are you? Additionally, this book takes away the need for the addict to spend his own money on the course itself, so that he can concentrate on the program and requirements of each lesson. So now I believe that the requirement to purchase this program is no longer a factor, and that *the book itself is the cure.* Yes, you heard that right; the cure for meth addiction is the content and execution of the program in this book. No more, no less.

If you want to clean up and finally kick this addiction, and you want the help you deserve, it's all here. Anyone who chooses to be a non-recovering addict and believes they can live with that, maybe that's who you are. This program is designed to help the addict who wants to kick their meth addiction. It is impossible to help an addict who doesn't want to quit using, but I also believe this program contains valuable information for those not wanting to quit as well, because it takes away the user's ability to believe there is no way out and teaches all addicts how to quit, even if they're not interested in quitting at this time. The content of this literature plants a seed in the mind of the user, weather they like it or not. The only question remaining is will they change their mind and start the processes to quit before their addiction ends up killing them or not. That said, this process is for those who want to kick their addiction now, at this time, while learning about meth addiction and following the guidelines laid out in these pages, as they are presented to you. If you are wondering if this program will fall flat and let you down, the answer is no. Not if you keep reading with conviction and stay on this path, and follow the guidelines. Do you need a guarantee with that? Okay then…

I will give you this guarantee right here, right now. *If you read this book from beginning to end and follow all of the instructions herein, you'll be drug free by the time you close the back cover. I guarantee it!* These are big words that nobody has ever said to you, and I know that. So what makes me so confident? What gives me the right to give you this guarantee? Why do I have the audacity to make this impossible statement that no other drug treatment program would ever dare say, let alone put in writing? Because this program is hope, and it is the truth, and it is the answer. Those are the three things I was searching for while I was trying to figure out how I was going to kick my own drug addiction. I wanted someone or something to prove to me there was hope, and I just wanted someone to tell me the God's-honest truth, and I wanted answers to all of my questions. No more lies and please, no more con-jobs. While doing my own research as I was looking for answers, I searched through all sources available at the time. This program is the culmination of many years of research, including existing drug treatment methods, Department of Justice studies, D.E.A studies, and interviews with drug addicts both on the streets and in the system. When I found the real answers I learned the truth, and when I learned the truth, I finally found hope.

The single greatest truth about a meth addiction is very simple. ***Nobody can help you unless you're willing to help yourself.*** Nobody really cares about you because you've already burned every bridge of substance in your life. *Not even God can help you* if you're not ready and willing to step up and help yourself. If you're ready, I'll teach you how. Trust me now and I will not let you down. I'm a drug addict who is now clean and knows why. This program will give you hope, because it is truth…and it is the answer.

The truth about me is that I can't even stomach drug addicts anymore these days…it makes me sick to see them struggling . They're a constant reminder of how I used to be, and of who I actually am. I am not in denial, I just carry around this truth about my past…of who I was, and it's not a pretty picture, as you know. The funny part is that you'll have these same feelings in the future. Once you finally realize that you've had the gift inside of you this entire time, you'll find strength in putting this behind you, and you'll grow to resent others who can't find the courage to take these simple steps. And trust me; you will grow stronger every time you see another drug addict who is still in the game. And there'll be nothing you can do. Because being addicted to meth is a choice, and you can't make it for them. But we are working on you right now. You can't save the world until after you kick your own addiction. And this is personal now. This is all about you. You have to be selfish right now, and concentrate on you alone. There is nothing in your world right now but you and this book.

So, I am cursed with the knowledge of how to fix your addiction and I believe that it's my duty as a fellow human to tell you there is a way, and to show you the path you must take to walk out of this nightmare you're living in. I am blessed with a writing style that will be easy to follow, as I know exactly who I am talking to. I hate you as you hate yourself, and I respect you for who you're about to become, as you'll learn to respect yourself once again. I am you, and soon you'll be whatever you decide you want to be, and not what this addiction has turned you into. This is a very exciting time for you, and the end is truly near. You knew that meth would either kill you or you would have to quit one day, and if you believe me and believe in my words, you'll finally beat this addiction once and for all. These are good times now.

The entire sales pitch for this program is in one simple question. *If they made a pill that would take away your craving for meth, would you want it?* I want you to think about this question long and hard. I want you to say it over and over again. *If they made a pill that would take away my craving for meth, would I want it?*

Of course, the answer is yes. That's exactly what you want. You want a simple and effective method to help you kick your addiction. If we could simply take a pill and all of the cravings would pass, we would jump on the opportunity and we would definitely take that pill. This program will show you how to use several over-the-counter pharmaceuticals, vitamins, and herbs to effectively create this missing wonder drug. This program is the missing link you've been searching for to connect you to your new drug-free lifestyle. I like to say this is a door-key program, and information is the key to kicking any addiction. You're now standing at the door and I will supply you with all of the information (the key) you'll need to walk through the door, back into the real world. You're learning about your addiction and you'll be learning what it takes to be clean and drug free, for the rest of your life. You can smile now because you can actually feel that you're getting close to the end of the addiction phase in your life. You can feel it in your blood and it should give you chills. The end is near.

So let's get on with the program…

The Quit Meth program
2-phases, 3-steps, 14 days

This program was made to be simple and easy to follow, in order to be effective and to hold your interest. I believe 12-step programs are ridiculous and so hard to follow that remaining an addict seems like an easier step. In the Quit Meth program there are 2 phases and only 3 simple steps you'll need to be concerned with. The two phases are basic and simple to understand. First you have to detox your body from the chemical you're dependent on by using the 14-day detox program, and then you have to learn how to stay clean for the rest of your life. Simple and easy to understand, right?

2 PHASES
Phase 1- Detox your body and mind from the dependent chemical (meth) by using the 14-day self-detox program.
Phase 2- Learn new techniques to gain control of your mind and stay clean forever.

Obviously you don't know how to do this yet or you wouldn't be an addict, so I'll guide you through these two phases as we get to them.

3 STEPS
I believe there are only 3 steps needed for kicking a meth addiction. Adding additional steps for the sake of making a program seem more valid or well-rounded is just a technique to make you believe that you're getting your money's worth, even when the added steps do little or nothing to improve the experience. You have enough on your plate right now in just trying to quit. You don't need to concern yourself with thin theories conceived by alcoholics, over a century ago. Just concentrate on the hard stuff, kicking your addiction. You can play in the sandbox later, if you feel the need.

Step 1-Say goodbye
Step 2- Quit
Step 3-Pay back

Step 1-Say goodbye

Step one is the foundation for your exit from the drug world. Telling you to just quit would be a ridiculous statement. You're a drug addict, you can't just quit or you would have done that already, right? (Step 2)

You have to plan your exit from meth on your own terms. You decide when you're ready to quit and how you want to go out. We'll discuss picking your quit-date in the next chapter. This is the most important day in your life and you must know all of your options. You're in total control in this self-help program and I'll show you how to quit when you decide it's time.

Step 2-Quit

After your quit-date arrives, you'll begin the 14-day detox program by following the suggestions in this self-help guide. You'll use the over-the-counter pharmaceuticals, vitamins, herbs, and other products as directed to make the self-help detox period as bearable as possible. *You'll need to purchase these items ahead of time,* and have them in your possession when you're ready to begin the detox period. I suggest you look ahead *now* to the chapter titled *'The list'* so you can begin purchasing these items now in preparation. This list is very important to you and the items included on it are all part of your self-detox program. There's a reason for each item on the list and we will talk about them later, when the time is right. There are other items which I will ask you to acquire but none of them are needed for the 14-day detox, and we'll talk about them as we get to each topic. Go to *"The list"* now and make a copy of the items you'll need to have before your quit-date arrives. All of these items can be purchased cheaper at your local big box discount store…usually the largest store will sell you the items much cheaper than anywhere else. These items were included in the original Quit Meth program, which was a significant portion of the cost of producing the packages.

In order to kick your drug addiction you'll need a plan that includes a quit-date and a 14-day detox period (to eliminate the chemical dependency). This is what makes this program the best on the market.

Step 3-Payback

I believe every drug addict who kicks their addiction becomes filled with an overwhelming desire to give back something to society, for all he has taken away. This is a very common feeling among clean addicts. I call it *restitution for the soul* and believe it's a vital step to walking away from the drug lifestyle you've become so accustomed to. I'll talk more about this later when you've already completed the 14-day detox period. That way you'll know and feel exactly what I'm talking about. You'll figure out if, when, and how you want to complete step 3 in the future. You just don't need this information at this time.

14 Day-Self detox period

We set the detox period at 14 days. After that, the chemical dependency is over and the program focuses on the psychological aspects of your addiction. There are many aspects of a meth addiction that will stay with you a lot longer than the 14-day detox period. Your body will be completely drug free after the first 14 days, and any odd feelings you may still have will simply be your body and mind trying to adjust to a drug-free life style, which it hardly remembers. I'll talk more about this later when you're starting to experience some of these feelings first hand.

Even though the chemical has been completely removed from the equation, you will have emotional ups and downs, as your body and mind begin to function in a normal state. It will seem at times that everything is great and life is perfect, and then there will be times when things seem a bit awkward. This emotional rollercoaster will work itself out with time.

How the program works

You will continue on and eventually read every word of this book, while trying your best to soak up all of the information provided for you. If you don't fully understand something, you'll read it again. It's not a bad idea to read every chapter in this book twice. This is your life here and you should do whatever it takes to grip this information. When you're not physically reading this book, you'll spend all of your spare time thinking about how it applies to you personally. Lay down on your couch or bed, close your eyes and think about everything you're learning and how it's going to help you change your life.

Remember that understanding this information is the key to your success. Read slow and easy and then when you think you understand what I'm saying, read it over again.

Chapter 4

Understanding the Literature

I would like to make it clear that this program is purposely designed to achieve a goal. I carry no burden of trying to be politically correct as long as the user understands that the information provided here follows a path which leads to the end-game of being clean and free from their drug addiction. There is nothing to be gained for me to be accurate on every subject for the sake of correctness, when a bend on the truth can sometimes be more effective than arguing any point to accuracy. Take the line 'drug addiction is not a disease' for example. We are not here to represent both sides of the argument or to cite the authors; we are here to present a path which allows you to understand how to walk away from your addiction. Understanding that drug addiction is not a disease will help you move forward to the cure, where trying to understand why some people believe drug addiction is a disease will only slow your forward progress, and allow the trigger of misunderstanding to block your path. It is for these reasons that all of the information shared with you has already been sorted out to your benefit. If you see information that causes you to pause, dismiss your minds attempt to get you to reconsider this program, as a trigger, because that is what's happening. You are learning here and not questioning the theories. This is the best way to get the results you are looking for. The information follows the path which you are on now. Understand the information provided and…follow the path.

As with many parts of this program, this is heavy in accuracy, and opinion. I believe strongly that repeating statements (and repetition itself) will help to drive these points home, as we set them in our minds as permanent replacements for previous thoughts. Like I've said already, it doesn't hurt to oversaturate you with this information. It's a better program for doing it this way. So, maybe these statements are all factual, or maybe some are factual and some of them are just my opinions or my philosophies. It really doesn't matter as long as it helps you to understand your situation, and helps you turn it around. Eye on the prize, my friend. Whatever it takes for you to understand how to kick this addiction is the right information. Whether you agree or not, with the facts as they are stated. So, here we go again;

Drug addiction is not a disease. Diabetes is a disease, Alzheimer's is a disease, cancer is a group of diseases, but drug addiction is not a disease. These are all facts. Disagreeing with this opinion is nothing short of a slap-in-the-face on someone who really does suffer from a serious illness. And do we really need any more excuses to be drug addicts? Do you realize that your entire life continues to be one long story of why you are addicted to drugs (things that happened to me, and things that I did because of such events). We act as if our drug use was a reactionary process to life's horrible realities, but these are just excuses we use along the way. Using our past as a doorway into our current addiction is just another trigger which we use to forgive ourselves for being addicts. As you move forward, this 'victim of our past' trigger has to be eliminated from your mindset. You just can't keep one foot in the past as you move forward down the path on which you are now walking, correct? It's time now for you to approach all of the excuses you've used so far in your addiction, and see them as triggers which you will need to identify as precursors to relapse, so that such memories will not have any strength to persuade you from this point on. You're stepping up now so that this 'victim mentality' which runs your life will no longer be a factor in your future. You can no longer afford to play the victim, so start thinking of yourself as the hero you are about to become. The only person in your life, who can save you, is you. You can get support from people close to you, but don't make the mistake of letting your friends and family members be factors in your recovery. I say this because somewhere down the road, they just may end up causing you grief. Family members can sometimes have a negative influence on your new positive push forward. This is you fixing your own problems, and others who enter the picture are just background noise to the song you are writing about yourself. Absolutely separate yourself from the opinions of friends and family members as you walk down this road. You are all alone, and you need to keep this perspective to complete the journey. This is only about you and how you are deciding to approach the end of your addiction.

I remember when actor Robert Downey Jr. (*Iron Man*) was arrested for possession of cocaine and valium in his Palm Springs hotel room many years ago…his mother was all over the media the next day saying that relapse was expected and accepted in his drug recovery program. 'Jeez, thanks Mom,' maybe she could do his time for him too. If you plant in someone's head that relapse is expected in their drug treatment program, then you're damning that person's future. In a real drug treatment program, there is no room for failure. When you kick your meth addiction, it's for the last time, period. There is no such thing as 'relapse' when you actually kick an addiction. When you clear the dependent chemical from your bloodstream, your body is no longer dependent on that chemical. You are drug free at that time, and it's only your mind that stays dependent on controlling you. And it's not because it wants the drug so badly at that point, it's just so used to controlling your actions and having everything it desires. Your brain enjoys its new purpose of running your life for you, so it's tough to cut the cord, but it's not impossible. In fact, once you understand how this process works, it's pretty easy to overcome the mind-control part of your addiction.

So, if drug addiction isn't really a disease, why do they keep saying that it is? And if relapsing isn't expected and accepted in kicking a meth addiction, how come they keep saying these things to everyone? Good questions, right?

You don't have to dig deep to realize that statements like these are built-in excuses for the failures of drug treatment centers worldwide. When someone puts all of their trust and hard-earned cash into the belief that their loved ones will be cured from a drug addiction, how can the weaker programs explain it when the addict is back on the drug a few months later? How else can you justify spending upwards of $10,000 only to have the program fail, except by saying that it's okay to relapse? Well, it's not okay, because that is a lie. A 70% success rate is nothing more than a well-padded 30% failure. Giving you the option to 'slip' is giving you yet another excuse to be a drug addict. When you quit using meth, there can be no trigger that you haven't thought of in advance, which will get you back to using meth again. You have to learn that there's only one thing that you can't do in your life anymore. Your entire life from this point on only has one rule that counts, so get it in your head.

Methamphetamine; you just can't do meth anymore, that's it. You can't do that one thing, because you're addicted to it, and it does nothing for you but ruin your life. This whole process is to get you off of that one drug. Once you are finished, there is no turning back. There is no chance for a relapse, because you only have to concentrate on one thing in your life; meth…the one thing you can't touch…and your life will be better every single day. Your one life has only one rule now. After you kick this addiction…you can't touch one thing for the rest of your life: meth. This is your one rule for the rest of your life, so you have to start to convince yourself of this right now. After you finish this program, your life only has one simple rule, from now on. No meth. You can do everything else that life has to offer…except for meth…because you're addicted to that drug, even after you kick the chemical dependency. Your brain loves meth now, so you have to address this every day hereafter. And all of that falls on you, indeed (repetition).

Are you tired of the lies yet? Then here is the truth, my friend. The world is content with you being a drug addict. Society needs to have built-in tier levels of success and failure. The many levels of poor and working class, middle class, or upper middle class, it doesn't matter. To reach any level of success you have to have someone on the bottom. People will smile and look you right in the eye and tell you they want to help you, but they don't. They really want to believe that they do, but they really don't. Meth addicts represent the ground level of human existence, and nobody really has to do anything to be better off than you are, as long as they aren't addicted to meth. Society loves those who live in the gutter because it gives even the poorest in any community the ability to pity and feel sympathy for someone else. As you climb your personal ladder of success (post-addiction) the first thing you will be, is better off than you were before, than anybody who is still addicted to drugs. Do you see how that works? That's why you're on your own in trying to kick this addiction, throughout the entire process. It's just you, baby. There's no one else left who really cares. You're on your own in every sense.

By seeking out this program you have now singled yourself out yet again. You are now the ultimate minority of one. To get through this program you must see yourself in this way. 'Me against the world' and that is the truth. At least until the time comes when you re-join your birthright, to live happily ever after. Did you think that was only in fairy tales? Because everyone who isn't strung out on meth is living a better life then you do. You see them every single day, everywhere you look. The world is full of happy people doing whatever they want, every single day...because they're not addicted to drugs. They have homes and cars and family...and you have every opportunity to walk in their shoes as well. You kick this addiction and then, with a little time, you can have everything you want as well (happily ever after).

Robert Downey Jr's Mom also publicly stated that she believed that her son needed to spend more time with his psychiatrist. While drug addiction is a psychological addiction in part, it's also a physical addiction. We play into yet another misconception when we rely on psychiatry to help us with our drug addiction. As with any other medical doctor, they simply don't know what to do with the meth addict. If you ask a psychiatrist how he treats a drug addict he'll tell you this; first you separate him from his drug and then you treat him with anti-depressants. Now, first of all, if we could simply separate ourselves from the drug, we wouldn't be drug addicts, right? And treating the addict with antidepressants is treating the symptoms and not the problem. Of course he's depressed. He's not getting his 'medicine.' The depression is absolutely caused by the addiction to meth, not the other way around. Never believe that you are addicted because you were so depressed that you started doing drugs to fight the depression. That is just your mind playing tricks on you, when you try to revert back to the beginning, and try to figure out why you started using this drug in the first place. It's just like the chicken and the egg puzzle, there is no real answer. You're only depressed now because being a meth addict is so...depressing.

There's an incredible amount of pressure being placed on the entire medical profession by deep-pocket pharmaceutical companies. The drug treatment industry is well aware of the fact that antidepressants and antipsychotics are of little value to the recovering addict. Always remember that pharmaceutical companies are shameful drug dealers who pour hundreds of millions of surplus dollars every year into keeping alive the lie that their goods are necessary in both drug treatment and dependency. Also, the psychiatric industry is in such a void as to their own intent, that they play follow-the-leader for fear of being put under the glass by developing any new strategies or techniques. Nobody likes to be wrong about the treatment methods for meth addicts. And psychologists are usually people who only know what they've read in books, written by other people who studied the profession before them. They fear establishing themselves as notable in their own Industry, and instead nitpick through other people's work looking for information they think may be false, so they can write a book discrediting someone else's work. But they will never try to discredit this program, and the reasons are quite clear; because this program actually works. It's current and it is effective, and there are no negatives they can point out. How do you discredit a drug treatment program that's already helped thousands of addicts kick for life? You don't; you learn from it and teach your own patients how to kick with these new methods.

Discrediting someone else's work is much safer then establishing theory but again, does nothing for those who really need their help. As an addict, you just have to believe you have the strength inside you to fix this problem on your own, because nobody is helping you from this point on. New theories in meth addiction treatment still go back several decades. So, remember that. The psychological industry does not even try to figure out what motivates you anymore. This book you are reading right now is the current information you need, and the best choice to help you at this point in time. And you should know that it's not only the psychological aspects of your addiction that's keeping you hooked on this drug.

Though it would appear your addiction is a psychological addiction, it's the physical addiction that we must fight off first to become drug free. *It's the addiction of the physical brain which causes the psychological dependency of the mind.* Think hard about that statement. When the physical brain is deprived of its 'medicine' it uses all of its resources (in your mind) to continue with the self-medication: hope, fear, pain, depression, guilt (you name it). Though they appear to be psychological in nature, they are caused by a physical addiction. Your brain is physically addicted to meth because of your chemical dependency to the drug. Your brain 'freaks out' when the chemical it needs to feel normal is depleted, and it uses your mind and all of its available data from your past, to trick you into finding and using more meth, so the physical brain can feel normal once again. This is the actual cycle of addiction, my friend. Your body needs the chemical to function in a normal state, and your mind is the tool your brain uses to make that happen, time after time.

With this knowledge in hand, it's much easier to treat the drug addict. If you can understand the relationship between your physical brain and your mind, as it applies to your chemical dependency, you are halfway home. Feel free to read that again, and take some time to thoroughly understand it, and let it sink in.

You are so close my friend.

First and foremost, you need to understand that there are thousands and thousands of people who have walked in your shoes who are now very clean. Grip it, hard, and always be thinking '*what one man can do, another man can do*'. The program you've chosen is a successful one, put together by people just like you who are now clean, because they have successfully used the techniques outlined in this program. Stay on course here and trust and respect the process. Your life will indeed change for the better, just like you always knew it would if you were drug free. The future is bright and you are now moving in the right direction. There are a few more things you need to learn so stay focused and move forward, always forward. Now, let's get to some of the basics...because there are a lot of them.

Know your enemies.

Rule number one on staying clean is to realize that you're a very different person now. In fact, you're not at all the same person who you've been in the past. All of the factors that turned you into a drug addict must be removed from your life. That was your old life and this is you now. You're not 'selling out' or being a hypocrite...but you must 'adjust-out' some of the people who used to be your friends. You know that already, don't you? You must *know your enemies*. Anybody who offers you drugs when they know that you've started a program with the intent to clean up for life...is now your enemy, straight up. A true friend wouldn't offer you drugs knowing that you're trying to quit, right? This is now your enemy number-one (in your mind) and should be handled as such. It's very hard to walk away from friends who have been there with you and for you for so long, but they are not on the same path as you are, and they will be there long after you are gone; in the same place, on the same day. This is also a big part of the cycle of drug addiction. Meth addicts only enjoy the company of other addicts because it helps them in their day to day belief that everyone they know is addicted to the same horrible drug. Hanging out with other addicts only completes the circle. It makes it seem like you are all in this together, but it's simply not true. You are all individuals, equally involved in your own demise. Separating you from your group is the first step in your personal recovery. This is not about your drug friends anymore, as they're not here with you on this journey, and they're not really looking for a way out. This is very personal because you are quitting the group now. Know your enemy; it's everyone still in the group, in your past. Sorry to have to tell you that but deep inside, you already knew. You are changing now, and that's a good thing. You owe it to yourself.

Put the hatred down.

In starting your new life you have to toss aside all feelings of hatred for yourself, as well as towards other people. There's no room in your new life for prejudging other people. It's very important you start thinking about people in only three categories. 1) There are drug addicts, 2) people who used to be drug addicts, and 3) people who have never done drugs before. You've heard that old saying before, that drug addiction is an equal opportunity employer which doesn't discriminate between the color of a man's skin or his religious beliefs. So now you must put the hatred down and give everybody a 'second chance' just as you will come to expect them to give you one. Put the hatred down and let it go. It's a burden that you don't need any more in your new life. Only then can you begin this program. Everybody starts new in your head. There are no heroes and no villains, just a bunch of people struggling with their own sets of circumstances, living their lives how they see fit. You don't hate yourself anymore and you won't feel hatred for anyone else. Everybody gets a do-over, including you. And this time you're going to take charge of your life and get this done. No more hate to rule who and what you are. Put it down now…let it go.

And....Begin.

This program assumes that you're a daily user who has not quit yet but wants to. Understanding this will assist people at all levels of addiction. It's very important that you listen closely to every word that is being said to you. These are words you need to hear and understand. Understand that 'wanting' to quit meth comes with many different tier levels of want, and only those who really want to quit and actually hate using will be successful. Remember this is a self-help program to assist you in quitting, and that using all of these techniques will get you off of meth and help to keep you off. It's time to start dreaming again, and from now on your dreams will come true.

Always remember and repeat these words; **what one man can do, another man can do.** It doesn't matter if you're male or female. What someone else has already done, someone else can do as well. Thousands and thousands of individuals have already kicked methamphetamines, cocaine, opioids, and heroin addictions, and that is a fact. And what one man can do, another man can do. I am living proof of this fact and I believe you will be as well. You need to start believing in yourself the way that I believe in you. Quit hanging around negative people who don't believe you have what it takes to kick this addiction forever. This movement is about positivity. Think positive and you will have a positive outcome. **Think big, be big**…I always say that; think big, be big (say it a few times). After you kick this addiction you're going to change the world, my friend. If for no other reason than to spite those who think that you cannot!

I will close this chapter with a quote from the movie The Matrix (1999) starring Keanu Reeves and Laurence Fishburne. The quote is pulled from the very end of the movie, just before the credits roll. It involves a phone call and the voice of Keanu Reeves. I use this as a valid message to you from the QuitMeth program and the world. I believe the truth is out there and you're finding it right now.

"I know you're out there. I can feel you now. I know that you are afraid. You're afraid of us. You're afraid of change. I don't know the future. I didn't come here to tell you how this is going to end. I came here to tell you how it's going to begin. I'm going to hang up this phone and then I'm going to show these people what you don't want them to see. I'm going to show them a world without…you. A world without rules and controls…without borders or boundaries…a world where anything is possible. Where we go from there…is a choice I leave to you."

I could not have said it any better, and I hope you take these words to heart. I think it speaks to the same situations that you and so many celebrities have lived through since this drug has become who and what you are. This is your program to change your world. It doesn't matter anymore what anybody thinks of you, it matters what you think of yourself. This is about change. Are you ready to change your life?

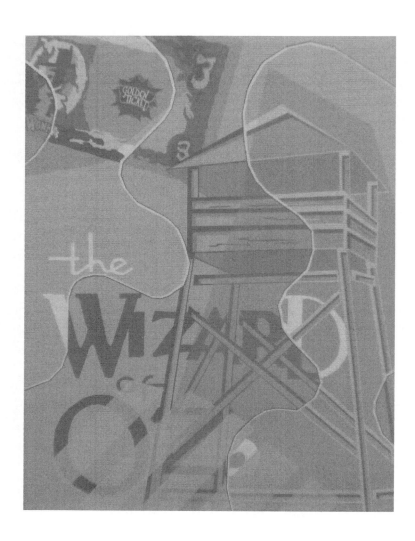

Chapter 5

Stylin'

At this point, it should be obvious that QuitMeth is a whole new style of drug treatment program. It conforms to nothing else on this planet, and most of the theories and techniques used here are fresh, current, accurate, and effective. As you can tell, I'm not a strong advocate of 12-step programs, and I don't believe in interventions either. I don't think people need to attend a series of meetings to share their stories, and we're not trying to save the world here, just you. This isn't about quantity, this is about you alone. This program isn't about a group of drug addicts trying to kick their addictions simultaneously. This is about your life, here and now…just you. Drug addiction is very personal and the treatment program associated with kicking a chemical dependency should be very personal as well. The focus here is one addict at a time, and you are the one. This is your time.

Although I understand there are exceptions to every rule and that 12-step programs have been helping people for decades, I absolutely disagree with many of their fundamental teachings. As you may already know, we can't insist that a meth addict put all of his faith in God or a 'higher power' to help kick a strong daily addiction. It just doesn't work that way. There isn't a drug addict in the world that hasn't gone down to his hands and knees and prayed for God to help him in any way, or to guide him out of his current addiction. You most likely have done exactly that at least a few times, as this is a natural move for an addict who is in a desperate search for a way out.

The problem is that most addicts believe one of two things 1) that God doesn't exist at all or that 2) he's turned his back on them in some kind of cruel and personal vendetta. An addict will always rationalize religion out of his belief system, because it seems like a God who would have the power to make it all go away, refuses to lend a hand. I've heard people say "I begged for help and nothing happened" or "I prayed for mercy and thought I heard a laugh." We cannot be forced into a drug treatment program which teaches us to believe in a God who we think has already abandoned us. If we start a program with such doubt, the user will only be waiting for the program to fail, as he believes his God has already done for him so many times in the past. For this and other reasons, addicts often fail the long and winding road of the 12-step program. I'm not here to try to persuade you to join any organization which looks at you as one person in a group of people. I'm here to teach you how to quit by yourself, without counting on any other single person as your partner in this redemption. Kicking a meth addiction is nothing but personal, and you can't do it in a group. You have to find the power which is inside you, in order to get the job done right.

Also, we must remember that making faith a fundamental piece of the recovery process and teaching an addict to believe that God or a higher power can help him cure his addiction…can be counterproductive, and can have an adverse effect when too much faith is substituted for one's own free will. It's very important that kicking your addiction comes from within you, and not from having faith in your God, your religion, or any other person or theory. Putting this type of faith and trust in other places too often leads to suicidal tendencies once the addict believes that even with such help, he is still failing the program. The program must therefore involve just one person at a time. Only you can fix you. It starts and ends with you and your motivations and commitment. Nobody else cares if you quit or not, so letting someone else into the equation just makes for bad math. You quit, on your own, at your pace, when you are ready. Nothing and no-body else is in the program with you.

As singer Sammy Hagar said in a Van Halen song, "Stop looking out and start looking in - be your own best friend - stand up and say 'Hey, this is mine' all mine." These are words to live by, my friend, as you stop pointing your fingers out and start pointing them in, at yourself. The secret to your success is within you. You broke it, you fix it…and that's what we're doing now.

If you are a religious person who puts your faith in God, please don't hear me wrong. Any true believer who is leaning on their religion to help them to kick this addiction has all of my support in this process. I only ask you to believe that when you prayed to God for help, he sent you here, where you are now, reading these words. Can I have it both ways? You betcha! This is your program, designed for and implemented by you and you alone. This guide is only here as a walk-through to the promise land.

For any non-believer who once had faith in a higher power, faith can be restored after an addict has figured out that only he can control his fate, and therefore his future. I think it's important to understand that you are kicking this addiction because you have found the power within you to do this, and that you have complete control over your own destiny. Insisting that God must be used as a third-step in a program, and to put all of your faith in God as a tool, only pushes addicts out the door and gives them even less hope then when they arrived. These 12-step programs haven't figured this out yet because they only track addicts who complete the steps. Their success rates are severely hindered because they don't take into account that they've failed, by-design, most of the addicts they've hooked into starting their programs.

You should also note that this is a very old program and in fact, the 12-step guidelines were written well over 100 years ago. And people in these programs are still reading from the same book! These guidelines were conceived for alcoholics, and written at a time when modern-day drug addictions didn't even exist. 12-step programs address those addicted to narcotics as if they were alcoholics and the approach falls short, because they do not understand the complexities in the mind of a drug addict. And we don't need 12-steps to confuse the already confused mind of the addict do we? If we take away the junk and the rhetoric, we can kick this addiction swift and true. Three full steps, with no baby-steps in the middle. That's all you need if you want to concentrate on the real problem; kicking your addiction to methamphetamines. The recovering addict needs to believe in self-empowerment. Placing all of your faith in a God that's already failed you supplies you with a trigger that you've already used so many times in the past. You must eliminate the opportunity to use that trigger again, by eliminating the belief that any God is helping you at all. If not, this backfires on your God, your faith, and your religion as a whole. God is not in charge of your addiction or your recovery. That's on you. No God introduced you to illicit drugs and no God will be involved in kicking this addiction as well.

I hope that's clear. I said it over and over to try to stick the point. Religion and meth addiction mixes like oil and vinegar. 12-step programs and interventions should be things you hear about, not participate in.

For the record, intervention is the name of the technique used for scaring the addict into quitting. It takes place when your family and friends have been witnessing your demise. Together they've concluded the best action to take to fix your problem will be to corner you in a room, as they take turns telling you how your drug addiction has been affecting their lives (and it really has). The thinking is that you'll feel so overwhelmed by the pouring out of love that you will have an epiphany, and 'change your mind' about your drug use. Furthermore you'll accept their help and advice, and your life will take a U-turn for the better. The problem is that they generally don't really understand a chemical dependency, nor any of the stages which leads to a drug addiction, or the better roads to treatment for such a dependency. The intervention is a staple in the belief systems of those who try to learn about how to help somebody they love, to overcome their addictions. But they really don't understand, or care about the fact, that the 'need' to kick has to come from within you, not other people. Perhaps it's true that an intervention can plant the seeds which will help you find the motivation to start the process, but if you are not self-motivated, there is no hope that an intervention will have a lasting effect on your intentions.

One of the problems with being a drug addict is that we've already become the world's greatest liars as a part of our own personal denial process. When we are forced into a corner, we already know how to talk ourselves out. We've already done it so many times before, in the past. The problem with the intervention is the drug addict will usually agree to whatever is demanded as soon as he realizes it's the only thing that will work at the moment, to put an end to it all. He will go through the motions and he might even attempt to quit for a while to show the 'loved ones' their efforts were successful in ending all of his real life problems. People love to think that they're some kind of hero, and drug addicts will feed into that need as soon as they realize they are being viewed as victims, which is actually a false narrative. There are no victims who are still using drugs, only winners and losers…mostly losers.

The counterproductive part of the intervention is that the intervened (that's you) is almost always guaranteed to relapse, and then the people involved believe the addict is just a loser who cannot be helped. Even if you quit for good, later down the road, they'll always think that you're just going to relapse again someday. I believe when put into this position, the meth addict will always agree to quit. But the addict will always leave a trigger in the back of his mind which will allow him to 'say goodbye' on his own terms. After he thinks he can handle it again (because he has been clean for a period of time) he will try a little on his own terms, with nobody watching. And the downward spiral will start up yet again.

The problem is that most addicts don't realize how much they're also addicted to the drug lifestyle…and if you're ever going to quit for good, you have to do it on your own terms, when and how you determine the process will actually work for you. You have to 'say goodbye' to your drug when you're ready or it won't be final and you'll be back on drugs without a doubt, in the near future. Interventions really only teach an addict who he needs to lie to in the future, or avoid altogether. A meth addict is already an expert on deception, so when he's cornered he knows submission (or the appearance of it) will be the quickest way to get back in the saddle again.

As we move towards the first step of this program, we find the intervention game plan is the exact opposite of how we need to exit the drug world. Instead of cornering the addict and forcing him to 'see the light' and have some sort or epiphany which sends him on the path to recovery, I'll ask you to do the opposite. I know you're still using and forcing you to quit will only lead to some sort of relapse in the future. So, you have to quit when you're ready, on your own terms, and on your own timetable. I tell you this clearly for one reason: a lot of people, who kicked their addictions because they were motivated by an intervention, relapse and feel such guilt after relapsing that they think about and sometimes actually carry out…suicide. I have to point out this fact here, because suicide…really is a 'thing' with drug addicts, and I always shake my head in fear when I hear the word 'intervention' because of this fact. Interventions therefore, must include speech which allows the user to know that family and friends will still be with them should they relapse (to avoid these suicidal tendencies) and therefore the addict reserves again, the trigger which allows such action. Again, full circle back to why this is just another failed system…that has indeed helped thousands of addicts kick in the past. So there you have it, the conundrum of the intervention.

So that's my anti-12 step and 'interventions are lame' speech. You can put that right there in the same jar with my 'you don't need counseling' speech. You counsel yourself if you really want to kick this addiction. You figure out what's wrong with you and you fix it. The entire success of the program lies within your own conviction to quit. Concentrate on your motivation to prove to yourself and the world, that you are indeed capable of such a task. You have within you the power to kick this addiction, while at the same time proving to those who doubt you that you can move on from this horrible experience and regain your social status.

I will always believe that drug counselors only prolong addiction by talking you through it, instead of teaching you how to quit. Most drug counselors have never even been addicted to narcotics and can't really relate to what you're actually going through. Besides, how can you trust the opinion of someone who makes their money as long as you need their help? Doesn't it make sense that it would be in their best interest if they could drag out your addiction to as many counseling sessions as possible? How does that help you if you want to quit right now? You have to believe that the best medicine is you, believing in yourself and your own abilities. That's all a counselor is going to try to teach you anyway. At some point you will realize that they hide no secret pill that reverses the process, and that you will have to do this on your own, without anyone's help. Again, I know the drug counseling business has helped thousands of people in the past, but at what price? It's not in your best interest to feel good about yourself, you're a drug addict. It's in your best interest to quit using drugs as soon as possible, which is the quickest way to regain your self-esteem, self-confidence, and self-respect. You can counsel yourself to kick your own addiction, and then you'll realize that you did it on your own, the only way it really works. This is self-empowerment in every sense of the term. Find the strength within you and get the job done.

I have been slammed hard for these words and my opinions on counseling, as I have stated them as fact in the past, but this is your program and I've already promised you I wouldn't be lying to you. The truth will set you free, right? On with the show....

To say goodbye to meth, you must pick your own quit-date. Sometime in the future you see as a perfect time for you to begin kicking your addiction. You decide when you'll be able to keep this promise to yourself and never use this drug again. It must come from your head, and from your heart. Then I'll show you how to detox your body during the 14-day period starting with your quit-date. No other program would dare say these words or use this risky technique, but I believe in this wholeheartedly. If you're using right now, how am I liable for telling you to keep using until your quit-date? I'm not, that's on you. If you need to throw yourself a big party to say goodbye to meth, it's not a bad idea to do just that, right? You decide when you will kick, and you pick the terms. You make sure you have nothing left when your quit-date arrives. That'll be the last time you ever use meth for the rest of your life, so make sure you don't overdose! The work is just beginning and you finally get that shot at that decent life you've been dreaming about. Stick around so you can see how good it really gets for you. Drug addicts who kick their addiction are super-humans who can do anything, and they usually achieve beyond their own beliefs. There are no relapses and there's no more involvement in the drug lifestyle. You decide when to quit using based on when you think you can handle it best. You say goodbye to the drug, all of your drug stuff and yes, all of your drug friends.

I know that parting with friends is one of the hardest processes of cleaning up. It was hard for me because you think that these are your closest friends and you can't live without them. You feel a sense of abandonment and you fear that they may think less of you or that you're feeling like you're better than they are, when you've all been using the same drugs for so long. The fact is that you are trying to better yourself. The whole process is difficult, and kicking this to better yourself has to include walking away from your enablers. The people you surround yourself with while you're using are only temporary friends anyway, no matter how close you feel to them. Friends never quit at the same time, never…and expecting to stay close to people who are not interested in quitting is impossible. The whole drug lifestyle requires that you live in a bubble, where everyone you know is also addicted to your drug. I'm sorry to tell you that after you clean up, you won't fit in anymore. You'd be a constant reminder of how messed up they are, and that a sober life is indeed possible. After you kick and stop hanging around with your old 'friends,' meth will be their only problem as well. You won't want to be around it, and you will find new friends when your life changes for the better. Good friends with good intentions and a new life with hope, where dreams actually come true.

So, your quit-date…big stuff!

This will be the most important day of your life when you look back. Picking the perfect quit-date for you is important and involves a lot of factors. The most important thing is that you have to believe this will be the beginning of your new life. You have to know in your heart and mind that you are strong enough to get this done now. You have to see this as a final step…an end of an era. And it will also be a new beginning. So your quit-date is very important as the two biggest things in your future will start on the same day, the day you picked. The end of everything that is wrong with your life and the beginning of everything good…when you finally walked away from the mess you got yourself into. The big day!

The idea to kick your meth addiction did not come from me, it came from within you. It has nothing to do with this book or any promise to help you. The promise came after you acquired this book and began reading it on your own. Remember this is a self-help guide for your decision to quit using meth by using this step-by-step plan to self-detox, after you've reached your quit-date. Yes, picking your quit-date is both personal and difficult. This is how you decide when you've had enough. If you're not fed-up with meth and all it has done to you, then you're not ready to quit yet, right? Think long and hard on this.

If you want to kick this on a memorable occasion like a birthday, New Year's Eve, 4th of July, a week from Tuesday…it doesn't matter. As long as you decide in advance when enough is indeed enough. That's your quit-date. The decision of when to quit is on you. Showing you how to detox and how to stay clean after you detox, that's on me.

So the first big step is picking your quit-date. After you finish this chapter, you'll close the book, lay down in a comfortable place with your eyes closed and you'll think about all of the factors surrounding your drug addiction. You'll try to see an ending, a means to an end, and you'll 'make ends meet' …and you'll try to decide when that last day will be…your quit-date. You may not come to a conclusion in one session, but you are introducing this new thought process into your daily routine now. And eventually you will make a choice and it will be in cement. Keep in mind, the sooner the better right?

Please remember the main thing you should know about the detox period is that some days are harder than others. It can all depend on how much meth you go through in a day. The more chemical dependent you are, the more painful the withdrawal symptoms will be.

Functioning addicts and non-functioning addicts

When it comes to planning a quit-date, there are two different types of drug addicts: the functioning addict and the non-functioning addict. The functioning addict is one who keeps up his social status by working and keeping his daily rituals, while the non-functioning addict is one who has already failed on most of these fronts. He has no job and has burned every bridge he's ever walked across. For the record, given more time, every functioning addict would eventually become non-functioning. Some just take more time to get there than others, but all roads lead to the addict being unable to function in the real world, be it a jail cell or a homeless plight.

If you're a fully functioning drug addict, (you still live with hope) you'll want to plan your worst and most painful detox days at home, so the people around you can't spot the obvious withdrawal symptoms you'll be suffering. In this case, you'll have to plan your quit-date around your work or social schedule. This is one of the main points I use when I refer to this as being an anonymous drug treatment program. The functioning addict has been able to fool most of the people in his life while at the same time appearing to be fully functional, even though we know the appearance of normalcy was maintained with drugs. You can keep this appearance without the drug by planning your quit-date around the days that would make your appearance at work or social functions less noticeable as you detox. This will help hide the fact that you are suffering and keep this program anonymous, as promised.

For this example, the average person who works Monday through Friday 9AM to 5PM would have to consider taking his worst detox days at the end of the day Friday and though the weekend. It would be ideal if you could go back to work on Monday with the worst behind you, correct? This can be done, but only if you're very headstrong. The worst part of the detox period can last 4 or 5 days so if you could take a few sick days in there, this would be beneficial to your general health and appearance. Only you know what your job requires and what you can pull off. So, when the time comes you'll have to decide exactly what your needs are at that time. Remember, people do get sick and you will be feeling horrible flu-like symptoms.

If you're a functioning addict who needs this type of plan, you'll want to pick your quit-date on a Wednesday. Typically your body won't miss the chemical too bad on Thursday because it'll still have so much left pumping through your blood stream from the day before. Friday would be a bit difficult but nothing you can't handle, as you've done this in the past, so many times. You may be tired and dragging a bit but a lot of people drag on Friday and it should go unnoticed by your co-workers. The weekend will be hard and you may want to call in sick on Monday, so keep in mind that people do call in sick quite frequently on Monday morning and it should go unnoticed, especially when you appear to still be sick on Tuesday and Wednesday when you do show up. You can always plan your vacation days around this period as well, if your situation allows.

I'm giving you these details for the sake of planning your quit-date so there'll be no surprises that you can use as an excuse to relapse. Nothing new you can claim as a trigger to start using again once your withdrawal symptoms begin slamming you to the ground. Yes, its hard work to detox but this is where you'll step up and take your life back. This is where you'll show yourself how strong you really are. This is when you'll tell your mind and soul that you've had enough and the end has come. This is the part you dread which has kept you addicted for so long, so expect it, accept it, and respect it…for what it is. This is the hard part and after you get through it, you will remember it forever. Eventually, you will even look back and think that kicking this addiction was easy. Trust me on that.

Non-functioning addicts can quit on any schedule they want. You can disappear from the world and nobody would miss you, right? You better believe it. For his reason, quitting is a lot harder for the non-functioning addict. You have no reason to be anywhere, and just about everyone you hang out with is a drug addict as well. Since most of your thought processes are hinged around drugs and the drug lifestyle, quitting takes strength from within, which you rarely find a need for. You have to actually pick yourself up and change everything you do on a daily basis, to things you would never do, or even consider. Don't get me wrong, you can do this…but not on your normal schedule. You'll have to make incredible changes in your life to run away from your current circumstances, to a mindset which holds for you a different fate. So…make it happen. Prepare for the ultimate changes in your life, the changes you always dream about. And start thinking about the steps you will need to take to affect such a change.

For the record, picking a quit-date is a lot easier then actually quitting on the day you picked, when it arrives. So, you have to be stronger in mind and heart then you've ever been in your life. Run far away from your current circumstances if you can. If you can't change where you sleep, you have to be able to change your thought processes. You have to be in a state of mind that's completely impenetrable. You need to get to a place in your mind where nothing can change your efforts to quit, once you officially start this program. This quit-date, this is it.

Cold Turkey vs Weaning (Tapering)

Before you get to your quit date, you'll have to decide if you are going to try to wean yourself off of meth, or kick the addiction cold-turkey. This is an important decision for a drug addict because both methods are valid techniques, and the choice has to be made by the user. People addicted to meth usually have to kick cold turkey, because weaning really doesn't work well for meth addictions, and such. Heroin is a different drug altogether, and many ex-addicts have had the ability to slowly taper their daily dose before their quit date arrives, making the horrible withdrawal symptoms associated with kicking an opioid addiction much easier to handle. Kicking your addiction cold turkey has a finish-line at the end which you aim for (your quit date), and the goal is to tough-it-up when you get to the end of the line.

In this event, kicking cold turkey brings out the best of who we are. You plan your quit date, you follow the process, you plan your escape…then you tough it up and quit, knowing the horrible pains of withdrawal will be addressed by this program, and you suck-it-up and take the hits that you have coming. Cold turkey is a wall at the end of the line and once you jump the wall, your drug addiction is in the rearview and you just follow the process until the pain subsides. You are left at the end of your addiction with a strong understanding of what addiction was, what it takes to get through it, and how it feels to walk away from an addiction forever. This makes you strong, in both mind and spirit. You grip hard the fact that you just quit one day, on your own, from inside you.

That said, weaning yourself off of meth is another technique that can work for you, if you plan it out and stick to the plan, focusing on the quit date that you have already thought about. Weaning can begin at any time, including tomorrow. If you are already in the process of weaning yourself off drugs, it may even help you to focus on picking your quit-date as you read through these pages. I like to think that each addict has the ability to put their own weaning program into effect, but that's just not true, as your mind won't always let you run the game. For this and other reasons, if you are thinking about weaning, you should concentrate on half-doses. What I mean by that is that I believe you are currently using twice as much as you should, if you are entering a program to kick for life.

This is easier for the opioid addict who uses pills because you can easily gauge your daily requirements, and cut them right down the middle. This may seem harsh but it's the best way to approach the beginning of the end. You cut all of your pills in half, and you take them as often as you always have, eventually extending the hours in between, to slowly wean yourself off of the drug, with your quit date in mind. When your quit date nears, you will cold turkey the drug on your predetermined quit date. The weaning will allow you to get through the detox period with far less withdrawal symptoms, as you will actually have started the withdrawal process with the wean.

Those who slam meth have a much harder time convincing themselves of what a half-dose actually means.

When you measure your own dose, the trick of the game is to realize that your brain doesn't really want you to cut your doses in half. You will have to watch for the triggers where your mind is always telling you that 'just a little bit over half' is probably better than a half dose. For these and other reasons, you will have to rely on your new found inner strength to make sure that your weaning process is on-course for actually cutting down. It does no good for you to believe that in the process of weaning, you can give yourself a full dose for just one day. You cannot do this. This is just a trigger your mind is using to get you back on the horse. Be careful to identify every urge you have to cheat, as a trigger that is working against you. Find strength in the next few chapters to help you with your weaning and cut your doses in half, if you believe that weaning would be better for you than kicking cold turkey.

If you find yourself failing on the weaning technique, you will be forced to kick cold turkey, against your will. Be clear with what I am saying here: 'against your will' because this whole program is your will, done by you alone. If you decide to wean and you find you don't have the will-power to pull it off, then you will have to figure out how to survive the horrors of kicking cold turkey, a feat that a million people have already pulled off. Always remember that '*what one man can do, another man can do*' as well. Say that over and over during the kicking process; *what one man can do, another man can do*. And remember that you are using the same process that a million people before you have already used to kick successfully, forever.

Be clear to yourself with the understanding that this is something you can do, no matter what methods you decide to use in your program. Addicts who use pills tend to have a better grip on half doses, but the strength to proceed with your personal treatment program involves you, and your understanding of your own mind, body, and spirit. And you don't have to figure this out right now. This is just another part of the process, you figuring out exactly how you will exit the drug world. You got this, my friend, chin-up.

Think big, be big!

At this point, you just keep reading and all of the answers will come to you at the right times. Now you know what's going on and what has to be done. You continue reading and you will think about all of these words when you're not reading them. And always feel free to go back and read the chapters again. There's so much more information in the following chapters that will help you to round out this program in your head. And don't worry; all of the answers are here in the following pages.

Like I said, you can plan your quit-date around any occasion or no occasion at all. *Quitting is quitting*. Yes, you can quote me.

Now, close the book and think hard about picking a quit-date. Peace.

Chapter 6

The human brain

The brain is the most complex organ in the human body. It is absolutely responsible for your drug addiction, and also holds the key to your successful exit from the drug world in which you live. Yes, it is the cause of your addiction, and it has the ability to provide you with the entire solution. When you let your mind control you like a puppet, you're purposely delaying your treatment, and when you learn how to control your mind, you'll be able to free yourself from all of its boundaries.

As we talk about your brain, we are talking about two distinctive entities which are the same, yet completely separate from each other. Your brain is made up of 1) the physical organ and 2) the mind; the complex computer-like mechanism which controls and memorizes all of your thought processes and patterns. The physical brain works like the other organs in your body. Your blood flows through it, and it provides the thought processes which maintain your body, to help you live a long life. Your mind works together and independently from the physical brain, to satisfy your short and long term needs and interests (among other things). You need to understand that both your physical brain and your mind are separately and collectively addicted to meth. In this case, your physical brain is addicted to meth by a chemical dependency…and your mind is addicted to meth because of its unique qualities, including the ability to persuade you into believing that you are at peace, and therefore the drug helps to convince your mind that it's running in a better and more efficient mode. Meth is brain candy, which feeds into its own belief that all is well, as long as you keep the candy flowing. Your brain loves its candy and your mind loves it as well. That's part of the reason you're a slave to the drug now, because of the physical addiction and because of the minds own ability to convince you that it needs its candy. You need to see this duel addiction and understand it clearly because both addictions are different and must be addressed separately.

To gain access to the mind, we have to go back and learn about the brain in a different way. Back to the beginning, as it applies to your current drug addiction. You can call this lesson *Human Brain 101* if you like, but I think we should talk about this as if you have no idea how your mind works. I think it would be a waste of time if I went on-and-on using scientific terms about the brain or to show you rhetorical information that has no meaning to you or bearing on your treatment. **Science has already failed the addict by producing data that documents the facts while offering no simple solution to the addict for overcoming the addiction**. We already know **the facts** so let's skip the confusing details. All you really need to know are the basics, like you might explain it to a curious child.

The brain as it applies to drug addiction

As you were probably taught in school, the human brain is a blank slate at birth. Most scientists believe we're born with no memory, just innate emotion and basic functionality. As you experience life, your mind learns and records images and data, and gains different cognitive abilities as you grow. Inherited personality and genetic traits, along with your personal intellect and the decisions you make in life, will mold who you are as a person as well as what makes you different from others. Although scientists may never understand all of the complexities of the mind, it's only necessary for us to figure out how your thought processes are influenced by both your addiction and chemical dependency. To do this we'll have to get a better view of the brain itself. *So, let's step inside...*

I want you to use your imagination here. I want you to picture yourself walking into a huge empty warehouse, so wide and deep you can hardly see the sides and back walls. When you look up, you can see that the ceiling is about 5 or 6 stories high and closes like a dome. On the ground level there are doors every 3 or 4 feet along the walls, all the way around, opening and closing in a helter-skelter fashion, at will. On the floor you see thousands of wooden pallets, all empty and placed neatly in rows, with 2 feet of isle space on all four sides. Thousands of wooden pallets as far as the eye can see, all the way to the back wall and all of them empty. As you look up to the ceiling you notice that above the doors are thousands of windows all the way to the top. None of them are in any order and they appear to be spaced at random in various sizes and shapes and angles.

This is how I want you to picture the inside of the brain of a newborn baby. This is your blank slate; an empty warehouse with no information to process and no memories to record and review.

In this scenario, the doors represent the brain itself while the windows represent the mind. Through the constant opening and shutting we can imagine how these doors represent the motor functions of the automated innate brain. How our bodies run on an apparent automatic flow of demands that keep us alive and well, even while we sleep. The doors control breathing, blood flow, heart rhythm, hearing, and all of your senses…and even dreaming. The windows on the other hand, that's where the magic begins.

I want you to picture the baby's eyes opening for the first time. It looks out into the world and the windows of the mind start opening and closing, just like the doors. Each window that opens sends a ray of light inside, as if the sun were directly above the dome and the angles between the different windows and the warehouse floor cause each window to shed light onto a different pallet. Stay with me here...

Each time a window is opened, a ray of sunlight hits a certain pallet and a box with information inside is created and now placed on that pallet. That box now represents a certain memory and will be forever in its place inside the mind. The eyes create video images that are recorded and stacked on the pallet where the mind has decided it should rest. Senses are recorded and placed on their perspective pallets and the boxes start stacking up. Smells and tastes, likes and fears, and all different types of emotions are being learned and remembered until there are enough to begin forming opinions. The boxes are being stacked and sorted for future reference…simple things like 'bananas are my favorite' and the memories of eating a banana, and the smells and tastes associated with that memory, all stored in different boxes for different reasons.

The mind just can't get enough. It starts saving everything, and it likes to sort the boxes and rearrange them so that certain memories can trigger a plethora of information on different topics in a moment's notice. It produces new pallets with new information as it sees fit. For instance, the pallet which holds the information about how much you enjoyed the smell and taste of the banana, is also the go-to location of all things you prefer to eat. The mind also creates a pallet full of boxes for the things you don't like to eat, and the smells which you have determined you hate. And so on, and so on, throughout your life.

These basic examples stretch with the minds own ability to grow and learn. By the time you reach high school, the boxes are stacked so high they almost touch the ceiling. Inside each box is a memory and each pallet is an organized thought or group of ideas, and your mind has figured out how you want everything categorized and you can re-stack any box or pallet at will. Memories are all dated with the most recent thoughts on top, easy to recall. And the past is full of faded memories that have been outshined and upstaged by newer, more interesting events. But they're all in there. All of your life's events, all of your past thoughts, and all of your trials and tribulations are all stored in your mind, forever.

Your mind knows everything you have ever done or thought. It knows what events have led you to your current circumstances and it also reserves the right to use this information for its own needs as well. And right now, with the introduction of methamphetamines into your bloodstream, and because of your chemical dependency, your mind wants meth every single day. And it knows how to persuade you to stay on course, using all of your past memories against you, to acquire…its candy. And it is as simple as that. Your brain is now physically addicted to meth by the chemical dependency and your mind is a spoiled rotten child, who just wants candy…and knows exactly how to use you to acquire it.

So, there you have it. Your brain is like a huge warehouse with doors and windows and data is stored just like your home computer stores data. Your entire life structure depends on the mental and physical health of your brain and body. To keep yourself healthy, you've developed a daily routine which involves waking up, eating meals, exercise, learning, interacting with others, doing things that make you happy and content…and eventually slipping back into bed for a good night's sleep. At the end of every day, the body and mind need to rejuvenate. The human body needs to rest and so does the brain. The windows and doors of your mind need to close so you can rest and rejuvenate for the next waking period. Resting the body keeps you healthy and resting the mind keeps you sane.

Remember that *your body and mind are all about sleep, and meth is all about keeping you awake in order to keep the windows of the mind open,* and to persuade you to acquire more drugs. This is now your daily routine and also one of the main reasons for most of your problems.

When a person is not addicted to drugs, the human body tires out at the end of the day and forces the body and the mind to rest up for the next waking period. And that's how it's supposed to work. Before you introduced your body and mind to meth, you would sleep every night and you functioned normally during the day. Sleeping was your rejuvenation period and while you slept, your brain would minimize its capabilities while your body got the rest it needed to function properly, again, during the next waking period. With the introduction of meth into your daily ritual, even while the body rests, the mind operates with most of its windows open all of the time. Meth is all about skipping sleep cycles as much as possible, and keeping the doors and windows of the mind fully functioning all of the time. You may feel like the drug puts you into a tranquil peaceful sleep sometimes after it wears off, but the truth is you never really approach the REM sleep that's required by the human body to fully recover, both physically and mentally.

Rapid eye movement (REM) sleep occurs in the last 1/3 of a natural night's sleep when your brain delves into the dream process, where the physical body eases all function while the brain enters a dream state, where the eyes are known to bounce around as you enter the deep sleep phase of your recovery period. This is a crucial part of the sleeping process most meth addicts never have the chance to enter, because of the inherent effects and side-effects of the drug. There are several terms devised for missing this crucial part of your sleeping experience including *REM sleep behavior disorder, REM deprivation, dream deprivation*, etc. But all of these terms refer to the same problem of how the human mind is affected by a sleep deprivation.

When your body and mind are sleep deprived, the long-term effects can actually change your body's metabolism, among other things. You have probably felt this for a long time now that you are walking around in a constant daze. You've probably thought this was because of the never-ending drug cycle, but it's actually caused by the lack of sleep, straight up. This constant wake-and-shake has changed how you think and who you are as a person, and the 'real you' is buried inside an abused mind that can't see the light of day because it never really gets the rest that it needs to function normally, or in a normal state.

Despite the fact that you may disagree or think this is not all true, you need your '8 hours of sleep' for your body and mind to function normally, and with all of the partial sleep periods mixed with waking up over and over, the natural feeling of being well rested and attacking the new day is completely missing in your life. And this partial on and off sleep (when you can sleep), which has become a huge part of your daily routine is literally driving you crazy. You have most likely felt this way many times, like you are literally going crazy, but what's actually happening is that you are suffering from extreme sleep deprivation.

Without reaching the REM sleep phase, which allows your mind a full recovery, you are actually sleep deprived…and because of that you now appear to suffer from a mental disability. You can't keep your thoughts in order, and you walk around in a deep fog because your brain is not working properly anymore. It doesn't have the ability to process information adequately because it's just so tired. You can't seem to get a grip on how other people are able to function and again, you've thrown in the towel and now believe you are different from other people, mentally.

I know you've felt this time and time again, but believe me when I tell you that this is not true at all. The mental problems you are suffering from are reversible. I hope you hear these words loud and clear. Where you may have been convinced that any mental problems were caused by your meth addiction, they're actually caused by the sleep deprivation associated with your meth use. When the chemical dependency on meth is eliminated, the sleep cycle of normalcy returns, and most mental disabilities caused by these processes can be reversed as well. You just need a good night's sleep. So let's talk about sleep deprivation.

Sleep Deprivation and the Human Brain

One of the main problems with meth addiction is sleep deprivation (now, think about that sentence for a minute). Despite what you may already believe, it is the single most problematic event in a drug addict's life, and meth literally guarantees the user will become chronically sleep deprived. Even when the addict's body shuts down in an instant, the mind can still keep up with its calculations, until it solves every problem the disordered mind of the drug addict thinks it has. At this point, most of the normal thought processes of the addict have entered a delusional stage, where the facts and figures, and the puzzles the mind is attempting to solve, are delusional as well. The addict has entered a new realm where fantasy and reality are intertwined and he can't tell the real difference between the two, which can often lead to depression, as well as a variety of other mental disorders often misdiagnosed by well-educated individuals who just don't understand what's really going on in the disordered mind of the addict.

To the addict, these twisted thoughts and images are all too real, and situations which present themselves need to be either addressed or ignored, by decision. Much of this has to do with how much meth the addict has, and how soon he will need more drugs. Above all concerns brought to the table by the mind, the addict will subvert all to obtain more drugs. The mind needs its candy and at this late point in the addiction cycle, the addict would do anything required to sidestep any task in order to obtain and use more meth. Hence, once the addict starts to suffer from acute sleep deprivation, all of the rules to the game have changed entirely. Sleep deprivation can be caused by a mental disorder, but when a person uses meth, sleep is being deprived intentionally, by design. Though this is not known to the user at the time, it's the long-term effects of sleep deprivation which supplies the addict the miserable life in which he lives.

Though hallucinations have always been attributed to drug addicts, meth is not a psychedelic or hallucinogenic drug at all. Meth use on its own does not make the user see things that are not there. It's the side-effects of sleep deprivation which cause the mind of the addict to start seeing hallucinations. It is also the side effect of sleep deprivation which causes the user to become psychotic, displaying symptoms which appear to mimic those often attributed to drug addiction such as depression, anxiety, withdrawal from family and friends, delusions, hallucinations, aggressive behavior, suicidal tendencies, and suspiciousness towards other people (and sometimes objects as well). Because of the sleep deprivation, long term meth use alters brain chemistry in the user and causes distortions in thought patterns, as well as an unrealistic perception of one's surroundings. It is these factors which separate the meth user from users of most other drugs. Besides methamphetamine, which is designed to keep the user awake as well, most other drugs include symptoms which would otherwise relax the user, eventually causing them to fall asleep. The problem is not the quantity of the sleep you believe you have, but the quality of sleep for which you are lacking. In this respect, you have to start believing that your outward problems do not lie on who or what you have become because of your drug addiction, but what has become of you because of your sleep deprivation.

I tell you this because you have probably never heard nor thought of this before. In this respect, meth addiction is a double edged sword which leads you into a chemical dependency, while at the same time causing you to suffer from mental instability caused by sleep deprivation. So listen closely to these words; in the case of your drug addiction, there are definite correlations to the causes and effects of your drug use and the horrors caused or created by sleep deprivation. Meth use is a different animal altogether, and sleep deprivation is the primary reason behind the insanity which can turn an ordinary person into a despicable human being, capable of all things, as you are well aware. Now take a breath and let that sink into your new thought process. I always say that the best thing you can give a drug addict is a good night's sleep. So, that absolutely is the goal here. We are working towards a new life that focuses on real sleep, with real waking periods. That's how you will heal yourself.

When you never achieve REM sleep your mind can't rest and it no longer processes information in a normal fashion. When you use these types of drugs, you speed up and slow down the normal functions of the brain, and the doors and windows begin slamming open and shut at record speeds…and then hardly at all. Information is stored and processed and reprocessed for no other reason but to keep the mind active, and at times your mind just gives up because of the introduction of a new fix. While you 'rest' your mind starts to dig deeper and deeper into your past memories, because it has already checked and rechecked all of the new information and needs something else to do. You become extremely dysfunctional because your mind can't process information normally anymore. Meth leads to the delusions of the mind, again by design. Soon, staying awake turns into sleep deprivation and the constant opening and closing of the windows starts to wear on your sanity. Your body shuts down and brain function halts altogether. This causes memory loss and the new function is now similar to the zombie that you are well aware of. He scavenges through the night with his brain functioning now in a half state of consciousness with a single goal; to find some way in the night to help you acquire the means to possess and use meth on the following day. Be it working or digging through trash cans for recyclables or other goods, or breaking into cars or homes, the goal is realized almost every day. Somebody hits the mother lode, and you are good to go for yet another day.

Your brain loves to do its job but with the chemical influence of meth, it tricks itself into believing it's still making progress on your future, but for the necessity of acquiring more drugs because of the chemical dependency. Yes, your brain loves meth now, which is a fact. This drug allows it to function like a super brain which controls your every move, capable of easing your pain and relaxing your spirit. Because of this super brain function, meth really does allow you to function in a quasi-normal state at times, and to some extent, even better than most other people. But eventually the whole process inches you closer and closer to insanity. With all of your windows and doors operating at a limited capacity, your mind is now confused as to how to identify and sort new information, and it gets lost as to where and when to store It, and when and how to recover it as needed. Because of this pattern of confusion, your mind has now become disoriented. It doesn't know how to relay to you basic signals which were used to protect you, and now has you feeling disoriented, perplexed, baffled, bewildered, and confused as well. And this form of indecisiveness is what leads you to believe that you are losing your mind. And when you relay these feelings to any professional, they will always see you as having one or many mental disorders. And they would be correct. But grip it hard...that all of this is reversible. The path you are on right now will take you out of this fog and deliver you to the promise land. Stay on the path and you will fix yourself. You just need to understand and respect the process.

The real problem is that you need your sleep. Your brain has to power-down to stay healthy but it really doesn't want to. So, the mind uses all of its influences to keep the meth coming and to keep you addicted, because it loves the feeling of complete control over you. Whatever it takes to keep the doors and windows open, the mind will figure it out and implement plans at all costs to your physical needs and social calendar. Your mind possesses an arsenal of weapons to use against your common sense. *It even has the ability to change your common sense* or any other sense you might use to try to exclude meth from your daily ritual. Always remember that your mind is all that you are, and all you ever were. Minor or major, every decision you've ever made is hidden in your mind, along with the deciding points you pondered to convince yourself of the outcome. All of your thought processes were conceived in your mind and decided on…in your mind. And all emotions involved in those decisions are still stored…you guessed it, in your mind. *Your brain runs your body and your mind...runs you. And that is why you're addicted to meth.*

As you live and breathe, the ever-powerful meth is now the wonder drug of your brain. The drug now gives you the ability to stay awake when needed, and to sleep when it decides the time is right. And all of these moments are now directly linked to your drug use. When you have your drug you can rest. Meanwhile, your body tries to rejuvenate for the next waking period, or zombie hunt, for sources of income to pay for your habit.

The power of the mind now includes a chemical dependency. It went from '*loves meth*' to '*needs meth*' as the chemical is now needed in your bloodstream for you to function normally. If you try to take the chemical away now, you will suffer from brutal withdrawal symptoms. Like it or not, your mind is up to the task. Needing meth makes it even more logical to teach you how to obtain it on a daily basis, right? The mind has no shame. Shame was one of your first personality traits it tossed out the window, along with a little bit of pride and honor and self-respect...soon to be followed by faith, dignity and hope.

Your mind is in control of all of your senses and emotions now. With the power to operate at this intense new level of consciousness, your mind finds it easy to convince you to keep a close relationship with all those around you. It wants to keep you around people with the same needs, while at the same time distancing you from those family and friends who would try to steer you down a better path. The people you used to count on slowly become your enemies, while your friends are a scattered group of rejects you would never have associated with in a million years before you became addicted...but your mind convinces you otherwise. You are convinced that you are also one of those rejects and being in this 'club' is a natural way for you to express yourself. If everybody you know is a meth addict, how can it be wrong? Like the old song says…"if loving you is wrong, I don't wanna be right"…and there we sit.

This is mind control, by the way. When you start to believe what your mind tells you as fact, without reasoning. When you reshape who and what you are to accommodate a drug addiction, you're giving in to the suggestions of a mind that has an ulterior motive. It wants to stay in control of you, and it wants its doors and windows open. Not that putting up a fight would work for you anyway, right? The mind is hard to control if you don't realize what's happening to you, and take a course of action to correct it. To kick this addiction you'll have to figure out how to convince your mind that you're no longer interested in being tricked into using drugs. You'll have to get past the attempts of a mind that knows everything about you, and all of the triggers which have kept you addicted up to this point. **You'll have to start giving orders instead of taking them.**

To figure out how to avoid your mind's attempts to persuade you to 'keep up the good work' you'll have to learn how to make it so your senses and your emotions have no bearing on your addiction. Since your mind has used emotional triggers to keep you addicted, you'll have to understand that bringing up old thoughts or emotions are easy for your mind to do. It sorts through your history to find these triggers and uses them to convince you that there is good reason for you to continue using meth at this time in your life. Since these mind techniques have been so successful in the past at getting you to seek out and obtain drugs, you'll be swarmed with this kind of mental pain, guilt, and emotion as a standard attempt to convince you to start using the drug again, once you have started fazing it out of your life. Once your brain realizes you're attempting to quit, it will pursue every trick in the book to get you to relapse, and always remember…*it wrote the book.*

What your mind needs to know is that this time things are going to be different. Real changes are taking place here and this is not an attempt to kick your drug addiction...this is the end. This end comes with a new beginning and there'll be no more war of words and thoughts and tricks. It's over and it will be done, and this will be another box on another pallet in a row, stacked as a memory of things that used to be. You must now teach your mind to discontinue all attempts at a relapse.

Easier said than done, right? You always knew your brain was in control of you, but having this information never came with a quick fix. So I'll have to teach you a few different techniques to gain control over your mind. The first and most important, I like to call "a ball of bad memories."

Chapter 7

A ball of bad memories

You'll find you hate meth the most when you're in possession of a nice quantity that'll last you at least a few days. The reason for this is because when you have a lot of your drug, your mind doesn't have to waste any energy trying to get you to obtain more. It only has to get you to use the meth you already have. You feel peaceful and at ease, if that's at all possible, right? This is when you think about quitting the most.

When you're running low or completely out of meth, your mind will never let you think about how much you hate using. It only reminds you of how great the drug is, and all of the good things you like about it, and how you need to acquire more, as soon as possible. If you could flip a switch in your mind that would turn off the cravings for meth when it was trying to persuade you to re-up then you wouldn't be an addict, would you? It's when you have no drugs that your mind works the hardest to persuade you, so this reoccurring moment is the frontline on your counter attack. You need to learn how to be strongest at this pivotal point, when your mind is in its best form.

The trick you need to learn is how to flip this switch off, so you can control the cravings when you're completely out of the drug, which controls your every thought. You can do this by learning a simple mind trick I call "*a ball of bad memories*" as a counter attack to your minds-own power of persuasion. You can do this by countering your meth cravings with a '*memory stampede*' of all of the horrible things this drug has done to ruin your life. With all of the powers your mind will use against you to make you crave meth, I want you to create a new file in your brain, and I want that file stuck in a bubble (or ball) and stacked on top of the tallest box, on the tallest pallet in your mind.

In that ball, I want you to put everything you hate the most about your drug addiction. Think hard about anything and everything in your life that makes you regret being a drug addict. Think about all of the hate, the pain, and the burned bridges, all of it. And put it all in the same place where you can keep it and recall it at a moment's notice. Include your memories of all of the horrible things you've done in order to support your drug addiction. This is your 'ball of bad memories'. It will always be easy to access because you're going to place it on top of every other feeling and memory you have. It's put there so you can recall it every time you have a craving for meth, after you've finally had enough. This is not complicated and having this tool will help you to easily counter the triggers in your mind that most often get you to relapse.

The easiest way for you to mount a counter-attack against your meth cravings, is to bring up your 'ball of bad memories' when your mind is trying to trick you into thinking you want more meth, right now. Using this ball of bad memories will counter the minds 'cheap tricks' with actual facts that remind you of why you're quitting, and what misery this drug has caused you in the past. If you stay firm and in focus, the stored bad memories will soften your minds attempts to get you to relapse, and eventually dissuade them altogether.

After you have built a strong and full *ball of bad memories,* you can recall it at a moment's notice, each time you feel the craving for meth. You'll remember that you have this weapon stashed in your mind and you access the ball and look through the files to remember all of the bad times, and the things that you hate most about the drug and yourself…and the cravings will slowly disappear. As you get better with recalling this ball, your glimpse through the ball will be quicker and the cravings for your drug will disappear at a much faster rate. As you become a pro at this form of recall, the cravings will fade as fast as you decide to go for the ball. Eventually, you can make the cravings for meth completely disappear in the matter of a few seconds. I know this sounds very hard to believe right now, but that's why this step is so important. After your mind knows that you are attempting to block the cravings, it will stop the attempts altogether and the cravings will fade away and then disappear entirely.

I know this sounds a bit lame, and way too good to be true, right? Trust me when I tell you that this mind exercise will change your life. This is a direct attack on one of the most vital triggers your mind uses to keep you addicted. It's important that you take this seriously, no matter how it sounds to you or how your mind will attempt to intervene in your thought process by telling you how this exercise just proves how lame the whole program is…because this is how the mind has fooled you into this long lasting addiction, which rules your life. Use this tool as a training mechanism to let your mind know that it is not intervening in this new action. You will learn to control your mind now, as your mind has been controlling you this whole time. Yes, this is mind control, absolutely. And it's very similar to the processes your mind has been using to control you all of this time. This is merely an attempt to alter your current thought processes; those which are keeping you addicted right now, against your will.

Believe it or not, this is the best mind control technique you'll ever use. And you can learn this important technique and apply it as a self-imposed trigger, and you'll see for yourself the power it has over your mind's influence. After a short period of time, your mind will stop tempting you with cravings and it will just give up, because it knows you're seriously trying to kick this addiction, and attempting to get you to crave meth through its normal channels just won't work anymore. The problem is that after you master this technique, your mind will start working on better solutions to its new problem: *baby still want's its candy.*

After you figure out how to get a handle on the triggers that use cravings to get you back in the game, your mind will start working to try to develop new triggers that don't already exist in its normal scheme of keeping you addicted. Your mind will soon work on new techniques to persuade you back to meth, techniques that won't so much use cravings as it will use well-thought-out plays on your senses, emotions, and memories. We'll address those issues when the time comes but first things first, right?

The first thing we need to do is work on you…*so, let's build this ball.*

This mind-game is so important you'll need to spend some real time getting this right. I want you to actually pull out a piece of paper and I want you to make a list of everything you can think of that causes you to hate your meth addiction, and your current situation. If you think you can skip this step, you're wrong, you need this. Get out a piece of paper and a pen, and start with number one, and then you keep going. Try to pick the top ten things that make you want to quit and write them down. I want to see things from your heart and your head. Make it count and you will make this work. I want to see things like;

1. My family hates me now

2. I feel like such a loser

3. I have nothing and nobody cares if I live or die

4. I hate jail and I hate being worried every time I see a cop

5. I'm always broke and I don't even have a car

6. I can't get a job and I can't get a bank account

7. I'm always dirty and my teeth hurt and I feel sick inside and out

8. I have screwed up so bad, so many times like…the time I…

9. I'm so tired of all the lies and thinking that I'm fooling people...and

10.   I ripped off so much stuff and I have nothing to show for my life

11.   I don't even know my kids, they deserve better

12.   I'm killing myself and nobody cares

13.   I'm hanging out with a bunch of losers and I know they ripped me off

14.   I lost everything and everybody that was important to me

15. I remember the time I was on meth and I...(remember all of the bad things)

16. I used to be so strong and now I'm so pathetic...

17. I'm going crazy because of this stuff and I keep doing stupid stuff...

18. I don't care about anything except meth and how to get it...

19. I tired of being a paranoid and schizophrenic junkie...

20. I hate needing meth to get through every single day...

21. I am so tired of being broke all of the time.

22. I have nothing...

23. I hate myself inside and I feel depressed all of the time..

24. I wish I was dead, I'm always thinking about dying

25. I sleep in filth and I'm sick all of the time

Now pick through your thoughts that are not on this list. Come on now, you write from your heart and your soul. Close your eyes and make it hurt. Make this list personal and accurate and if it doesn't bring tears to your eyes, start over and look deeper into who and what you've become.

Yes, this is a soul search. Close your eyes and dig deep and put it on paper...it has to be on paper. Do not move on in this book until you believe your list includes all of the things that you think about, when you wish you knew how to quit. Remember all of the bridges you've burned and take a good look into your soul and figure out why you hurt...and put it on paper. When you are positive you have it all, and not until that moment, read on. Take a day or two if you need it, but make this list full and complete. This is a very important step in your full recovery from meth. Dig deep and write it down. Remember everything, all of the horrible memories you have that make you hate being hooked on this drug.

Continue on until your list is full and complete.

Now we're making progress. Now we have something to work with. These are the bad memories that will help you kick this addiction…so here we go.

I want you to hold that list in front of you and I'm going to ask you to do another strange thing. I want you to close your eyes and picture a round clear bubble about the size of a large softball and I want it to be floating about six inches above your head, but over to the right side when you bend your head a little bit to the left. Now try that. Picture the ball floating above your head.

This will be your ball of bad memories after you fill it with the memories on the list. When you picture the clear ball with your eyes closed, make it always appear above your head, about six inches up and over to the right. That's where it belongs…it just keeps popping up there when you think of it. You will learn to produce this ball and everything inside it, when you need to, at a moment's notice…and that moment is when you feel temptation. When you feel a craving for meth, you will produce the ball and everything inside of it.

Now, fill the bubble. Start with the first thing on your list and add it into the ball. Picture each memory in order on your list, and place them in the ball, one at a time. As you place these bad memories inside the ball, you will be able to see each of them individually, and eventually you will be able to see them all at the same time, as a group of memories. And all of them together have extreme influence on how you really feel about your meth use. This will become one strong memory of why you don't want to be a meth addict anymore, because of all of those reasons, grouped together collectively. And you'll be able to recall all of the memories you are storing in this ball. You are actually pulling these memories from different boxes in your mind, from different pallets, and placing them on a new pallet on top of all of the old pallets, in a new box you are creating right now. This new box will contain only your *ball of bad memories* and you will store it on top of everything else you have in your mind, for easy access. It will be the most important memory you have, easy to recall in a moment's notice.

Learning this technique begins the process of your personal take-back of your mind and how it controls you. Now you're taking all of your powers of memory and putting the worst ones on top, so you can remember the most important things about your addiction without your own mind trying to blur the process. Whatever your mind tells you from this point on, you do not allow anything (any memory) to replace the information you have re-sorted and stored on the top of all other memories. This ability to recall the horrors you have lived through is a powerful tool to combat the addiction cycle. This is your new hope; focus on the *ball of bad memories*, focus on the truth. This is your new best friend. Treat her right.

I hope all of this stuff is making sense to you now. Ok, let's move on. Read the list and place all of the memories in the bubble above your head. Try to picture them as a group, and try to see them all together at one time. Collectively and individually, all at once, inside the ball you've created, above your head, to the right. Whenever you get a chance, try to pull up the ball and look inside it to see the images that you've now created. This ball is your first and best tool, so practice and imagine that you are pulling it out, and then sticking it back in your head. Do you get that? Practice pulling the ball out of your mind and placing it in its spot above your head and to the right, and then put in back inside your brain. This is your exercise. Pull it out, and put it back in. And learn how to be able to do that at a moment's notice, when you have a craving for meth. You crave and you pull it out to remember, at a moment's notice, everything you hate about the drug and how it has affected you. The goal here is to pull it out every time your mind starts craving meth. This is a deterrent to stop your mind from tempting you into wanting your drug. Every time you feel the need, remember the ball of bad memories and picture the memories you have stored inside.

As you practice this technique, you will see the power and how it makes the cravings go away. And with time and practice you will teach yourself to pull this up so fast that it won't even matter anymore. The cravings will vanish as fast as they appeared, and eventually your mind will just stop making you crave meth at all. And that's half the battle right there, correct? If you didn't crave meth, you wouldn't feel the need to acquire and use the drug. Once you've knocked out the cravings, you can concentrate on beating your chemical dependency problem. You've always believed that if you had no cravings, you wouldn't be an addict, right?

For the record, I'm teaching you this technique now because it'll be used after your quit-date and will be one of your main weapons after you have actually quit using meth. It's important you work on this now so that when you actually have to use it, you'll know exactly what it is, what it's for, and how it works. This technique is for you to use after you quit, but it's so important that you put this in place when you can still feel the pain and abuse of the drug you're trying to kick. After you quit using, these painful memories will fade, and your mind knows it has more power over time. So, work on this now and you will use it later. On with the show…

Defining your motivation

Defining your motivation is a lot like *a ball of bad memories* in that both of these techniques contain lists that could be posted on your refrigerator, like a child's school drawings. I'll even go as far as to say that if you are in a private setting where you feel comfortable, posting these lists on your fridge is not a bad idea. You can memorize them or you can post them where you see them all of the time, as a reminder. This is important stuff so no need to minimize unless you're in a situation where you have to hide things that are private.

Defining your motivation is the basic first step in achieving anything of value or substance in your life. Like the list you just created, there are so many things in your past you wish you could change, and these are the things you're working on now, so let's make another list. The big difference is this list will be all positive. Positive motivation is a powerful tool, as you'll see.

One of the main problems with any addiction is that the user can't seem to find the motivation to quit. Therefore it's very important that your reasons for quitting are clear and personal to you. The factors which have kept you addicted for so long must be taken away and replaced by new factors that are your personal motivation for completing this program effectively. I want you to think long and hard about all of the reasons that brought you to this program. Then I want you to write them down on a piece of paper and put them in order, according to how important they are to you.

In the future, when you are clean, people will ask you questions about your addiction like "How did you become addicted?" and "Why did it take you so long to quit?" Your answers will change almost every time you reply. They're not easy questions with easy answers. They're deep, long, and involved conversations and the reasons are many. I don't want the same thing to happen when you're asked questions like "How did you quit?" or more importantly "Why did you quit?"

Defining your motivation should leave you with a straight and focused answer with only a few reasons. You need to know in your heart and in your mind, what this is all about. This is a big part of the process.

"I quit because I hated the lifestyle" or "I quit for my kids" or "I got tired of going to jail" or "I couldn't stand looking at myself in the mirror and I wanted a better life" and such. There are as many reasons to quit as there are days in the year, but I want you to take a deep hard look inside your head, heart, and soul - and start writing down all of the reasons that **you** want to quit. Putting this all on paper is a very important step for your mind right now. You'll write this list and then break it down to the strongest points, so you can focus on your motivation for quitting throughout this program. You won't need this list in the future because it'll be so short and important to you, that eventually you'll have it memorized.

First, I want you to write down everything you can think of. Define your motivation on paper. List all of the reasons which have been haunting you so that you'll always remember that your short list was once a long one. Write it now. Include things from my list if you like.

---I need to change my life now.
---I want my pride and dignity back
---I want to be trusted and counted on again.
---I want to quit for my kids. They need a better parent.
---I want my family back. I want them to look up to me again.
---I want to contribute to society and my family.
---I want a house and a nice car and a great job and extra money.
---I want my life back.
---I don't want to be a slave to a drug anymore.
---I want to feel hope and pride and success.
---I want new friends who believe in me for who I am.
---I want to be happy, all of the time.
---I want to be in charge of my destiny and leave this life of self-destruction.
---I want to hold my head up high because I know that I kicked the most addictive drug on this planet...and I did it by myself.
---I want my kids to love me for who I am and how much they need me.
---I want to prove to myself that I have the power to quit.
---I want to be in a relationship where neither partner is a drug addict.

Defining your motivation will help you focus on your real life goals and make them a reality. For those of you who fit in a different category and feel that none of this motivation stuff has any meaning to you at all, I have something for you a little more twisted as a back door motivator. I also believe in a more powerful tool that no drug program or counselor or psychiatrist would ever dare mention...spite. Spite can be a powerful motivator as well.

Spite comes from the word despite, meaning that ulterior motives can also help keep you strong. You can actually use spite as a weapon of motivation to help you kick your drug addiction. Spite is a powerful tool that can cause death, destruction, and war (as it has)…but it can also be used as a mind tool in your fight to kick your drug addiction. Spite can actually help you win your war with meth, believe it or not, if you want to do it out of spite. As I've said so many times before, you can kick meth…"if for no other reason than to spite those who say that you cannot."

If you are so angry at methamphetamines and the people on both sides of the table, then you can gain strength with spite. If you are tired of people who tell you all of the time that you cannot kick your meth addiction, you can absolutely focus on these people and kick your addiction to spite them; to prove them wrong. You can do this because of the power in you to prove to yourself and to everyone in your world that you can do what you say, when you say it, and how you said it would happen. You can do this to spite those who say that you can't. Those who say that you'll always be a loser drug addict junkie and that you'll never change. You can prove them wrong by gaining strength from within and from mastering the power of simple…spite. Pull in your power of hate and redirect them into simple spite, and you will be the master of your own reality. No more hate, but plenty of spite…will turn you into a productive drug-free winner. This is the power of a true conversion towards setting things right.

If you're so twisted that normal channels of drug addiction treatment will not work for you, then step up to this table and harness this power, and concentrate on your new motivation: to prove everybody wrong. This you have the ability to achieve; anything but meth, right? Do it out of spite.

Defining your motivation is personal to you and we're all different. Design your program with every twist you need to make this work for you. Now, make your list, write it out…and read it…and learn it. Just like with the ball of bad memories, do not hurry through this list. Take your time and get it right. Do not move on until this task is completed. Take a day or two if you need it but get this part of the program completed correctly. Define your motivation on paper, and then start putting them in order from the most relevant to the least relevant. Rate your own work.

Continue on when your list is done.

Starting right now, you will begin the program by deciding when you will make your big exit from the drug world. You have already decided that you want out, and your decision to quit is in cement. So now, you have to work on your quit-date. As you read through the remaining chapters, eventually you will come to the beginning of the 14-day detox program. At that point, you will stop reading until your quit-date has arrived. You'll be given instructions at that time and you will know exactly what to do and how to do it.

When your life is consumed by a meth addiction, you see things through a tunnel that denies you of living your life like a normal person. When all of your focus is drugs, consuming drugs, and getting more drugs, and not getting caught, you're missing out on everything else life has to offer. You're not living your life at all, you're just dying slowly. Like I said before, meth addiction is a death wish, straight-up.

You live for meth and the drug lifestyle, and you pass on all of the great stuff that life has to offer. Life is not a bad thing...life is a good thing. If you can remove your focus from meth, you'll be able to see that there's more out in the world for you then you ever thought possible. You can make decisions that will fill your life with love and happiness and a true sense of being a part of a bigger picture. After you kick this addiction, your feelings of depression, anxiety, helplessness, and your thoughts about suicide...will slowly be replaced with happiness and a feeling that you can do anything you want in this life (except meth). Life will offer you a new gift, a second chance, if you will. You can go out into the world and find yourself...and live a new fulfilling life which makes you feel better about who and what you are. It's all there, just outside your reach.

Now it's time to let go of the pain and the anger and walk toward the hope and freedom that a drug-free life allows you to experience. Who knows, maybe you'll screw that up too. There's only one way to find out, right?

You need to understand that while I am explaining this program to you, you will begin the procedures necessary for planning your exit from your drug addiction. We are working up to step 1 of the program which is to 'say goodbye' to your drug entirely and to enter phase 2 which is to begin your 14-day detox period.

So now you have to think about the last time you will ever do meth again. You have to plan your exit from the drug world. You need to think of it as a retirement, just like someone who has worked his whole life so that someday he can retire and never have to do that kind of work again. You have earned this. You'll be picking the time and the day and after that, you're out. You're out of the business, you're out of the game, and you're out of the loop. From here on out, when they go to call someone, they'll have to call someone else.

Now figure out that quit-date…and read on.

Chapter 8

The List

As I mentioned before, the QuitMeth program was conceived by drug addicts just like you, searching for a process to kick their addiction, with a strong desire to eventually become a major source itself. While putting together this program, I was constantly interviewing addicts and asking each one what they thought was the most important element in kicking a meth addiction. Everyone had a different answer, which made the puzzle extremely complex and very interesting. The solution would therefore require a significant influx of opinion and fact. Through years of research and study, there seemed to be a pattern evolving in successful techniques. I was only interested in those which took the daily addict all of the way through the detox period and on to a life that was absolutely free of addiction. A successful program would have to supply people with the ability to resist the urge to use the drug ever again. Once a pattern was determined, a solution for kicking could be charted and mimicked by others, like you.

Along with technique, there had to be pharmaceutical intervention to address the ever-changing effects of a body and mind that were detoxing from a chemical dependency. *Ironically, the key to kicking a chemical dependency would have to involve the use of new chemicals, herbs, and vitamins in order to reduce the pains of withdrawal*, and also to address other common withdrawal symptoms. Also, the needs of the user would change from day to day, as the dependent drug was being cleansed out of the body. Therefore, besides the techniques in this program which will teach you how to forget about meth altogether, there'll also be a list of over-the-counter pharmaceuticals, herbs, and vitamins, along with several other 'items' which you'll need to acquire before starting the detox period.

Always remember that this is your recovery program and what you decide is relevant always takes top priority. The processes outlined for you here have been designed by others like you, as the best path for you to take to get to the end-game. Any modifications you make to this program are to be considered as relevant to you, and are changes you will make knowing who you are and what makes you tick, as an individual.

The obvious reason for using over-the-counter remedies is the fact that I am not a doctor and I can't prescribe medicines. Also remember that having a doctor's opinion when you're trying to kick on your own defeats the whole purpose of anonymity. Over the counter pharmaceuticals are tested and safe and all have the manufacturer's instructions and warnings on the labels. If you read the labels and follow the manufactures suggestions, you won't have to worry about any side effects or negative or unexpected results for using such an item.

So, here is a list of the things you'll need to have at your side when you approach your quit-date. It's important that you purchase these products *now* or as soon as possible, before your quit-date closes in. You *need* this stuff. The list is laid out below and a further breakdown of each item and why it is needed will follow the short list.

1) **Excedrin PM's** – 80 to 100 counts. As this product is sometimes hard to find, feel free to substitute for the active ingredient which is the sleep aid: diphenhydramine, an antihistamine and sleep aid sold under the brand of Benadryl…Benadryl knock-offs are easy to find now and are usually much cheaper. You can find this in bulk and Costco, Walmart, Target, or any pharmacy under the stores generic brand. It's the little pink pill that will change your life.

2) **Excedrin migraine** – 24-count or more. Again, this great product is not always available in all areas, so if you have to substitute a migraine pill, make sure you get one that has 60-65 mg of caffeine. Read the labels.

3) **Caffeine pills** – w/200 mg caffeine (popular brands include Jet-alert, stay-awake, etc.) Any brand with 200 mg per tablet will work.

4) **Ginseng** – Any quantity will do, in pill or caplets.

5) **Ibuprofen** – 200 mg, 24 count or more (Advil, Motrin or any generic brand)

6) **Aspirin** – 24 Count or more- any brand, full strength.

7) **Acetaminophen** – 24 count or more (Tylenol or any generic brand is fine)

8) **Ginkgo Biloba** – 24 count or more (use any brand you can find)

9) **St. John's Wort** – 24 count or more (use any brand you can find)

10) **Multivitamins** – 100 count or more (buy the best brand)

Bonus items!

There are several items that you can 'take it or leave it' as needed. I call them 'bonus items' because they're recommended but not completely necessary as with the list above. This is what is meant when I said that you're designing your own program, as you can decide if you want to include or exclude certain items or techniques in your personal detox game plan. These include anything you can think of, along with the following items:

SAM-e Complete by Nature Made – 200 mg capsule which is clinically proven for healthy mood and joint comfort. This is a great addition to your personal detox plan, but it is a bit pricy and not a required element of the program. It is extremely beneficial, if you can afford it.

Gatorade – to supply your body with needed fluids throughout your detox period with the inclusion of electrolytes. This is the perfect liquid for hydration during your detox period, and after.

Energy drinks and 5-hour energy – To help you gain a little energy as you detox from your addicted drug. 5-hour energy shots and most energy drinks fall into the same category. (Not to be used ever again after you detox)

Marijuana – To help keep your mind relaxed and lose focus so you don't feel the urges to use meth. We will talk more about this later...

Pepto-Bismol – To relieve some of the flu-like symptoms associated with a major meth withdrawal.

Prescribed pain medicines – In moderation as needed. Use ONLY if your doctor has already prescribed them to you. Use your best judgment.

Coffee – A great caffeine supply that you should drink every morning for the rest of your life (or tea if you prefer).

Cigarettes – They will help you keep calm and to give you something to do to keep busy with your hands and mouth, if you already smoke cigarettes. Don't take up smoking if you're not already addicted to cigarettes.

So, there you have it. The famous list of items you'll need to start the 14-day detox period. It's important you obtain these items before your quit-date arrives. You'll need all of them and buying short will only make the suffering during withdrawal more intense. Fill the list as if it were your top priority to a smooth transaction into a drug-free lifestyle. Don't worry about when and how to use these items. The entire process will be laid out for you later in the program. Trust the process.

Now I'll give you a quick explanation for each item on the list so you can begin to understand why they're needed. These comments will be short and quick to the point, as the reasons for each may be way more involved than you need to know at this time. Just trust in the fact that you'll need these because I'm telling you this right now. And please don't think that you can just take this list and run with it. Though this list contains all of the products you'll need in your detox program, during the 14-day detox period you'll be told which products to take at each part of your detox, as a recommendation. The methods for taking these products are based on the different levels of withdrawal you'll be suffering from each day after you quit. You will not be taking each and every item on the list, each and every day. You'll move from one item to another, as instructed in the program, during the 14-day detox period, as it becomes necessary.

I am explaining each item now only so that you'll have a better understanding as to why you need this once your quit-date arrives. Please don't worry or fixate on any one item or try to figure out in advance what the protocol will be. It's just a lesson for the future right now. So, here we go.

Excedrin PM's, (or the little pink pills sold as Benadryl), are probably the most important item on this list for a couple of reasons. Since the withdrawal of a chemical dependency includes a lot of pain and discomfort, these pills can help to relieve this with the combination of pain relief medicines and the addition of a strong sleeping aid. More than anything else in this program, getting long periods of sleep while you're detoxing is going to be your top priority. The more you sleep, the less pain you'll feel. As I've mentioned before, sleep deprivation caused by a meth addiction can drive the addict towards insanity and can lead to several other conditions including anxiety, schizophrenia, and even depression.

The best medicine you can give a drug addict is a good night's sleep. Not only does it help the body and mind rejuvenate, but once you start getting the proper amount of sleep, your thinking will be clearer and you'll start making more sound decisions. Also, once the withdrawal symptoms start kicking in strong, it's best if you can sleep through the toughest parts.

I'll also recommend keeping Excedrin PM (or the Benadryl pills) in your medicine cabinet for the rest of your life. There'll be times when you'll need a pill to help you sleep better and in my opinion this is the one you'll need.

As with everything else, you're in charge of what you take and if you believe that using another PM pill is better for you then feel free to substitute. Always remember that *reading the instructions on PM tablets is mandatory* as you'll never want to consume more than the manufacturer is suggesting, unless you decide you can handle it and you need a little more. That's on you and part of your own personal game plan. Also remember that taking Acetaminophen or Tylenol with this pill is not recommended since you're already taking the same dose (500 mg) and too much Acetaminophen is not good for your liver and won't reduce the pain you're feeling by any noticeable amount anyway. But if you're taking the pink pill instead, feel free to add some acetaminophen to help relieve the pain as well. Only the PM brands add the pain reliever as well.

Excedrin Migraine serves the same purpose as a pain reliever, but the caffeine content is the main reason for including this product in the program. Unlike Excedrin PM which gives you 500 mg of Acetaminophen in each pill, Excedrin Migraine only uses half of that at 250 mg combined with 250 mg of aspirin and 65 mg of caffeine. Being that the average aspirin contains about 325 mg, you should once again consider what other pain relievers you're taking as they may already be in these other brands. Read the labels and know your facts.

The main reason for using this great item is the inclusion of the small dose of caffeine. Once you take the meth away, you'll find yourself to be a little sluggish and taking 2 Excedrin Migraines (130 mg caffeine) as instructed, will add a little caffeine to the pain relief, which will help you function better in the earlier days that follow your quit date. You'll learn this as you use them when instructed, trust me.

Caffeine pills are included to help you function during the worst days of your withdrawal symptoms. With your average caffeine tablet being 200 mg, be sure that you experiment slowly with this item and know how much you can handle. The goal is to mimic the effects of your drug addiction as well as possible during the withdrawal period, to fake your body and mind into believing that it might be getting some stimulation, as the caffeine enters your bloodstream instead of the meth it's used to. Mimicking the side effects of your chemically dependent drug with caffeine pills, vitamins, and herbs can soften the blow of a total withdrawal, and help you get past a few of the hardest and most important days, when the goal is to complete the 14-day detox period.

You will not be using this product during the first few days of your detox period, and you will not continue to use after a certain point, which I'll be telling you about later in the program. This is not a permanent replacement for hard drugs and this will definitely be one of those things you throw away at the end of the detox period. You're not trading narcotics for caffeine in any way. It's just to help you detox.

Ginseng is an herb that'll help you get through this in many different ways. Although it's not good to use in the first few days after you quit using, ginseng can not only mimic some of the effects of your drug, but it can also reduce stress and keep you from feeling depressed while you're detoxing. It's also very helpful at keeping you calm since it has many properties which actually counter the withdrawal symptoms in your brain by improving concentration, enhancing memory, and making your brain feel like it's not missing some of the abilities that meth now provides for you. You can feel the calm come over you when your mind is scrambling over the lack of meth in your bloodstream. Great stuff!

Ibuprofen is the ultimate pain reliever for the aches and pains in your muscles during detox. You'll need this when all of the muscles in your body start to ache as the meth no longer stimulates your nerve endings, and your muscles and skin start to feel the pain of withdrawal (yes, even your skin will hurt). Not only will this be a great tool in dealing with your withdrawal, it's also a nice item to keep in your cabinet for the weeks that follow. There are so many different things that'll go crazy inside you once you change the chemical makeup of your body, and simple Ibuprofen can help to relieve some of the misery and help you to feel whole again.

A little known fact about Ibuprofen is that pain relief does increase with each dose. Unlike most pain relievers which hit a maximum pain relief level (where taking more of the pill is useless) Ibuprofen will have added relief if you increase the dosage. That's why doctors prescribe it in doses with 600 and 800 mg's. The more pain you feel, the higher the dosage you require.

You can do the math on that as most ibuprofen tablets sold over the counter come in a dose of 200mg's. Therefore taking 3 or 4 of them would equal the dosages given by doctors when extreme pain is involved. If more is needed, you can always trust that it would help relieve more pain. As with any of the other items listed, make sure you read the manufacturers warnings on the label and don't abuse this drug just because you know it has a better effect in a higher dose. And always take ibuprofen with food or milk, as designated by the manufacturer. Again, the inclusion of this item into your personal plan is on you, and it's up to you to know what you're putting into your body.

Aspirin is a simple pain reliever. It works in the body in completely different ways then Ibuprofen and other pain relievers, and also helps to keep your blood healthy and thin, which you will need for pain relief in your bloodstream. Aspirin is the world's wonder drug and many have forgotten its basic value with the creation of so many other pain relievers we now have to choose from. Read the directions carefully, as Aspirin is not to be taken in large doses and can cause stomach problems if abused.

Acetaminophen is the actual drug we used to refer to as Tylenol. It's now the most commonly used pain reliever on the planet. It's taken for pain relief and it is different from all of the other pain relievers mentioned here, because its kind to your body if taken in moderation and it will help relieve your pain. Since you will suffer from so many different types of pain during your withdrawal, we attack this with as many different pain relievers as we can handle. Acetaminophen is a basic staple in your recovery.

Again, remember that this drug is also included in many other over-the-counter and prescribed drugs. Please be aware that mixing pain relievers of different kinds is not always recommended and that the amount of acetaminophen in your system is the total amount included in all of the items you take in a short period of time. Also remember that certain prescribed drugs like Vicodin, for example, use acetaminophen as a buffer additive to increase pain relief, so read the labels and do the math.

Ginkgo biloba is an herbal supplement that can help you with your mental health while you're in the detox mode of this program. It's been known to increase mental alertness while minimizing depression often associated with detoxification periods. It's been reported in many studies to help with nerve cell function and blood flow to the nervous system, as well as the brain. These are areas of concern for you as your nervous system and nerve endings can make kicking this addiction a painfully uncomfortable experience. This great item combined with the ginseng already mentioned makes a great combination of herbs to keep your mind positive when normally negative thoughts and feelings would be present. This is good stuff!

St. John's wort is an herbal supplement which can also help to provide you with a positive mood while detoxing, and can help take away any moments where you may feel a bit depressed. Like with the other herbs in this program, the combination of these herbs is the key that will help you realize you can live without the meth in your bloodstream. You'll learn that you can operate in a new normal mode as these herbal supplements help to replace the strange new feelings in your nervous system and brain. You'll just be replacing the need for meth, as your doors and windows will now be opened with the help of these all natural herbal additions.

Multivitamins are necessary on every day of your recovery and can benefit your mind and body if you continue to take them for the rest of your life. Not only do they supply you with needed energy, but they also help the recovering addict by replacing the lost vitamins and minerals you've deprived your body of while you used your drug. Vitamins and minerals are essential supplements in your recovery.

Bonus items!

The bonus items should be included as extras if you can afford them. They are not as necessary as the main items mentioned, but if you can see past the additional expenses, they will benefit you in your program. You can take them or leave them accordingly. You can also add any other supplements as you see fit. Remember that this is your program, and you know what makes you tick better than anyone else. Do what you have to do and feel free to modify the details where you see fit.

SAM-e Complete is a great item that does not come cheap. Any time you can find a clinically proven item that helps with something you are suffering from, you should take notice. Since you will be suffering joint pain as well as mood swings during your detox, this great product by Nature Made seems to be a product that will help you with your goals of relieving some of the withdrawal symptoms you'll be suffering during your initial pull away from your addicted drug. If you look around, you can also find this product as a knock-off for about half the price.

If you can afford this product, please note that the manufacturer is posting that the product may take 7-14 days to reach full benefit so you may want to start taking this supplement as soon as you see fit. This is also one of those things that can stay in your medicine cabinet after you have detoxed. Even though you've physically detoxed your body from the chemical methamphetamine in the first 14 days, the mental anguish that can accompany any about-face into a new lifestyle may have adverse effects for many months after detox. This supplement, along with anything that helps you through this dark period, is going to be beneficial to your overall wellbeing, correct?

Gatorade – To supply your body with needed fluids throughout your detox period with the inclusion of electrolytes. As detox often includes strong flu-like symptoms, you may find yourself in need of fluids that help you hydrate such as Gatorade or any of the many copycat drinks. This way you can keep them close to you and have refreshing fluids at an arms-length.

Energy drinks and 5-hour energy – This is to help you gain a little energy by mimicking some of the effects of your drug as you detox. I am not a big supporter of these big name brand energy drinks, but if you can purchase some of the cheap knock-offs and keep them close, I can't sit here and tell you not to do just that. I know that some people believe in energy drinks whole heartedly, and if you're one of these people, you may already have this item in your normal diet. But energy drinks do scare me a little. As a recovered drug addict, I just don't want to ever find myself addicted to anything else for the rest of my life. Personally, I believe these drinks are bad-news and that they were brought into this world before anyone realized the addictive qualities they contain.

You and I have addictive personalities (like everyone else). We have to watch ourselves and make sure that we don't trade one addiction for another. Even though I always teach that anything is better than meth, I want you to consider energy drinks as a temporary fix to help you through this detox period. Please don't find energy drinks as a replacement for the void of your daily drug use. Try to get these out of your life as soon as you can. (But anything is better than meth).

This other item that calls itself a 5-hour energy drink is the same thing in every way. Just because it comes in a shot form that makes you believe you are limiting your intake, it's the same as just about any energy drink on the market. If you read the ingredients, you'll find that it may contain a few different vitamins but the active ingredients are the same and I feel exactly the same about this item as I do with any 'energy drink' out there. It may even be more deceptive, since it tries to convince the buyer that it is different.

Again, if you are hooked on this item, you can kick it after you kick your current drug addiction. This is just another part of the program that you'll have to design to fit your own needs. Energy drinks and 5-hour energy is a touchy subject with me…but anything is better than being a drug addict, and don't ever forget that. If you can kick a meth addiction (and you can), everything else in your life will be easier. You can kick any secondary addiction down the road, when you see fit.

Marijuana – To help keep your mind relaxed and to lose focus on the moment, so you don't feel the urges to use other drugs. Yes, pot is a touchy subject. You will not find a single other drug treatment program on the planet that tells you that it's okay to use marijuana in your treatment plan. Besides absolutely believing that it can help you relieve some of those nasty withdrawal symptoms, I have two theories about smoking pot as it applies to a meth addiction.

One is that it's not a bad idea to reverse your history if you used to smoke pot before you became a meth addict. A lot of people believe that pot is a gateway drug which may have been the catalyst that turned you into a drug addict so long ago. If this makes you go back to your roots, so be it. You can quit the pot later, if you like. It is a fact that smoking pot during the detox period will help you get your mind off of meth to some extent. This makes it a valuable asset in your arsenal to combat the ill effects of withdrawal as well as its ability to take your mind off of the cravings.

The second theory would be a warning to anyone who didn't smoke pot before they became addicted to meth. *Don't start now!* I don't want to be the reason you smoke pot, so don't blame me. If you think you can handle it and want some of the benefits, I caution you to move slowly. The marijuana available these days is getting more and more potent and you should start small, if you start at all.

There have been so many studies, and some which are current, that actually prove that smoking pot does help the addict in kicking their addiction. Smoking pot really does take the mind off of the cravings for meth. These studies are very interesting because they all say what most of us have known to be factual for so long. Pot can take your mind off of meth while you are in the detox period, and it's definitely a major tool in your new toolbox. Feel free to try it every day that you are off of meth, and figure it out for yourself. Like I said, if you can kick a meth addiction, you can walk away from pot when you feel like it. This is your program, so do as you feel.

As a side note, if smoking pot makes you crave meth more, discontinue this from your program. Use your common sense throughout each step of your program.

Pepto-Bismol – This has always been the staple go-to item for typical flu-like symptoms. Since kicking a drug addiction involves detoxing from the addicted chemical, your body will suffer withdrawal symptoms very similar to when you having the common flu. Pepto-Bismol is not a requirement for this program but it is highly recommended if you can afford it. Keeping this item in your medicine cabinet is a good idea when the time comes where you may feel an upset stomach or nausea associated with any withdrawal.

Coffee – A great item that adds caffeine to your daily diet. I have no problem with substituting caffeine for narcotics. If you're not already a daily coffee drinker, I want you to make coffee your new best friend. I don't care if you like the taste of it or not, eventually you will learn to love it. You can add cream and sugar until you find the right combination that helps you with the taste, and eventually coffee will become a part of your new daily ritual. For those who already drink coffee, you may find it interesting that most meth addicts don't drink coffee, as they have never felt the need.

Coffee is good for you because it helps to wake up the body and mind (and they don't arrest you for drinking it, or throw you in jail for having it). The world is flooded with coffee and coffee drinkers, and a big part of normalcy can involve seeing what most people are doing, and taking note that there are reasons for such things. Society likes a coffee drinker, and our mind and body likes coffee as well. Besides the caffeine, there are many proven benefits to drinking coffee every day.

Even though coffee drinkers have less of chance of developing type 2 diabetes, certain types of cancer, strokes, Parkinson's disease, heart rhythm problems and certain types of dementia...the ever changing scientific proof of these benefits has no real bearing on why the recovering drug addict should take on this wonder drug. Coffee should be seen as a significant benefit to your new daily routine because it replaces so many of the actions of your daily meth ritual, with real similar moves which take you through the same types of motions, and still offers you mental rewards for your actions.

The daily ritual of making coffee and drinking it can replace certain parts of the missing elements which cause you to think that some good things are missing from your new life. Coffee is a cure that can remove future triggers from ever forming in the first place. Important triggers that work on your mind can be removed by replacing basic needs that can benefit you throughout the day, and replace the need to think of new ways to get your fix. Coffee should be your new fix. Invest in your coffee future and make it part of who you are. This is strong advice for you that you won't ever regret.

Cigarettes – If you smoke cigarettes, I've heard it on both sides of the argument. I've heard people say it helps them kick, and I've heard people say that it makes them crave meth even more. I'm on the fence here so this one is up to how you feel personally. Your personal drug program involves you working out some of the details. But if you've never smokes cigarettes, don't start. A recovering drug addict will easily become addicted to cigarettes so, don't do it. If you do smoke and you think it helps you kick, by all means use it as a tool in your program, but if you think it makes you crave meth, figure it out and don't smoke during this period. Maybe now would be a good time to kick that addiction as well.

Prescribed pain medications – If your doctor has previously prescribed you pain medication, use it cautiously as needed, and follow the instructions on the label. Never use more than the bottle recommends, especially when you are detoxing from a meth addiction, and using several other over-the-counter techniques as well. I can't stress this enough; I am not a doctor who can recommend prescribed pain medication. This is not what I am doing here. I am only trying to bring attention to the fact that prescribed pain medications can be a powerful relief option if you have personally been prescribed them by your doctor. Do not attempt to purchase pain pills that are not prescribed in your name. If I told you to do that, I would be committing a crime. Always note that people are dying now from pills that they bought on the streets that are laced with fentanyl. Be careful how you proceed in life at that pivotal point where you are finally kicking your meth addiction.

Let's be real here. You've been self-medicating with a dangerous illegal drug for so long that you've become chemically dependent to it. You can make big-boy decisions about the temporary use of pain pills but do not trade a meth addiction for any other addiction. This happens a lot and it's a fool's move. Stay clear and be wise.

Chapter 9

Sights and Sounds

Originally, I wanted to call this chapter *Another List,* because you'll need to get a few more items in your possession before you reach your quit-date. These items will not assist you with the pain and agony of quitting or the withdrawal symptoms, but they will be needed to help re-program your brain as you detox. This is not about emotion so much as it is about *sights and sounds.* It's important at this time in your life to change your subconscious thoughts as well as things which you already believe you know to be true. If you can change the sights and sounds which you are accustomed to as a drug addict, you may be able to address some of the triggers your mind will use (from your past) to try to get you to relapse in your future.

These theories again, are not part of any other traditional drug treatment plan. I believe (as you do) that meth is in your body, your mind, and your soul. You can't just shake-off the desire to use because it's part of everything you do. So, in order to kick this addiction completely, you have to change as many factors in your drug life as possible. This includes all of the things that make up your normal day, including what you watch on your television, as well as the music you listen to. Everything you see, smell, and hear in a normal day needs to change, as you begin to change.

Changing the way your mind perceives your daily ritual has to include actually changing the ritual altogether.

The goal here is to force your mind into a new train-of-thought using the *whiplash* effect. Subtle changes in the art surrounding you can go unnoticed, but *drastic changes* in what you see and what you hear from the minute you open your eyes in the morning, can cause your mind to take a second look and question your new surroundings. It's time for you to look at new things in your life, and to hear new things and to smell…new things. This is something you should be able to easily understand. It works on the theory that certain songs or types of music, TV shows, or even certain smells, may trigger you into thinking about your meth-days again. This is a real thing, a 'phenomenon natural' of your drug quest. Your meth memories are tight inside who and what you are, and the best thing you can do now is to start changing everything in your life. Change it all, change everything. Like David Bowie used to sing *"cha-cha-cha-changes…look out you rock and rollers!"*

So here we go…out with the old and in with the new. The plan will be to *reformat your senses.* As meth and other drugs have now taken over the majority of all that you think and feel, you'll now take back your senses, one at a time. Your favorite music, out! Your favorite TV shows and movies, out! Your favorite pictures and paintings on the walls, out! Your favorite smells around the house including scented candles, incense, potpourri, or whatever makes your nose send messages to your brain, OUT!

It is a fact that if you can c*hange the look and feel and smell of your surroundings, your mind will be shocked into submission.* That these things which used to be a part of your 'normal' life…are a-changing. Change is the 'new you' and it's important that you leave this old life behind and start inventing the 'new you' as you progress past this life of addiction.

Well, I wish it was as easy as it sounds, but there are just a few more pieces to this puzzle we're putting together in your honor. I know that changes in music can be a bit upsetting, but you'll soon find the change soothing and interesting, and when the time comes where you think you can handle it again, you can slowly go back and start over, as you see fit. As you rediscover your old music as a clean responsible human being, your old music can also become a part of your new drug-free lifestyle as well. But for now, it has to go. I'm not begging you to throw it away, just to set it aside for a while until you get a grip on your new life. Believe it or not, this is big part of the 'stuff' that's holding you back right now. These are musical 'cues' that can trigger you into using again. These triggers are a very real part of your addiction, and eliminating them entirely throws a brick into your minds plan of keeping you 'on the pipe' for a few more years. For now, you put it away, or you throw it away. Like the old saying goes 'out of sight, out of mind', but for reals. You hide or toss your music and your visuals as you see fit (trashing them is always best), and you replace them with items which are new and interesting to you, so that while you detox, your mind is getting a whole new picture that things are truly changing and that your normal day is now different in every way. Now, let's get into specifics.

MUSIC

First, let's talk about your music. Music is the heart and soul of who and what you are. We love our music and it defines our life and lifestyle. The music we each listen to is personally picked from a large repertoire of everything available from different music styles, cultures and history. We each have unique preference of what we like and dislike. Our personalities have shaped our music preference, and our music preference has also shaped our personalities as well. This should be easy for you to understand as you are subconsciously telling yourself right now that changing your music is off the table. But that's where it needs to be, off of your table, literally. Your music is who you are now, and if you are truly interested in changing your life, you will have to change 'who' it is that you are. And you are your music, and your music is who you are. Get it?

Like I said, all change has to be drastic and changing your style means that it's time for you to change the style of music you listen to on a daily basis. It's time to start listening to music you would never have listened to in the past, and keep in mind that this is probably the best thing you can do for your new daily ritual. For so many of us music is our life, and the move to eliminate your entire music collection and replace it with musical nonsense will blow your mind, man! Yes, I'm being sarcastic but I don't know how else to stress this point. You're changing…everything. Listening to new music genres will shock your mind into believing that everything has indeed started to change. The goal actually is to 'blow your mind' as you change the 'who' and 'what' you are.

So, you will need to acquire new music…CD's or downloads of music genres you're not familiar with, or different stations on the radio, or groups you have never heard of on your phone apps. New music styles that you would have never listened to in the past will be the goal here. Maybe sounds that you heard other people listening to and thought you might like it but never pursued, or something completely different from anything you would ever consider. Who knows, you may find something you like. I always say "try bluegrass" because it's great music and a lot of addicts are not too familiar with the genre.

Imagine the shock to your senses when you listen for the first time. Try new music that's extremely different from your normal sounds. The more you experiment with different sounds that you're not used to, the better it'll be for your therapy. This is to replace the pleasant relaxing feelings you're used to with a confusing new style. Like a musical mood swing to remove the belief that today is just like any other day. There's nothing normal about kicking a chemical dependency, right? All change is for the better.

So, if you are into Heavy Metal, you'll need to change into softer music like Country, Rhythm and Blues, World Music from new cultures, Bluegrass and yes, even Symphony Orchestra music and the classics your parents used to listen to when you were young, before you started using drugs. Your first thought is that this will drive you crazy but there is a method to my madness, as you already know. Your *new way of thinking* should be a clarification that you are already aware that you are going crazy from the meth, and the new music will bring with it a sense of sanity. Remember, subtle changes are fine as long as you're not too familiar with the new music, but big changes will produce big results, and that's what we're looking for here. Drastic changes are needed for these drastic new events in your life.

I'm not saying to ask your Mom or Grandma for suggestions (not that it's a bad idea) just take the time to prepare your own new set of musical madness. If you like the slower more melodic types of music, it's time to experiment with harder and faster and newer music. *Snap your fingers-snap your neck* and *shock the world* and stuff like that. This new music therapy technique is vital to your success in this program. I cannot stress this point enough. I would give you a list of my personal suggestions but the drug addiction client covers the entire music entertainment spectrum. I put this one in your hands. You pick the new music for your recovery and you shock your brain into submission. Please get these new music items ready, and cover a broad base to saturate yourself with so much new music style that you will not run out of material. Make it so that no matter how many times you pull a CD, you always have more to try.

I believe this is a major addition to traditional theory and practice, so you should take this one to heart and do as I say here. Put in the time and get this one done right.

Art and your surroundings

Art is what you see when you open your eyes in the morning, and everything you see during the day. If "beauty is in the eye of the beholder" (and it is) then recognizing that "*everything you see is a picture of your life"* can help you understand why you need to consider changing what you're used to seeing throughout the day. The pictures on your walls that are not of your family are 'art' which you have chosen to live with day to day. The trinkets and other items you have stacked on shelves, your refrigerator, your coffee tables, your desks, and around your sinks are just a conglomeration of art that needs to be reevaluated, rearranged, and removed. Now is the time for a '*new look'* in every part of your life. It's time for you to put up new art and to 'lay-out' new things which will help your subconscious mind believe that changes are truly happening all around you. Art can come in many forms, so pay attention to what you see every day, and consider getting new art for your new life. Think positive and change the entire image of your surroundings.

When you see new art in the new life you are creating, your mind will know it's intentional. It's time you stared into other people's art and looked for the meaning of what was in the artist's mind while the piece was being created. Find magazines and books with pictures and keep them around you. Look at new things that stimulate your thought processes. Take down the garbage that currently hangs on your walls and doors and get rid of it (throw it out with the trash) and replace it with new art to stimulate your mind and thought processes. Shock your eyes, shock your mind, and shock your world.

You can do this as a project on a continuing basis throughout your recovery. You need to clean up your messes and replace them with art that represents who you will be after you're clean. If you can get some of this stuff before you quit, you can get a jump on the game and this will help you. "Art is art"...you can quote me on that. As you go through the recovery process, anything that stands out to you, that absolutely reminds you of when you were a slave to your drug, get rid of it. It hurts you to constantly be reminded of how low you reached in this game of life, and throwing out the junk is like tossing these memories to the wind. You'll be reminded of these lows everyday throughout your life, but you'll also possess the knowledge that you figured out how to rise up from the ashes and become a better person. After you kick this addiction, you will be a rock...with new art in your world.

TV and the movies

What you are accustomed to watching on television (or your phone) can be a big part of who you are as a person. Just as television and videos have influenced your life to some extent, you are also influenced by the movies and shows you choose to watch. Being as how movies involve both sight and sound, watching films and TV shows while you're detoxing is very important to your recovery. In the early days of self-detox you'll feel weak, tired, and lazy...and if you can just lay there and watch TV, the time will pass with much less of a struggle. It's important that you watch new shows that your mind has no memories of when you were using, and I can suggest some shows that may influence you as well, during your recovery. Yes, the object is to incorporate new, thought provoking material at a time when you are vulnerable to suggestion.

These suggested movies and shows will help to change your thought processes and therefore have influence on your new life. Most importantly, what you are watching and hearing is being fed into your mind at the most crucial point in your life: as you are actually kicking your drug addiction. This you must take seriously. The stress levels involved with a self-detox can be relaxed by sights and sounds which take your focus away from your current condition, and refocuses them into concentrating on a visual drama or comedy that has special meanings to you, or is simply there to help you laugh. Remember the old saying that "laughter is the best medicine" because it is absolutely a fact.

You need to have a certain type of thought provoking cinema in place and ready to watch as you're physically and mentally detoxing. You need new audio and visual art as well, as some of the things mentioned may already be familiar to you. You'll watch these constantly while you're awake and it's important that you understand that certain movies have a theme or message which may make you believe they're talking directly to you. This is good stuff.

The following is a list of movies I would like you to watch during your detox period and after you're clean. Watch them more than once and you can double the therapeutic effects they'll have on you during your recovery. Take the list to heart as a lot of time went into making sure that this list would be beneficial to you. It is the list…that binds us.

- **Magnolia –Tom Cruise, Julianne Moore (1999) New Line Cinema** – Even if you 've seen this film before, I want you to watch it again and figure out where you fit in to the message of this great movie. This is not Steel Magnolias, the chick-flick…
- **Final approach- James B. Sikking, Hector Elizondo (1991)** - If you can get ahold of a copy of this great movie, the 1991 version, enjoy trying to figure out what it's about. I hear Netflix has it on steam now.

- **O Brother, Where Art Thou?-George Clooney, John Turturro (2000)** -This is a Coen brothers film. Anything the Coen brothers made is recommended so feel free to search for them.
- **Vanilla Sky-Tom Cruise, Penelope Cruz (2001)** - A great film that will dig deep into your critical thinking and perceptions.
- **The Fifth Element-Bruce Willis (1997) -** This is for entertainment purposes.
- **Enemy of the State-Will Smith, Gene Hackman (1998)** - Great movie to keep you busy and make you think.
- **Sling Blade-Billy Bob Thornton (1996)** - This one, you just have to watch. It has a lot to with perceptions.
- **WALL-E- (2008) -** A soft thought-provoking animated masterpiece.
- **Minority Report (2002) Tom Cruise, Colin Farrell (2002) -** Science fiction at its best.
- **Scarface- Al Pacino (1983) -** I'm sure you've seen it…time to watch it again. A film about the drug life and where it can lead.
- **The Edge – Anthony Hopkins, Alec Baldwin (1997) –** A classic film of human nature and survival. Great lessons taught in old-school style of modern film making. A must see, in my opinion.
- **The Matrix-Keanu Reeves (1999) -** A great film that brings you into the inner workings of the mind.
- **South Park; Bigger, Longer and Uncut–Trey Parker, Matt Stone (1999) -** Quite possibly the funniest movie ever made. Laughter is the best medicine. Watch this, even if you've seen it already.
- **The Cable Guy-Jim Carrey, Matthew Broderick (1996) -** A look into annoyance and interactions.
- **The Big Lebowski-Jeff Bridges, John Goodman (1998) -** Just a cool film to relax you, with deep philosophical flair.

- **Waco, the Rules of Engagement-Great Documentary (1997)** - Maybe the best documentary ever made. A look into actual events on American soil. A film everyone should be aware of.
- **Inception- Leonardo DiCaprio (2010) -** A mind bender.
- **Saving Private Ryan-Tom Hanks (1998)** - Probably the best war movie ever made.
- **Stuck on You – Matt Damon, Greg Kinnear (2003)** – A great comedy that has a lesson about living life with someone who you have to live with, and then the complications of moving on when the chance arises.
- **The Departed-Leonardo DiCaprio, Matt Damon (2006) -** Great film making.
- **The Green Mile-Tom Hanks, Michael Clarke Duncan (1999) -** Again, great movie to help you pass the time.
- **3:10 To Yuma-Christian Bale, Russell Crowe (2007)** - This is a great movie start to finish. Art, at its best.
- **Heat – Al Pacino, Robert Di Niro, Val Kilmer (1995)** - One of the best films ever made. Great story, direction, production.
- **Fargo- William Macy, Frances McDormand (1996) -** Another one to pass the time. Shows how stupidity can travel in different circles and accomplish different goals.
- **No Country for Old Men- Josh Brolin, Tommy Lee Jones (2007)** -Always good to remind you what you are getting away from.
- **There Will Be Blood – Daniel Day-Lewis (2007)** - Good movie to pass the time.
- **Good Will Hunting - Matt Damon, Robin Williams (1997) -** This is a 'great white hope' type of film where the underdog climbs the social ladder.
- **Dinner for Schmucks-Steve Carell, Paul Rudd (2010)** – Great light comedy with a message about people on different levels.
- **Slumdog Millionaire-Dev Patel (2008) -** Another film to inspire those who think they don't have a chance in this world.

- **The Shooter- Mark Wahlburg (2007) -** Just a good story to help you pass the time.

This is a list of films that I would start with. Some have deep meaning that I need you to view so you come out of detox with hope and inspiration. Some are just to help you pass the time so the shock and pain of detox with pass, as you keep yourself busy with new things. If you see a recommended film that you have already seen, I encourage you to watch it again, for the sake of this program. This is entertainment, and change is built into the lesson.

The next list is a group of shows that appeared as a series, mostly from cable channels like HBO or Showtime but also available on Netflix and other steaming networks. If you have the ability to watch any of the following TV series from the beginning, this will help you pass the time also. These are all great episodes with lessons for you, as well as to help pass the time as you detox. Again, a lot of time went into picking these perfect episodes for you to watch, to gain from the lessons being taught. All of these are the best efforts of some of the greatest artists ever to pick up a camera. This is their gift to the world and also for you. Check them out and if you've already seen them…not a bad idea to watch them again during this critical time in your life.

- **Breaking Bad-** One of the best series ever made for TV. The story of Meth manufacture and sales as you know it, and on to big time scary stuff.
- **Ozark-** An incredibly brilliant series on Netflix about dealing with drug cartels.
- **Narcos-** and **Narcos Mexico-** The real stories of how it all began. I prefer that you would watch 'Narcos Mexico' first and then go back to the original Narcos after.
- **The Shield-** Along with Breaking Bad, this is probably the best series ever made for TV ever. The Shield will keep you

watching and you will not believe where it takes you as bad cops play in the hard life of crime.

- **The Wire-** A great series which deals with drug dealing and the ghetto life.
- **6 Feet Under -** A great series which deals with death from the eyes of a mortuary.
- **The Sopranos-** I doubt there's anybody who doesn't know what the Sopranos did to change TV forever. It's because of this series that most of the others were able to be made. This is roots.
- **Family Guy-** Anything Family Guy is funny and will keep you laughing all the way through to a full recovery. This series comes to you from one of the funniest people ever to have a forum to show his talents.
- **South Park-** Same thing…anything South Park will help you fully recover while laughing your way through the pain.

The rest is all up to you. Your ability to gather these items and to prepare yourself for these major changes will be the test of how serious you are in kicking this addiction. This is a huge part of your program and these are serious suggestions. If you jump in with both feet, I guarantee you'll get the results you're looking for. Trust me again when I tell you to do as I say. Prepare to change the art in your life. Prepare for the arrival of your quit-date. The proof is in the pudding, right? Well, this is the pudding.

Chapter 10

The Three Stooges
(The good, the bad, and the Ugly)

There are certain times when the explanation for a technique I want you to use sounds far worse than the actual exercise itself. When we insert mind-control techniques to counter the control that your drug addiction already has on you, sometimes the reasons for the exercise might be enough to convince you that the technique is not a valid one. Trust is the only issue at this point. Now that you have read this far into the book, do you trust me enough to take a few more steps down this path? I'm hoping the answer is 'yes' because these new techniques are as simple as they are affective. At this point you've come to the understanding that this program is attempting to corner all angles for addressing the triggers in your mind which have caused you to relapse in the past, and those that are keeping you addicted to this very day. Some of the information is easy to understand and some is complex and takes effort on your part, to learn and complete the tasks. This chapter covers a few new techniques that are very easy to understand, but the actual reasons for the tasks are very complex. This again, is something I want you to know, but there is no point in tying up your mind with the why's and the how's and such. Just go with the flow and follow the path.

The secret now is to work the process, and not dwell on the fact that some of the tasks just seem so lame. A lot of this program may seem odd and pointless, but it's all a part the process that gets you to the end-game, which makes this such a full and complete program. Being as how this part of the program is 'out there' by any standard, I like to call these great mind control techniques "The Three Stooges" since there are 3 simple techniques here that may seem disingenuous, and there is almost a comedic resemblance to the old black and white TV shows. If this makes you feel awkward, it's supposed to.

There are 3 phrases that I'm going to ask you to say over and over again throughout your recovery, to remind yourself exactly where you are and what you need to be concentrating on. Along with your *ball of bad memories* these simple mind tricks can help to mold your perception of the drug-free lifestyle you're about to start living. The three stooges are these 3 statements which you will say over and over again, throughout the rest of the course;

"I'm Robbie Long" (I'm where I belong)
"You're on your own, you know"
"Fat is good."

The purpose of these catch-phrases is to directly attack the most common triggers you'll be dealing with, as you fight through the worst parts of recovery. Like I told you before, triggers in your mind that tempt you into believing that you can use meth again without consequences, must be addressed in full before you can put an end to these attempts for good. Triggers are weak-spots hidden in your mind that wait for certain emotional cues, to convince you that all hope is lost and you would probably feel better if you just reverted back to where you started, addicted to this horrible drug. These hidden triggers need to be identified so you can learn techniques to eliminate them in advance, so that your mind loses its ability to control you in this way. By addressing these 'emotional cues' in advance, your mind losses its ability to control them in the future, thereby eliminating some of these triggers altogether. Remember that your mind will always think of new triggers after you stomp out the old ones, but when you can see them coming, you'll gain the strength of knowing you are in charge of your life now, and any new trigger will be red-flagged as 'dangerous thinking', and will not be enough to convince you to go back to your old drug lifestyle. This technique is to make you stronger and strengthen your belief in yourself, while at the same time convincing you that this is the only way for you to win this war inside your mind.

Simple techniques such as repeating catch-phrases can remind you to stay strong because you have important goals now and you have to stay focused. When you feel a trigger in your mind trying to trick you into using meth again, you just recall which catch phrase is set up to reduce the particular trigger that is tempting you. This will get much easier for you with a little time.

So, let's get started with the simple phrasing and the explanations, and hope that you'll take my advice and use these techniques to gain strength as you get this grip on your mind's control over you.

I'm Robbie Long! *(I'm where I belong)*

The saying *'I'm Robbie Long'* is based on the theory that you've taken every step in your life to end up exactly where you are today. It's the old belief that every decision you've made in your life so far, has determined that you would end up a drug addict, in your current situation. It also includes the fact that you are reading this book at this very moment, because at some point, you knew that you'd eventually start taking your life back into your own hands. This whole thing is on you, just as mine was on me. Everybody has a path in life, and every path is taken one step at a time. You ended up exactly where you were headed. Grip that as fact. This is not something that happened to you, this is something you did to yourself. You became a drug addict because at some point in your life you took all of the right steps to be where you are at today; this is where you were going to end up. You did everything it took including convincing yourself that you were not at fault...but here you are, where you belong. You're a drug addict, addicted to methamphetamines, because you did everything it took to end up here. And now, you're looking for a way out, because you don't want to be a drug addict anymore. You're starting to believe there's more for you in this world than chasing meth and the drug lifestyle that's been torturing you lately. You're starting to believe that you are destined to be drug free, and that you don't belong where you've ended up anymore.

But today, you are where you belong. Where once you were a drug addict with no way to kick your addiction, you have now decided that there is a way out (this program), and you're going to take it. You are where you belong now, just as you have always belonged exactly where you were. This is a profound moment for you; the realization that you are a meth addict because you have done everything to be just that, and the realization that kicking this addiction right now is exactly where you belong at this very moment as well. Say it out loud *"I am where I belong"* because now you're exactly where you belong, working on kicking this addiction, once and for all. When you started introducing drugs into your system you thought you were only 'experimenting' with drugs, just like everyone else…but you were destined to become a drug addict. It happens to almost everyone. Right now, today, you are where you belong…and when you become clean and fully recovered, you will be there because that's where you belong as well. You will take every step to get there and you will belong there. Agreed?

So, say it again out loud, over and over…*"I am where I belong"*…*"I am where I belong"*…*"I'm where I belong"*…*"I'm where I belong"*…*"I am kicking this addiction now, because I belong in a better world"*…*"I'm where I belong now"*…*"I am where I belong"*. Say it again over and over, until you understand it, and convince yourself of this new fact; *"I am where I belong."* Because all of your actions brought you to this very place, right here. Reading these very words and saying these very things. You are exactly where you belong; right here and right now, actually taking the steps needed for kicking this addiction. You are where you belong; because you did everything you needed to do to get here.

To add a twist to the obvious statement, I want you to say it as "I'm Robbie Long" because it plays a trick on the mind that intensifies the need to understand what's going here now. This approach only changes the spelling of the words, not the statement itself. Funny thing about the English language is that we have these types of tricks that only fate and destiny and irony can explain. When you say *"I'm where I belong"* (and I want you to say it) our mouths and tongue do exactly the same things as when you say *"I'm Robbie Long."* Take the time to figure that one out and use it as your own little inside joke towards your recovery.

I'm Robbie Long. I'm where I belong. I'm Robbie Long. I'm where I belong. I'm Robbie Long. I'm where I belong. I'm Robbie Long. I'm where I belong. They are exactly the same, right? Do you feel it? Can you hear it? Say them both out loud and say them over and over.

I'm Robbie Long.

I'm where I belong.

You can see why I call this one of *the three stooges*, right? It's lame…but it works to repeat these lines as you move forward. This is definitely a part of your program. You wanted to know, and now you know.

Again, the reason I want you to say "I'm Robbie Long" is to change it up, to make it significant and personal to you. Now you'll join the *Robbie Long club* in your mind, which reminds you that you're different from everyone else. And that you know the reason you're different is because you're fixing yourself now, and that is exactly where you belong. You are where you belong right now, and after every step you take to finish this program. I'm where I belong too, my friend. NEXT!

You're on your own, you know!

This next step is the most important of the entire program. If you don't know that you're on your own here, you're missing the point completely. There is no one in your fan-club right now. The decision to quit and the execution of that decision are entirely on you and your efforts here. There is nobody out there who can help you and frankly, nobody really wants to. **You're on your own, you know?**

You need to get this point inside your head so deep it becomes a part of who you are. You need to say it over and over until it sticks. Nobody cares about you but yourself, and you won't be of any worth to anybody until after you quit doing meth and kick this addiction completely. Way after! So, say it out loud right now and say it often. *You're on your own, you know? You're on your own, you know? You're on your own, you know? You're on your own, you know?*

Lucky for you though, you're right where you belong and things will be better in the future. You are guaranteeing that at this very moment, aren't you? Now say them together because you know they will help you.

I'm Robbie Long *and I am where I belong.*
You're on your own, you know?

The inclusion of these exercises is part of the reason that counseling is not required in this self-help detox program. As you can see, you are counseling yourself as you learn to use these simple mind tricks to your advantage. Now…on to the never, we must go.

FAT is Good!

Fat is good, my friend. Say it often as a reminder and get used to it. We cannot be swayed any longer with such a simple trigger as the fact that you will be gaining weight soon after you kick your meth addiction. For those of you who have convinced yourselves that you were using this drug to lose weight, I want you to hear this loud and clear; give me a break, I don't believe you. It didn't happen that way.

Nobody tries meth for the first time because they heard it was a great way to lose weight. You tried meth because you hung out around people who have it and do it. If you've used the excuse that you only tried this drug to lose weight, you're telling the rest of us that you're better than us, when you're exactly the same. If we're all in the same boat, what use do we have for believing that worrying about weight gain is a real excuse for becoming addicted? It's not, it doesn't float…but it can be a trigger nonetheless.

The fact of the matter is that you do need to know that you will most likely be gaining weight during this drug recovery, and you need to understand that this is a good thing. You can worry about losing the weight later, if it really bothers you, but for now you must believe the facts. **Fat is good!** If you're cleaning yourself of a drug addiction and the only worry that sticks in your mind is about getting fat, then you have to reprogram your mind into believing that fat is good, because it is. It's the best thing you can do for your physical well-being. Fat is good. Say it over and over..."*fat is good. Fat is good. Fat is good. Fat is good*".

Again, we're talking about a trigger that can get you to relapse if you gain a lot of weight after kicking, which you probably will. So get this fact clear in your mind right now. *Fat is good.* Say it!

The reason for weight gain during drug recovery is because of the way we deplete our fat cells during drug use. Through time, as you used more meth and found yourself eating less food, you deprived yourself of the basic nutrients your body needed to function normally. When your body has a vitamin deficiency it turns to your fat cells for the vitamins that have been stored there in the past. As you continue to live on less food then you need, eventually the fat cells in your body begin to run out of the nutrients which are vital to your health. That's when you start to develop health issues along with your drug addiction, and everything in your life takes a turn for the worse.

The problem is that your body is now full of empty fat cells. These empty fat cells are waiting for you to start eating again, so they can begin to store these vital nutrients back in your cells. The farther you get away from your drug addiction, the more control your body will have on your mind and soon you'll start to feel hungry all of the time. When the taste of meth is no longer affecting your taste buds, food will taste amazing and your fat cells will insist on storing everything, in the belief that you will eventually succumb to the desire to use meth again someday, because you always have in your past attempts to quit. This is self-preservation. Even your fat cells will run on the belief that you'll not have the strength to overcome your minds-own powers of influence. So, your fat cells keep storing the fat back where it belongs so that if and when you start using meth again, it will have enough energy saved up to get you through long periods of drug use in the future. Your fat cells will grow and they will swell up to hold more substance, waiting for the fall. So, you will gain weight but you have to remember that fat is a good thing.

That's why people who quit using meth, over and over, and keep relapsing, get fatter and fatter. Because they have trained their bodies to store fat and release it, then store and release, until the fat cells are so big, they're like balloons that have been blown up and deflated over and over. You can't win with the fat. You have to believe that **fat is good** or you will never break the cycle. Fat is good, it really is. The best way to stay thin for you now is to quit for the last time, right now. If you really don't want to get any fatter, than this is it and fat is good. You can get fat and get healthy and then you can get smart and lose the weight later. It can be done without drugs, so you have to believe that fat is good.

Say it again out loud, over and over. *"Fat is good…fat is good…fat is good"*…because you need to believe that. Now give me all of the three stooges at once.

Fat is Good!
I'm Robbie Long!
You're all alone you know!

Say them out loud and say them often, and keep them close and in your heart. The three stooges are so lame…and they will help you win this battle. You're all alone, you know? Fat is good! I'm Robbie Long!

The three stooges are the good, the bad, and the ugly. Along with your *ball of bad memories* and *defining your motivations*, you now have a handful of simple mind games which can have heavy influence over your minds ability to control you as it has in the past. With your ability to learn and execute these odd powers, you can have relief that you can actually feel, from your minds attempts to get you to relapse. These are trigger-softening-devices which will take away the cravings you feel when your mind is trying to trick you into using meth again. When used properly and often, you can feel the cravings disappear as you use these simple techniques, over and over again.

When you feel any craving for meth, just think of your ball of bad memories and the three phrases you just learned, and use them as a mind trick of your own. Simple as they are, you'll learn to use them as weapons to help keep you clean. Take it seriously and take it to heart. This is your life we're talking about.

Oh, and don't forget about spite. You can always quit out of spite.

Chapter 11

Meth Facts…and Stuff

The main reason for learning the mind techniques used in the previous chapters was to help you get a grip on the triggers your mind will try to use to get you to relapse once you've successfully quit using meth. These mind-games are important inclusions in this program, as you've already agreed wholeheartedly to quit using forever. Digging into the inner workings of the mind is essential for curing any kind of drug addiction, and any additional information you can cram into your brain will always be beneficial. Being that you already grasp the position that there is no such thing as relapse in this program, you should feel a huge sense of relief inside of you, because you know now that you're kicking here for life. From this point forward, you can do anything you want in your new life, except methamphetamines. You have one single rule you have to live by and focus on, and your entire messed-up world will begin to repair itself. After you quit, you just can't use meth anymore, that's it. Your life will now consist of one-thing, one-rule to live by; no meth.

When you think of it this way, it seems like a simple tradeoff for a way better life. You trade your horrible drug-induced existence for one simple rule in your new life, and it's easy to remember; "I can't do meth because I'm addicted to it." Relapse is no longer an option because in the past, you've become re-addicted every time you thought you kicked this evil drug. No more games, no more lies. You only have to learn how to avoid one thing on this planet; everything else is still on the table. You have one rule for yourself that nobody else has to worry about, and you're learning right now how to pull it off. No meth, ever again. You can do this one thing, right? You've already lived through everything horrible about this drug and you've learned that you no longer want to be a part of this anymore. So, after you kick it, there's just one rule to live by from this point on; no meth. And the world is yours…

You should know as a fact that many addicts will kick their meth addiction and simply trade it off later for another addiction down the road. This scenario happens all of the time, and sometimes with very tragic results. The ex-meth addict, who starts messing with other narcotics, may eventually convince himself that he can use meth again at some point. But he can't, because of the one rule he lives by, right? This is a real phenomenon and it kills thousands of addicts every year. At this point in the game, his return to meth is similar to a death-wish because many addicts who return to meth often lose hope, and sometimes their lives. The ex-meth addict, strung out on meth once again, may be putting one foot in the grave, so remember that always. Yes, you heard me right; you can die with this failed game plan. It happens all of the time and maybe you have examples of that in your life. Maybe that's why you're looking for a way out at this moment. And that's why this program teaches you how to quit forever, without even thinking about relapsing. No valid drug treatment program would ever teach the addict that relapse is a part of the process. It's not. Life is good and there is a lot to live for. This will become much clearer once you start thinking much more clearly as well.

It's very important that you hear these words clearly, because I stand by the fact that you can trade anything for meth and you would be doing the right thing. It will ruin you and eventually send you to your grave. Fear the meth, as you will learn to fear the thought of ever using it again. For this reason, I am going to get into the history of the drug, so you'll get a keen understanding on what has happened to you, and what to avoid in the future. So, let's move on...

After you've learned to use these mind techniques to gain control over the triggers in your head which are trying to get you to relapse, this next step follows the 'knowledge is power' model. I believe the more you know about your enemy, the stronger you'll be in defeating it. This chapter will attack the basics, so that all factors of your addiction will be addressed and understood. Knowledge is power, and the power to kick this addiction involves understanding all of the concepts which got you addicted in the first place.

Although I believe these facts to be accurate and true, there are many versions of right and wrong when it comes to explaining the facts about the history of meth use and production. Again, these are my theories, my facts, my program, and my book. And I've designed this program for you, based on these theories and facts. Debating any of these is wasted time. They're here to give you knowledge, that's all. Anybody who wants to pick apart my words to try to prove me wrong, at any point, is wasting their time, not mine. This isn't about picking apart relevance in the perfect drug treatment program, since everything I say here is true and accurate. Trying to prove me wrong affects me not, and gives you no justice. When you hear the history of these drugs here and learn these facts, you'll understand more clearly that your addiction was only avoidable if you had been warned in advance, that using these drugs would cause you to become addicted. If you were forewarned, then shame on you, right? That was a historically bad decision, repeated so many times by generations of people before you as well.

As you read on, you'll begin to understand how drug addicts get sucked into addiction by designer drugs that were made to keep you coming back in the name of quid pro quo economics, with absolutely no relevance to your personal well-being, or whether you live or die. These were not supposed to be recreational drugs for partying all night with your friends. Drugs are produced and distributed to control you, and meth was invented to keep you awake so that you could produce products in factories beyond the normal working hours of the human body (and to control your mind so that you would be willing to kill other people in times of war).

Meth History

Methamphetamine was invented by scientists who were studying the minds of people who were already addicted to stimulants such as amphetamines and cocaine. The goal was to figure out how the drugs opened the doors and windows of the mind, and to see if they could produce a chemical similar or more powerful, without the negative side effects associated with such a dependency.

Although the invention of methamphetamine is always credited to the Japanese, the dates and time periods are completely irrelevant to the recovering addict. Some like to believe that it was invented with no predetermined use or function, but the obvious across-the-board use patterns by the Japanese as a whole would suggest otherwise. Meth was invented to win wars. It was synthesized from ephedrine in a laboratory in hopes to find a way to keep soldiers and factory workers awake and alert, for the common good of the nation-state which produced it. It was manufactured in large quantities and forced onto its citizens for the good of the nation's longevity.

Although the Japanese invented methamphetamine prior to the First World War, it was equally perfected for use by both the Japanese and German fighting regimes during WWII, when the two nations became allies. Both used brutal long-winded fighting tactics that went out of the box of normal war strategy. But it was Adolf Hitler's regime that experimented further and managed to create the crystallized version in pill form. The same twisted thinking that people experience today while using meth went into the minds of those who commanded large armies packed with meth users who had no fear and no feelings of wear and tear.

These early Japanese regimes were so brutal that even the Koreans and the Chinese still hold a bitter taste for Japan to this day. They don't trust the Japanese because their earlier tactics involved occupying foreign territories, killing all of the men, and using rape as a weapon. Women were made into sex slaves for the Imperial Japanese Army, and over a long period before and during World War II, millions of Chinese and Korean civilians were murdered by soldiers strung out on meth. These brutal war strategies involving the sex trade (as a weapon), include a style of thinking which can only be explained by wide spread meth addiction and abuse.

Maybe you can relate to some of this history, as you know first-hand the miseries that a drug addiction can cause, and the wicked, twisted mind tricks involved in a drug induced and sleep deprived marathon. This is the kind of mess that parlayed itself into a long and brutal World War II, where even the U.S. soldiers were using different types of speed for their fighter pilots (some are still used in different forms to this day). You've heard of the Japanese Kamikaze pilots ramming their planes directly into the flight decks of our naval ships, right? Believe it or not, that was meth induced suicide as a weapon of war. In the untold real history, Kamikaze pilots were given meth in rituals, mixed into their Sake (a Japanese form of alcohol), and taught that suicide was some form of national honor (altruism). They were treated as heroes before they died, and just before their last flight, they ingested sake and meth in a ritual to help focus on their final conquest.

We all know that the Japanese and Germans became allies long before the Second World War, and it seems that part of the deal included tactical information sharing where Germany soon began to produce its own version of methamphetamine for its soldiers as well. Crystal meth tablets were mass produced in Berlin under the name of *'Pervitin'* and distributed to factory workers and most of the troops. In fact, it was Pervitin that was actually distributed to the Japanese armies and the Kamikaze pilots, proving that the alliance between the two nations was indeed 'crystal clear', as the Japanese were making their own brand of the drug before the nations merged with common goals. Imagine the strength of an army that needed little sleep or food, and a civilization which could keep its factories open day and night. Just like the initial affects you felt when you first started using meth, spirits were high and production was at its peak.

This eventually leads to a burnout which can take down the very people it was meant to inspire. People who used to clean everything and work in double time, eventually stopped trying, and the messes started piling up. The long-term effects of drug addiction eventually led to the Germans losing the war, with armies made up of tired and burned out soldiers, eventually not willing nor having the abilities to carry on. Japan was woken-up with a stern slap in the face, as the United States dropped a series of Atomic bombs in retribution for the attacks on Pearl Harbor. Personally, I will always believe that the twisted planning and execution to bomb Pearl Harbor were born in the minds of sleep deprived meth addicts...but I digress.

It's my personal belief that there may not have been a World War II at all, had it not been for the invention and dissemination of methamphetamines. It is well documented that Adolph Hitler had a cocaine problem as well, and new evidence points to him being an intravenous meth addict, if you can believe that. Though history would have us believe that he was suffering from a mild form of Parkinson's disease and was given meth injections as kind of a cure, it's obvious to anyone who's ever been a meth addict that the twitches and shaken nerves he displayed in public were most likely caused by the meth, not because of a Parkinson's disease. There's also proof that towards the end of the war, Hitler had somehow become addicted to heroin as well. With or without his knowledge, it was his inability to acquire heroin after our allies had started to bomb Berlin, which caused him to go crazy in his bunker, from withdrawal symptoms.

Can you imagine what pressures a world leader would have while suffering from extreme withdrawal from cocaine, heroin, and meth at the same time? It would be impossible to function at all, let alone make rational decisions. The inevitable collapse of a nation based on the irrational thinking of its lead commander, hooked on narcotics and suffering from withdrawal, is more than a cause for alarm. This is now a part of human history, at the hands of drug addicts. Nothing good could have come from it.

This would show us as proof that Hitler was well involved in meth before the beginning of World War II, and could make it easy to believe that a man on meth with such power could supply a nation with this drug as well. Meth addiction in an army of soldiers can absolutely fuel the kind of hatred that killed countless millions during his regime. At the heat of production, the factories in Berlin were producing and disseminating 860,000 crystal meth tablets a day, every day, and 7 days a week. These are facts, not theories. They don't tell you this kind of history when you're first introduced to cocaine, heroin, or meth on the streets. It's an integral part of society and history, but when they tell the stories, only a drug addict would understand what really happened. A natural historian would tell you such stories and throw in meth, cocaine, and heroin use as a side-note, without understanding the gravity of his own statements. You know as a drug abuser, that it was most likely the drugs and the power combined, which made these horrible atrocities real. These drugs have moved mountains, murdered millions, and ruined your life as well. Use this history as a tool to help push yourself as far away as you can.

Since the defeat of these two meth infused fighting regimes at the end of World War II, governments have taken precautions to insure that meth would be studied closer and eventually regulated. Although the end of the war did spawn a new meth epidemic in Japan (when they released their military stockpiles to the general public), the world is learning first-hand about the devastating effects of the meth model.

Amphetamines (another form of speed) were the drug of choice during the Vietnam conflict as well, as the US armies consumed vast amounts of the drug. Meth had taken a back-seat to a slightly milder form of amphetamine and still, we learned again that new strategies would have to be implemented. Governments are now passing new laws to curb the production of meth globally, and most of the meth available to the public is produced and consumed illegally, as you are well aware. The chemicals to produce this drug are being ever regulated, at the same time that illegal meth use has reached record epidemic status. Every country on the globe is infected by cocaine, meth, and heroin epidemics, and the use of these drugs has now labeled them all, individually and collectively, as the most addictive drugs on the planet.

As far as I'm concerned, that's all of the history you need to know. The rest is your own personal history, and you already know how that turned out for you. Now we have to focus on the cure, as you learn how to kick your addiction. And soon, that'll be in the past as well, and kicking your meth addiction will be your personal history. The buck stops right here, with you…right now.

If you believe in citing proof of these facts as I have laid them out, feel free to read the following link to my personal research on the topic, citations included;
https://escholarship.org/uc/item/70s7k6rs

There is one more fact here that I want you to pay close and special attention to. While doing my research for this program, I asked recovering addicts a series of questions, face to face. I was amazed that almost every single person I asked gave the same answer to this one question: *What's the biggest change in your life since you've been clean?* Keep in mind that I only interviewed ex-drug addicts who had been clean at least 6 months, who were firm with the fact that they were finished with drug use forever. The answer always came with a smile and a glow that I can't describe. Everybody said the same thing; "I can't believe how much money I have now".

I was floored by this answer. Who would have guessed that? Drug addicts with cash always buy more drugs, right? Bigger quantities of cash always equaled less down time. It is therefore a fact that if you take away the need to acquire drugs, you have money that has no predetermined earmark. And so begins your climb to the top. People always say that money can't buy happiness, but most of them have never been poor. Money does buy happiness, and you can quote me on that. Focus on the dream and the dream will be real. It's called hope, and it is real, and this is the path you are on now. Soon you will have more money than you will know what to do with, and all you have to avoid is buying drugs. That's why other people have nice cars and homes; because they don't know what else to do with all of the money they have. This is your future, a few years after you kick, when things start coming together. For now, focus on the prize.

A non-functioning meth addict always has meth, but never has any substantial cash flow. And a functioning addict pays his bills, provides for his family, and spends a lot of money on drugs, but sees it as necessity. Although he may have extra cash in appearance, he doesn't see clearly the suffering involved with the missing funds because the mind blocks that out, for the good of the drug dependence. Yet in both cases, if you take away the need to acquire meth, the appearance of extra cash is upfront and personal. Not only does quitting meth change your life for the better, it comes with a cash reward.

Since your survival involves living in the lifestyle of .99 cent burger deals and Top Ramen lunches, you've already designed your life around basement bargains and that habit will continue for quite some time after you kick. As long as you don't reward yourself with drugs because of the new windfall (and that's the first thing that crosses your mind) eventually you'll have better things. That'll be how you reward yourself for your efforts. You can replace the old drug addicted life-style with new things that you've always wanted but couldn't afford. I'm telling you, your life is about to change in a big way.

Meth Facts

The following facts are written as I want you to understand them, not because I think they're all bonafide truths. It's important, for the program, that you believe every word here to be factual. They may be disputable but not by you, as they are written this way to help you understand meth from the standpoint of the recovering addict. You should see these as facts and remember them as truths. Again, anyone who wants to dispute this part of the program is wasting their time, not mine. Picking apart these words doesn't change the fact that I believe wholeheartedly in every word, as I think you should do as well.

- Methamphetamine is the most addictive drug on the planet.
- The main difference between drug use and a chemical dependency is addiction. A casual user may not be chemically dependent...yet.

- You are both physically and mentally addicted to meth. The physical addiction is the chemical dependency. The mental addiction is caused by the physical addiction.
- There are 3 discernible levels of meth use. 1) Snorting or swallowing which is the easiest to kick. 2) Smoking meth, which is highly addictive and much harder to treat and...3) Slamming or injecting meth, which is the worst method of use, as you know, and involves a deep commitment to kick successfully.
- Meth addiction is not a disease. If you've bought into this lie, your treatment begins the day you acknowledge to yourself that you are not the victim of an incurable disease, but a willing participant in your own addiction.
- A meth addiction can kill you. Scores of meth users have died from heart failure, overdose, stroke, murder, suicide, and accidents. It can cause brain damage, schizophrenia, depression and several other mental conditions, as well as early death by unnatural causes from deterioration.
- Meth addiction often comes with a death-wish.
- Kicking your meth addiction can reverse most of the problems you are dealing with as a drug addict, if not all of them.
- Science has failed the meth addict by producing data which documents the facts without providing any cure to the recovering addict.
- Crimes committed by drug offenders while high on meth can never be calculated accurately, but are the bulk of all court cases.
- A drug treatment counselor who has never been addicted to meth does not know what it's like to be addicted to meth.
- Most addicts who quit using meth kick it on their own, without the help of in-house drug treatment centers or counselors.
- Being a meth addict is the easiest thing that anybody can ever do. It requires no effort, and supplies you with all of the necessary excuses to be a failure.

- The best medicine you can give a meth addict is a good night's sleep. Sleep deprivation is the cause of almost everything that's going wrong mentally with any drug addict. If you take away the meth addiction, the problems will go with it.
- Meth use is an epidemic in almost every nation, state, and territory on the planet. Where it was once believed to be a problem in third world countries and the slums of the inner cities of America, it has now spread like wildfire around the globe.
- Most meth addicts say they want to quit, but they really don't. Wanting to quit and quitting are two different things. You are actually quitting now because you actually want to.
- You are not the victim of a meth addiction, you are a willing participant.
- Nobody can help you kick your addiction unless you are willing to help yourself. Kicking comes from within you. There is no other way.
- The treatments for kicking a cocaine or methamphetamine addiction are virtually identical. The treatment programs for heroin are completely different.
- *The cure* to meth addiction lies within **the understanding** of how your body and mind are simultaneously influenced by a chemical dependency.
- Trigger is a word we use to describe **the action** which takes place in your mind, which can cause a relapse.
- Understanding how the triggers in your mind are manipulating you softens the attempt, and eventually frees you of the urges to use meth altogether.
- The psychiatric industry has failed the meth addict by not developing any new strategies or techniques for kicking the addiction. They are at a void as to their own intent.
- Quitting is quitting. It is finality. There is no such thing as relapse in quitting. When you quit using meth, you win the game. It's over.

- QuitMeth is the world's first and only absolutely anonymous drug treatment program. You don't show up, you don't sign in, and nobody knows you're following a program unless you tell them personally.
- Thousands of people have already kicked their drug addictions by using the QuitMeth program. This is a fact and you must grip this information hard.
- Always remember; "What one man can do, another man can do." This is a fact, as well.
- If you read this entire book and follow all of the instructions provided in the content, you will be drug-free by the time you finish this book.
- Kicking this addiction is your destiny. It is who you are now.
- You are exactly where you belong at this very moment.

These meth facts are laid out for you here to help you focus on the truth about your addiction. Feel free to go back through the list at any time to fully understand exactly what is being said, and as a reminder that repetition is a vital key to your success in this program. The facts were not weighed down with rhetorical information that have no bearing on your recovery. Rather they were hand-picked and written by me and put in the order I wanted you to understand them.

This whole process is calculated and executed in a fashion that trains you to respond with reaction that moves you towards your goal. This program is an algorithm that takes you from one end of the spectrum as an addicted drug addict, and processes you through a series of separate and simultaneous systems and methods into a drug-free recovering addict for the rest of your life. I like to refer to this program as an algorithm because it simplifies a word that was invented with mathematical and scientific intent. What could be more scientific then curing a meth addiction, right?

So now you've completed the main lesson and you know more about meth addiction and treatment then you ever thought you would. Where at first you were hesitant that this may be some backwards attempt to try to understand the drug addict, you now know that the book has been written directly with you in mind. This is your book and your time to shine. Your head is now full of new information for you to consider and process, as you weigh in on the last days of your addiction. You now realize that this is something that is within your reach and that kicking your addiction is only a heartbeat away.

The remaining aspects of the program require you to fully understand everything that you've already learned here, while practicing the mind techniques that will eventually make it easy for you to let go of drugs altogether, as the cravings and the allure of the drug will fade into the past. Like I said before, it's not a bad idea to go back and read every page over again before you proceed from here. Information and repetition can provide you with a better advantage going into the next phase of this program.

This is your life we are talking about here, and anything you can do to guarantee a smooth transition into your new lifestyle, the better your new life will be. It's hard to believe that changing a few minor events in your daily ritual can change your rituals altogether, but that's exactly what your life is made up of right now. I hope that you're absolutely committed to this program and that kicking this addiction is almost a done deal in your mind. The basic tools have all been laid out for you now, and all that's left is the implementation of the recommendations during your actual meth-free days to come. You'll learn a little more each day as you read through the recommendations, and you'll come out of this clean and ready to take on the world. The next section involves the detox period after your quit-date has arrived. Take it all to heart and know that the words are talking straight to you, personally.

I put this into your hands now. Good luck, my friend

STEP 2...QUIT

STOP! ...And Begin

I know you remember the promise I made you when you started this program. I guaranteed if you read this book from cover to cover and followed the instructions, you'd be drug-free by the time you were done. The instructions in this self-help guide are the key to your success. I remind you of that fact because it's very important you follow this instruction absolutely. After you start the 14-day detox period, you will not read ahead and you'll stay focused on the day you're on and nothing else. Reading ahead can only hurt you.

When you get to this point in the book, it's all about making sure you have your list of items complete and that your quit-date is coming up soon. I cannot say this too many times. **You do not start reading the detox chapters until after your quit-date has come and gone, and you have quit using meth forever.** Detoxification means that you are cleaning the bad chemicals out of your body. You can't do that until you stop taking the bad chemicals. Clear?

I will say it one more time; DO NOT read the next page until the day after your quit-date has come and gone (repetition). You start day #1 on the day after you've quit using meth for the last time. You do not read ahead, you just read the one day that you are on. Your quit-date was picked by you and you alone and you cannot proceed until you have actually quit. This is your program and the quit-date was designed by you. The 14-day detoxification period begins as **DAY 1** - the day after you have used meth for the last time.

Keep your head on straight and always remember that quitting is quitting, and you will not be starting this detox period until you have quit for the last time ever. This is where the real work begins and the pain starts. This is where you show that inside of you is the strength you always knew you had; the strength to kick this addiction on your own. Yes, it takes 14 days of living hell to fully detox your body from this chemical dependency but after that, it's downhill all the way. The daily torments of being an addict for so long are much easier to handle once the chemical dependency is behind you.

So, strap on your big-boy pants, use meth for the last time ever, and do not increase your dose (you can't kick if you overdose)…wait a day…and BEGIN!

Chapter 12

DAY 1

Hi, *I'm Robbie Long* and welcome to Day-1 of the self-detox part of the program. Congratulations are in order, as you have now quit using meth forever and have moved on to the second step of the program, kicking your chemical dependency through self-detox. I like to say here that you have quit using drugs altogether and now you're kicking it, so you understand the clear difference between the two terms. Kicking is the detox period and you are now starting the process of reversing the chemical dependency. Now your body will start feeling the withdrawal symptoms that occur when you take away the crucial chemical it requires to function in a normal state. Your goal is to get to the new normal, which is to actually feel normal again.

Kicking is to say that you've decided to quit using meth forever now. You picked your quit-date (which was yesterday), and you've decided that you're in total control now and that methamphetamines will no longer play a part in your life anymore. You quit yesterday, and today will be your first day ever as a non-meth user. You haven't *"kicked"* the addiction yet because the chemical is still in your blood steam. It's a part of the chemical make-up of your body right now, and kicking the addiction involves eliminating the chemical 'meth' from your bloodstream, and adapting to life without this chemical in your body. This adaptation will only take place once the meth is entirely out of your system, and then you'll have to adjust a few basic skills to adapt completely after you're clean. Sometimes this can be a slow process, where the mental anchor that meth has on you takes time to set a new pattern of normalcy. For some people, this can also be a quick transition and walking away completely can be as fast as the 14 days go by. Time will tell how your personal experience may differ from someone else's, but if you stay strong and focused, you'll be on the other side before you know it. They say that *time heals all wounds* and indeed it does. The further you get away from the drug that rules your every move, the better your life will be.

After the 14-day detox period you will be drug free. You will have quit using meth and kicked the addiction altogether, and all you'll have to concentrate on for the rest of your life will be to stay clean by avoiding meth with the techniques you've already learned in this program. You'll become a drug addiction and treatment expert who kicked your addiction to meth by yourself. Good stuff, my friend. Today you start your drug detox…wow!

Remember that old saying, *"Today is the first day of the rest of your life?"* Well, that was all stupid stuff until today. I'll always regret saying this to you but I have to; *'Today is the first day of the rest of your life'*. Remember I said that, and always remember this day, as it is the true beginning of the end. You used to be a chemically dependent drug addict and starting today you're changing who and what you are. As you start to detox your body from your chemical dependency, I'm going to supply you with all of the tools you'll need to kick this addiction forever.

Before I get started, I need to remind you that this is a self-help detox program. For the sake of liability and the law, these are recommendations and not requirements, and this self-help program is specifically designed by you and for you, to treat your addiction. It's completely up to you to decide if you want to accept any or all of these recommendations, and administer them to yourself. Although I have to point these out as facts, it would be ludicrous to think that someone who has self-administered a dangerous drug over a long period of time cannot be responsible enough to do the same with the over-the-counter medications, herbs, and vitamins recommended in this self-help program.

Nonetheless, for safety and health reasons, please read and understand all of the printed material on all of the labels on each individual product used, and follow the manufacturer's warnings and recommendations. They're printed on the labels for a reason and you should be well aware of what you're taking and what the manufacturer has determined as their own recommendations and warnings of their products.

You also have to realize that each of these 14-day installments is a stand-alone article designed for you to read at the beginning of each day, on the day corresponding with the day you quit using your drug. You have to read it on the day that it applies to you, and never read ahead to see what's coming tomorrow or next week. This is an important rule of the program so please, follow this simple instruction. This is the only way for you to get full value from this program. There are points made later in the program that are critical to your continued success which cannot be laid out for you until your head is clearer, and your body is completely detoxified.

First I need to address a few key issues that involve this 14-day detox period. One issue is cigarette smoking. I'm not qualified to advise you about smoking or not smoking cigarettes during the detox period. Including cigarettes into your personal drug treatment program is a chore I have no say in or opinion of. I've heard logistics on both sides that contend that smoking cigarettes during detox can make it harder for you to detox, and I've heard from the other side too, that smoking cigarettes for a person who already smokes, can ease the pain of detox to some extent. I'm going to put that one in your hands and let you decide how cigarette smoking affects you in this program. You do what's best, you decide.

The other thing I'd like to talk about is alcohol. I purposely skipped this topic up till now because I know that some addicts are going to have a real tough time with alcohol, and I didn't want to scare you off early. Alcohol consumption is a major problem with people as a whole and not just drug addicts. Just so you know, trying to kick a meth addiction while continuing to consume alcohol is almost impossible. Alcohol weakens the mind and can easily lead to relapse as your weakened spirit is a big trigger that your mind will use to convince you that a little meth wouldn't hurt you at this time. Remember that you've already quit for good, so if having a drink weakens your resolve to kick this addiction, then the alcohol must be eliminated from the puzzle to avoid relapse. There is no such thing as relapse in this program as you have already quit for life. You cannot substitute hard alcohol, beer, or even wine for meth because it's a trigger that weakens the mind at a time when you're learning to be strong.

As I've already pointed out, smoking marijuana is just the opposite for a meth addict who is kicking. New studies by top organizations have proven that pot can get you through some of the hardest parts of kicking this addiction. This again is part of the program where you decide what you need, and you execute knowing that it may help you, or supply you with a trigger to try to get you to relapse. So, pay attention to your minds own response, and if you feel more vulnerable to relapsing when smoking cigarettes or using pot, you'll have to eliminate that as well. You have to address the triggers in your own mind, when you feel them trying to trick you back into the addiction process. You are the new king of what controls you now. Tread lightly as you learn about yourself and your personal actions and reactions to marijuana and cigarettes. Is it helping you or hurting you?...and react accordingly. Always be aware of your minds own diagnosis of your current events, as it tries to figure out the easiest steps to get you to relapse. This is exactly what we mean when we say 'mind-games'...your mind is playing a game with you right now. But this time you beat the computer, correct?

This is the most important 14-day period in your life and you'll have to control everything in your life during this time. You'll have to figure out what it takes to look inside yourself and find the courage to make changes, and the strength to commit all that you can, to your own future and the future of those around you.

You will not be able to do this program while drinking unless you're a full-on alcoholic who needs just a little bit to get by. If you can separate the issues and really take charge of the cravings for meth, then you'll be set. If you cannot separate the issues, do not trade one for the other. You cannot start drinking to put distance between you and your drug addiction, because it will send you right back to the meth. They are partners in crime, so to speak.

So, now it's time to let go of that piece of skepticism that you're holding onto. That shadow of a doubt that you're keeping in the back of your head, as to whether or not this program is going to work for you. It's a very dangerous trigger that you're keeping in place. It's time to take control now. Release the element of doubt. Believe that you are finished. Believe it. *You're all alone, you know* and you can do this.

It's time now that you start attacking these triggers with logic and to let your mind know that you've decided that meth is no longer a part of your life. You have to believe that you are strong enough to break this cycle and that now is the time. You quit yesterday and that was the end…that was it. Do not listen to the voices in your head that are trying to convince you that this program has holes in it, and that it may not work for you. This is the best program in the world and thousands of people have already proven that this works. Focus on your life now and focus on your inner strength. Use the ball-of-bad-memories technique as often as you can, when you feel the urges coming on. The strength is within you because the strength is you. You are running the show now and you have all of the power. You finally quit using meth and now you are working towards a better life. You did this, you stand firm and you will win this battle, I promise you that. You are where you belong right now so let's say these things out loud.

I'm Robbie Long...I'm where I belong…Fat is good…you're on your own, you know? And "what one man can do, another man can do."

Are you ready to begin your detox now? Do you really believe in your heart and soul that this is your time, your new life? Can you do a lousy 14 days without complaining about how bad you feel, so that you can live forever after without the pain of a meth addiction? Can you grip the pain of withdrawal for 2 weeks if you never have to feel this pain again? It's time to focus on the fact that you will be drug free within a 2 week time period, period. It's time you believe in yourself and step up to the plate and take a swing at a better life. It's time for you to learn how to grow stronger every day so that you can make this dream a reality. You knew this day would come and now it's here. You are making this happen because you decided that you had what it takes to do this. Now, you are making it happen. You can do this easy now.

The first day of detox is something that you are very familiar with already. It's just like the day you can't find any meth because your contacts are unavailable…or can't get any until tomorrow. It has a bit of agony but it's nothing you haven't felt before, more than a few times. Try to plant a seed in your head that you are only out of meth for the day. That will help soften the minds ability to tempt you with hardline tactics. Even though you will never do the drug again, the mind can still be tricked at this early point into believing that you're not so serious about this yet. Stay serious but convince your mind that you're not. This is something that can be done, and at this early stage, it will give you confidence that you do possess the ability to talk to your mind as if it's really listening to you, and taking your thoughts into consideration…because this is a fact. This is where you start to learn that mind control is not just something that controls you, it's also something that you can use to control your own mind. Fascinating stuff as you'll see.

So you get through today with hardly any of the goods I made you purchase. You bought all of that stuff, right? Go over the list and make sure you didn't miss anything. The only extra item I will mention here is the SAM-e. If you did buy this great item, make sure you take your daily dose all through this program. I will not be reminding you of this anymore since most people will see this as an extra expense that they cannot afford but if you have this item, just take it every day as it says to. That, along with the multivitamin, will help keep your body supplied with necessary supplements that your body needs to function through these tough times.

Please remember that I want you to drink a cup of coffee first thing in the morning from now on, if you're not already in that habit. Coffee is a huge part of your new life and a few cups a day will help you find clarity at times when things may be unclear. Coffee will benefit you greatly as you walk away from the meth. I don't want to sound like a broken record but coffee, coffee, coffee...coffee. My intentions should be clear now. Coffee is your new wonder-drug of choice.

Today's focus will be primarily on ending the day with a good night's sleep. Since it will be one of the easiest days to get through, as far as chemical withdrawal symptoms go, I will skip to the end and remind you about the importance of a full night's sleep. Remember that if you were a heavy user, meth will run through your bloodstream for 3 full days, though it will thin as time goes by. It is the withdrawal symptoms that keep you addicted, by causing so many painful feelings and emotions at the same time as you separate yourself from the drug that is still in your system, as it dwindles and after it's gone completely. This is a *process*, please don't forget that fact.

I want you to get through today as soon as possible and concentrate on getting yourself where you belong, which is home. I want you to end this day earlier then you are used to, by taking the Excedrin PM's (or substitutes like Benadryl) way before you feel the need to go to sleep. This is going to be a long night where you are going to possibly wake up some time in the night and perhaps you should consider a second dose, according to how you feel and the manufacturer's suggestions on the label. Today is about maintaining your presence and feeling normal, and tonight is about sleeping. Eight hours is not enough anymore so, *'think big, be big'*.

If you're a functioning drug addict, these are the recommendations for the day. If you're a non-functioning addict, just try to sleep as much as you possibly can. Remember, Excedrin PM is your friend. If you could sleep through this whole fourteen-day program you'd be set for life, but you can't. Functioning addicts will have a schedule today as follows;

- Wake up with a cup of coffee and feel free to enjoy coffee throughout the day.
- Have a nice breakfast and remember to take your multivitamin with food if you can.

- Get home where you belong as soon as you can and avoid people, so you can focus on your needs.
- Excedrin PM's after dinner as soon as possible to induce sleep.
- Relax and enjoy the rest that you need so badly.
- Remember the marijuana speech. It's not a recommendation for everyone, it's a tool…for you to use if and when and how you decide it will help you.
- Remember to schedule enough time in the morning so that you can wake up and read the next chapter before you leave the house.

Now it's up to you. Follow the instructions as you are told and you will be successful in this program. These next 14 days are the most important in your life, so please take this as serious as it is intended. Be strong and make it happen! I will talk to you tomorrow morning. Have a nice day!

"If you're going through hell, keep going"

Winston Churchill

Chapter 13

Day 2

Hi, I'm Robbie Long (say it) and welcome to Day 2 of your QuitMeth program. Normally, I'd say this is where we separate the men from the boys, but that's not the deal in this program. This is a 'no man left behind' program, where you find the power inside of you to complete the process, no other options. You just do it. You suffer when it's time to suffer, and you promise yourself that this is the last time you will ever have to go through this torture. Then you keep your promise to yourself, every day from this day forward. It really is that simple. This is your day-2 of not using meth and things can get a little bit rough today. This is where you start to use the mind techniques you've learned earlier, and grow stronger with faith in this system you're using. This is a program to kick your drug addiction and you knew it would get difficult, and this is where the pain begins. Not so much withdrawal today, as you need to begin to conquer the cravings. Your body and mind want their medicine and they're not going to get it, so they'll start to make you suffer for that decision you've made.

So, are you up for a little agony? I hope so. It's time you prove to yourself that you can do this…*'if for no other reason than to spite those who say that you cannot'*, right? Its crunch-time and you knew when you took on this feat that there would be a time for pain and a time for relief. This is where the pain begins, where you learn about yourself and what you're capable of doing. It's time to 'find yourself' like you always said you would, and all of this is in your lap now, and you'll kick this addiction because you decided it was within you to do just that.

Keep in mind these 'two days off of meth' is also something that you are very familiar with. You've done this before, more than a few times, but probably never with the intention of quitting altogether. So, this is the same and…this is totally different. Again, you can separate the issues or you can use the fact that you've experienced this before to your benefit, and just get through the day. The only difference is that this program is going to show you ways to lessen the blow, and to ease the pain and agony that you would normally feel.

Remember the Methadone game plan? I talked about it earlier in the lesson. If we can mimic the effects of the drug that you're addicted to, it will help you to keep your concentration, while at the same time detoxing your body from the chemical dependency. You still have meth in your bloodstream but the content is growing thin, your body is sluggish, and your mind wants to convince you to fix the problem. It reminds you that the easy solution to an unsatisfied mind and body is a meth-fix, just as it has been for so long. It wants its candy, real bad. Since you're not giving it the drug it needs anymore, you have other options that the mind is not so familiar with. It's time to implement a few new strategies.

To mimic the effects of the missing chemical, you have to work on making it through the day by stimulating your nerve endings and neurotransmitters with other forms of…stimulants. These will include techniques that'll help soften the pain so you can get through today without even thinking about using your drug. Meth is not an option in your life anymore, and this is where you grow strong and start to really believe in yourself. There's nobody on your 'team' anymore except you, and the personal belief that you can do this on your own. Remember that the strength is within you because the strength is you. **You're on your own, you know**…and you are where you belong (*I'm Robbie Long*) because this is day 2 of you kicking this addiction, and you are absolutely in charge of what goes on in your life today. You won't be doing meth today just because you think you're so addicted that you have to. Those days are over because you've left them behind. You'll be kicking today because you know it's time to step up and these are the rules. There is pain, there is agony, and after the chemical is out of your system, there is reward. There is a better life for you. Now, focus on the prize.

I want to mention again that all of the recommendations here are flexible. If you're a functioning addict who is not on a day off of work, this will be the perfect program for you to follow today. If you're a non-functioning addict, or a functioning addict who has the day off of work, perhaps you can get around the stimulants for now and wait until you feel the need. Like I said so many times before, sleep is the best medicine for the recovering addict. Although there will come a day where you'll find you just can't sleep anymore, today will not be one of those days. If you don't have to function in society at all today, remember the Excedrin PM's are your best friend and listen to some of the new music, and watch the some of the recommended shows. The object is to make it through the day and get on to tomorrow drug-free. One day at a time, right? You've got this now, my friend.

About this time, you'll begin to feel extremely hungry. If not today, by tomorrow you'll feel the need to eat a lot of junk food and snacks. This is a normal reaction to kicking any narcotic, as the body has been deprived a normal eating cycle for some time, and needs to replenish your fat cells. My advice for you is strong; eat as much as you feel like eating. Remember the motto '*fat is good*' and apply it to your new way of thinking. It is this inclusion of food and nutrients that will cause people to tell you things like "you look great" and "I can see the change" and "you look so healthy now" as they get a first glimpse at the new you, once you are clean.

What they're saying is that the sick way you used to look is now gone and you look better, over all. It's the food that you're now eating that'll cause this effect. Please do not fight it and enjoy the food, as it'll taste better than you ever remember. This is because your mind realizes that you're consuming for the better of the body and without the taste of meth, your senses will actually make the food taste better to convince you to keep eating. This is a natural occurrence and a great trade off. Please don't worry about rapid weight gain at this time. You can lose the weight in the future, when you get back on your feet. *Fat is good* and very important in your life right now. It goes hand in hand with kicking your drug addiction. Out with the meth and in with the food. *Fat is good,* so eat when you feel hungry and get healthy again.

Today begins with the introduction of a few more items from the list. Besides having your morning coffee (which I hope you're drinking as you're reading this), today you'll be experiencing a slight increase in withdrawal symptoms as you have now walked 2 days away from your drug addiction. To help relieve the pain and discomfort, today you'll introduce a slight increase of caffeine into your bloodstream to cautiously stimulate you into feeling better about the deal. The goal here is not to over-caffeinate but to add just enough to make a difference so that the withdrawal won't be so painful.

To start off, I would like you to understand how quantities of caffeine compare to the average cup of coffee. I do this because you'll need a perfect gauge to understand where to start and stop on caffeine intake. Too much caffeine at any point in your detox will make you sick to your stomach and possibly cause you to vomit. Being that normal meth withdrawal will look and feel just like flu-like symptoms, you don't need another element to upset the course, so charting your caffeine intake will help you stay aware.

The average cup of coffee contains anywhere from 100 to 200mg's of caffeine, depending on how strong the coffee is made. Starbucks is always going to have more caffeine then any coffee that you would make at home. Their 16oz cup will be closer to 300mg's of caffeine, so remember that as a guide to compare with some of the items in this course. Despite the fact that caffeine is caffeine, it can act completely different when administered to the body in pill form than when you drink a cup of coffee. The caffeine in pills can be more of a shock to your system than the caffeine diluted in a cup of coffee. Also, you usually don't drink the coffee all at once, so the effects are more gradual and less invasive.

Today, I want you to consider taking 1 or 2 of the migraine pills first thing in the morning. You can space them out if you want, by taking a second pill 30-60 minutes after the first. The migraine pill has 60-65mg's of caffeine each so compare that with your coffee intake and adjust accordingly. I want you to use this migraine pill in the morning for the rest of the detox period. Not only is it the caffeine that you are using as a benefit, the pain medication in the migraine tablet will now be used to soften the agony of the withdrawal, as it will be starting to cause you pain. Although the pain associated with chemical withdrawal will be worse in the days to come, if you can concoct an over-the-counter solution using all of the pain medications mentioned in this program, you can figure out what is best for your particular needs and be ready when things get tough.

Throughout the day you should keep the ibuprofen, aspirin, and the acetaminophen handy for when you decide you need the benefits of these pain relievers. Remember the simple rule that ibuprofen is for when your muscles ache, and aspirin and acetaminophen are for headaches and pain in general. The three combined will interact well with each other but try to keep the aspirin to a minimum as the side effects can outweigh the benefits if you take too much. You can still use it, just watch how much you take and like everything else, know and follow the manufactures suggestions. These are for pain relief, so use them for pain relief. Remember the game plan is to make it through the day with as little agony as possible, to get back home to go to sleep.

The only other thing I want you to concern yourself with today is the caffeine pills. Remember that I want you to take the migraine pills in the morning but you can leave them in the same spot as they are just for morning use. For stimulation that you may feel the need for later, you can use the caffeine pills that you bought for the program. Being that the caffeine pills are typically 200mg doses, you're talking about the same as a large cup of coffee. But remember how I said that the effects were different from drinking coffee? I would like you to split the pills in half if you can and take them in 100mg doses. This will get you the caffeine you need to function normally, and won't be such a large dose that it makes you sick. You can regulate your caffeine intake better in 100mg doses.

If the pills you purchased don't have a line in the middle to help you break them in half easily, they sell an item at every drugstore called a pill-splitter that cuts a standard pill right in half for you. You could use a razor blade, which I'm sure you have, but please be careful and don't cut yourself at this fragile time of recovery. The pill-splitter is a great item, costs only a few dollars and you may need it down the road anyway. The pill-splitter is a great invention for the recovering addict as you'll want to regulate everything that goes into your body in the future, so as not to ever become addicted to anything ever again.

If you keep all of these medicines within reach, you should be able to fake your way through this day. The caffeine is a great way to fool your senses into believing that you're not so far away from the meth yet. The mind will still think it's getting some of its 'stimulants' but won't be able to figure out that it's not meth for another day or two. The pain medicine will help you to relieve the common pains of withdrawal, and this should be a perfect program to get you through the day. Please remember that if you are using energy drinks or that 5-hour energy junk, read the labels and know the total amount of caffeine in your system at any given time. This is so you don't add caffeine when you already have too much in your system. Don't whack yourself out and make it obvious to other people. They may think you're on drugs or something.

Today is the day where you "find yourself" by keeping your commitment to this program, by being strong no matter what happens. Your mind will be trying hard today to convince you to use meth again. You have to keep reminding it that you have changed and that using meth is not something that is happening anymore. Use the ball-of-bad-memories technique often and chase the temptations away. Craving meth is a mind-game and now you're using your own mind to fight for your life back. This should be easier each day, as you can make the cravings disappear faster each time you use this technique. Soon it'll be as easy as searching for the ball, and the cravings will disappear in an instant. Your mind will sense what you're up to, and just stop trying to temp you (with the goal of making you slip later). This is a real and substantial weapon in your tool box, as you wouldn't be addicted if not for the cravings, right? Without the cravings, the battle is half over. Perfect your ball-of-bad-memories recall, and you will feel a quicker relief each time you use it.

Remember to be strong and fight for yourself, and focus on your motivation. If you made the list to define your motivations, remember clearly why you're doing this at this time. You are where you belong (I'm Robbie Long) so be where you want to be, and who you want to be. Make it through today and there's only 12 days left. You can do a lousy 12 days, right? This is for you now, and for the rest of your life. You can do this easy, so stay focused.

Drink plenty of fluids as mentioned before. Gatorade is your drink of choice and any of the cheaper knock-offs will work just fine. Remember to keep the food and drinks flowing all day, if you can. Finish up the day and get yourself home and take the Excedrin PM's as soon as you can. Listen to your new music and watch the programs that were recommended for you.

If you're a functioning drug addict, these are the recommendations for the day. If you're a non-functioning drug addict, just try to sleep as much as you possibly can. Remember, Excedrin PM is your friend. If you could sleep through this whole fourteen-day program you'd be set for life but you can't. Functioning addicts will have a schedule today as follows;

- Wake up with a cup of coffee, and feel free to enjoy coffee throughout the day.
- Take your migraine pills as soon as possible. Split the pair by taking one at a time, if you think the caffeine will be too much at once.
- Have a nice breakfast and remember to take your multivitamin with food if you can.
- Keep the 3 pain medications handy and take them as needed. Remember that ibuprofen is for pain in the muscles, and aspirin and acetaminophen (Tylenol) are for headache pain and body pain in general. Use as needed.
- As the day draws on, count your caffeine intake and if you need the caffeine pills for extra energy, take them with caution to help stimulate your nerve endings. If you can, use a pill-splitter to cut them in half so that you can regulate the caffeine 100mg's at a time.

- If you use energy drinks, be cautious and know the caffeine content.
- Drink plenty of liquids and eat well, all through the day.
- Get home where you belong as soon as you can and avoid people so you can focus on your needs.
- Excedrin PM's after dinner as soon as possible to induce sleep.
- Relax and enjoy the rest that you need so badly.
- Remember the marijuana speech. It's not a recommendation for everyone, it's a tool…for you to use if and when and how you decide it will help you.
- Remember to schedule enough time in the morning so that you can wake up and read the next chapter before you leave the house.

Now it's up to you. Follow the instructions as you are told and you will be successful in this program. These next 13 days are the most important in your life so please, take this as serious as it is intended. Be strong and make it happen! I will talk to you tomorrow morning. Have a nice day!

Chapter 14

Day 3

Hi, I'm Robbie Long and welcome to Day 3 of your program. I wish I could tell you that today is just going to whiz on by, but it's not. Today is going to be quite the experience for you, as the meth is almost completely out of your bloodstream, and the fight from inside your body and mind will be one set on convincing you that it's time to forget about this program and get back to the meth lifestyle you're trying so hard to walk away from. Your minds influence will be strong today, and all of its reasoning will make perfect sense. That's because your mind knows exactly how to talk to you in logical terms that make sense to you, and appeal to your needs. Remember that this game of mind-control is a fight between the real you, and a mind which has been controlling you since the first day you started using your drug. Your mind is now suffering from withdrawal because you have removed the drug it needs to function normally. It will use all of its powers to convince you that this program is bunk and that you should just start using again, to end the pain. But things are different now and you are taking back control of your own mind. You know that all of the pain will be gone forever if you stay on track and finish the program. Be strong, because you really are stronger than a few suggestions planted in a mind which could care less about your good will. It just wants its candy. But you got this.

Today you'll work hard on some of the mind techniques you learned earlier in the course, and quite possibly perfect your ball-of-bad-memories exercise. Today, you will feel pain and you will be sick. As the meth in your bloodstream wears thin, your entire chemical makeup is changing and the effects will be just as obvious as the first time you put that chemical into your body. If you can remember that far back, your body and mind were instantly shocked the first time you used meth, and the doors and windows of your mind were thrown open all at once. You went from a 'normal state' to a completely different person within minutes, and you could feel the adrenalin pumping throughout your body, letting you know that this drug was exactly what you needed to feel right (I call it 'the big lie').

Though this may sound like a great time to someone who isn't addicted to drugs, you know first-hand how this drug has since ruined your life, and all of the horrible atrocities that you've lived through. The goal is to get back to that 'normal' state, although the appeal of being normal can be bitter-sweet. You have to remember that the normal you're going for here, is one that removes the chemical dependency and gives you your life back. Normal is good and normal is the goal, but feeling normal will never be the greatest feeling on earth, or you would never have tried to escape it in the first place. The lesson you learned was that being normal is way better than being strung out on meth all of the time, hating your life, and hating who you have become. At this point, getting back to normal is a shot at seeing where your life would have taken you, if not for the paths that you did choose. Normal is your big second chance, and take it from me, it is way better than a chemical dependency.

This is not some trick that puts you back into a stagnant boring life, but rather a key which opens the door to a brand new lifestyle, made up of dreams and visions that your chemical dependency has led you away from. A huge wall was built around you with meth, and now you're tearing down that wall, and the world will be yours once again, to live in, explore, and to become a part of.

Though you will go through ups and downs which will make the day-to-day monotony of normalcy seem at times to be boring at best, you will embrace the silence in your head with a new found love which will take the place of the everyday static you now live in. You will thank your lucky stars for the ability to approach meaningless activities with the smile of an accomplished human being, who took the initiative to tackle one of the hardest feats known to mankind. This feeling of exuberance will flow through your veins every time it hits you, that you are clean and that you did so on your own…and that everything else in this world is easy now. After you kick this addiction for good, I promise you that your new life will be far more exciting than this mess you're leaving behind. You will embrace the change for all of the good that it brings.

Unfortunately, today you'll be jumping through hoops to make that dream a reality. You knew there would be tough days ahead, and this is just one of them. If you planned your quit-date correctly, this will be a day where you can stay out of the world and concentrate on making the transition as painless as possible, to get you through today and into tomorrow as quick as possible. Like I always say, if you could sleep through the entire day today, the better for you and those around you. Today is supposed to be a day of rest. If you were needed at work, you are supposed to be thinking about calling in sick. Remember, people do get sick and most likely today, so will you. If you think you can make it because you feel you are tougher than the average human, than you probably can. This is all about strength and mind control, and if you have your mind set, you can do anything, even if it hurts. I know I can, so I know that you can as well. *What one man can do, another man can do also* (say it twice). What one man can do, another man can do. Thousands of people have kicked this very addiction with this very program. What one man can do, another man can do, as well.

For the functioning addict intent on keeping up your work presence, please remember that it's okay to tell people that you're feeling a bit under the weather, as they may notice you dragging some anyway. This will also set you up if you have to call in sick tomorrow or the next day. There's nothing wrong with stepping up and taking the bull by the horns. It does make you stronger and it does enlighten you more clearly that the pains of withdrawal are nothing that you can't handle. More power to you, literally.

If you do press on, please remember to keep your schedule just as we have talked about. Hopefully, you're drinking a cup of coffee as you read this, and remember to use the migraine tablets in the morning as suggested. Keep your pain medicines close by, and remember that today you may even need more of the caffeine pills as you will be running on empty about half-way through the day.

Remember to calculate your total caffeine intake so you know exactly where you are at, when you gauge the next step. If you're drinking any of those energy drinks or the like, this is an important step to make sure you don't go off the deep end.

Remember to eat whenever you are hungry today, which may be quite often as your body is now trying to save up nutrients and vitamins that it's been deprived of for so long. *Fat is good* and food is what it takes to cure the body of the malnutrition caused by a meth addiction. Even if you're a big boy, food is vital at this stage when kicking any drug addiction. Keep your body hydrated with plenty of liquids today and remember the drink of choice is now Gatorade or the like. What you put into your body now is just as important as what you are keeping out of it. All of this is to change the daily ritual to a positive experience altogether.

Concentrate on the fact that this choice to kick your meth addiction is a choice which you made on your own, in your mind. It doesn't matter if others in your life wanted you to quit or if they preferred you addicted for their own selfish reasons. When it came down to action, you took this one on by yourself and for yourself. You are the only one interested in getting this done and that's why it's finally happening. *You are on your own* in every way now, and the strength is within you because the strength is you. You can look yourself in the mirror now and you can see that you are different, and you can see the strength in your commitment. Stay on target and stay the course. *You're on your own, you know.*

Throughout the day, I want you to remember about the earlier statement that art is everything you see when you open your eyes in the morning. Think about it when you start to feel depressed or anxious. I hope this is making more sense to you now that your life really is changing. The art that you surround yourself with is a picture of who and what you are. If you can change a little part of the art in your world every day, you will begin to see your old life as it transforms into your new drug-free lifestyle. If you would take the time to remove something that reminds you of your drug days and replace it with something that is new and fresh, you will be winning a battle against your mind, which you might not even know is taking place. Change your art, change your life.

Like I've said before, if you can shock the senses into believing that today is indeed a brand new day, then things are really beginning to change. Art can do just that. If you change the art in your life, you will indeed change your life. Please work on this step with the idea that the new art you are adding to your life with be with you always, to remind you of the days that you fought back, to take your life into your own hands. The new art will always make you feel better. Out with the old, in with the new, right?

A new addition to today's menu will be the Pepto-Bismol I included in the extras list. If you decided to purchase that item, keep it close today in case you may need it. In the case of an upset stomach or feelings of nausea, one shot of Pepto-Bismol (or the cheaper knock-off) can take away those feelings and move you towards your next withdrawal symptom. Pepto-Bismol is also used if you should happen to experience the joy of common diarrhea, which can be a part of your reaction to removing any chemical from your body. We always call these 'flu-like symptoms' because the body reacts exactly the same to the common flu and chemical withdrawal.

Another new addiction for today will be the St. John's Wort pill. This herbal remedy will lift your spirits a bit at a time that may normally swing the recovering addict into a mild depression. This is again, one of the items meant to relieve a withdrawal symptom before it appears, making it easier to get past this pivotal point of recovery. None of the other herbal tablets mentioned in this program should be used at this time. They have a tendency to make you sick to your stomach during the worst days of withdrawal. I will let you know when to start using the other forms of herbs mentioned.

The focus for today is to not give up the fight just because the going is getting a little tough now. You knew it would get rough, and this is just one more day that you can put behind you as you walk away from this horrible time in your life. Feel free to add these 'new memories' of the agony and pain of kicking meth into your ball-of-bad-memories. It's a good idea to include the memory of this pain when you start thinking about using meth again after you're clean. This is just another piece of the puzzle that you won't have to relive in the future.

The goal of the day is to make it home without any incidents which may alter your goal of a smooth transition into a drug-free lifestyle. There is no need for you to visit anybody or do anything outside of getting home, where you belong. If you find your mind racing through a list of places you need to go or friends that you need to see, remember that it's just a mind-game to trick you into 'accidentally' running into someone you know who uses meth. Just bring up the ball-of-bad memories until these types of urges go away. These are the normal brain-games from four days off of your drug. You've experienced them before, but you had the full intention of finding meth. This time it's different as your life now involves a new path void of all illegal drugs.

Leaving your home today comes with one quick and clear message. You have to return home as soon as you possibly can. No detours and no getting side-tracked. Stay focused on your motivations for quitting, and don't give into the pathetic tricks from your mind, that misses its candy. Since you have cemented your efforts to kick this addiction, your top priority is to get back home, as if it's some kind of 'safe zone' where you can be trusted. Focus on the end of the day and get yourself home, where you belong.

The goal, again, is to have a nice meal while the Excedrin PM's are already in your system and to get to bed. Remember to listen to your new music and watch the recommended shows. Hopefully you have found peace and calm in the stories that can help you get through today and into tomorrow.

As these lessons progress day to day, some of these techniques should begin to become more automatic to you, and seem more like common sense. That's where you need to be, as you work your way through this program. Keep your eyes on the prize and never look back. The future belongs to you because you've earned that. You are where you belong now…kicking your meth addiction and changing your life. Say it…"I'm Robbie Long!"

If you're a functioning drug addict, these are the recommendations for the day. If you're a non-functioning drug addict, just try to sleep as much as you possibly can. Remember, Excedrin PM is your friend. If you could sleep through this entire fourteen-day program you'd be set for life but you can't. Functioning addicts will have a schedule today as follows;

- Wake up with a cup of coffee and feel free to enjoy coffee throughout the day.
- Take your migraine pills as soon as possible. Split the pair by taking one at a time, if you think the caffeine will be too much at once.
- Have a nice breakfast and remember to take your multivitamin with food if you can.
- Take the St. John's wort pill today as part of your regimen.
- Keep the 3 pain medications handy and take them as needed. Remember that ibuprofen is for pain in the muscles, and aspirin and acetaminophen (Tylenol) are for headache pain and body pain in general. Use as needed.
- If you decided to purchase the Pepto-Bismol, keep it close in case feelings of an upset stomach or nausea start to make you feel sick. It's also used to relieve common diarrhea as some addicts will experience this from time to time.
- As the day draws on, count your caffeine intake and if you need the caffeine pills for extra energy, take them with caution to help stimulate your nerve endings. If you can, use a pill-splitter to cut them in half so that you can regulate the caffeine 100mg's at a time.
- If you use energy drinks, be cautious and know the caffeine content.
- Drink plenty of liquids and eat well, all through the day.

- Get home where you belong as soon as you can and avoid people, so you can focus on your needs.
- Excedrin PM's after dinner as soon as possible to induce sleep.
- Relax and enjoy the rest that you need so badly.
- Remember the marijuana speech. It's not a recommendation for everyone, it's a tool…for you to use if and when and how you decide it will help you.
- Remember to schedule enough time in the morning so that you can wake up and read the next chapter before you leave the house.

Now it's up to you. Follow the instructions as you are told and you will be successful in this program. These next 12 days are the most important in your life so please, take this as serious as it is intended. Be strong and make it happen! I will talk to you tomorrow morning. Have a nice day!

Chapter 15

Day 4

Hi, I'm Robbie Long (say it) and welcome to Day 4. Meth is now completely out of your bloodstream, as far as you're concerned. Although there'll always be small trace amounts to be found, you could probably pass a drug test right now for meth, even if you're in law enforcement, where testing standards are inflated. Day 4 is a day of learning basic motor functions, without the aid of meth to push you through the motions. Some of the horrible things you will feel today involve your body and mind relearning how to operate without methamphetamine as a crutch.

Remember that flu-like symptoms are normal at this point, and there will be physical pain in places where you might not ever remember feeling pain. Your skin may even hurt in several different places, as your nerve endings are being deprived of the normal stimulations they are used to. You might feel an odd sensation on your arms and legs where your skin can crawl or just plain ache. This is the reverse affect to being high on meth, as you eliminate the chemical from your physical makeup. Your body's reaction is to try to figure out what's going on and to send new messages around your mind and body questioning if you are aware of this missing element, or wondering why the normalcy of your drug addiction is missing. Your mind will, of course, try to correct the mistake it thinks you're making, by letting you know (with all of its might), that the quick-fix to the agony you are feeling is to add the chemical meth back into your bloodstream.

You will be reminded constantly that your normal flow of 'medicine' is not being received and as you ignore the signs, the temptation will grow in persistence. You can counter in part, by saying to yourself (or out loud) that you quit, that there will be no more drugs coming in. This bold and stern commitment will help you focus on your goals and often lowers the craving as I've mentioned before. Your job is to talk to your brain and to be a constant reminder that meth is no longer a factor in your daily ritual. Talk to your brain and let your mind know that you have taken control. Its efforts will no longer be required. You are where you belong today (I'm Robbie Long), kicking a serious drug addiction once and for all, and your mind should now be trained to accept this as fact. The party is over, were going home!

Today isn't going to be a great day to be practicing your social skills. If you can stay at home and sleep through most of the day, with the help of your Excedrin PM's/Benadryl's as a sleep aid, that would be good advice, and the easiest way to make it through to tomorrow. Remember that the purpose of each day is to get you through to the next day, with as little turmoil as possible. You don't need to be out in the world, where meth lives; you need to be hiding at home as you find the cure. Nothing good can come from meaningless trips outside for the sake of socializing. Today would be a great day for a movie marathon from the list I gave you, and when you're not physically watching television, your new music catalog would provide a nice change for you while you rest your eyes and listen to the changes that are taking place inside you. Remember that these techniques, and the art around you, are the signs of change while you're looking forward to starting your new life. As you struggle through these, the hardest days of your journey, they'll be the memories that you will take with you when you come out the other end. Stop, drop and roll, my friend. Stop, drop and roll.

This is a day where you 'find yourself' and figure out what you're really made of. The cravings for meth will be intense and your fight to stay away will prove to you that you do indeed have what it takes to kick this drug addiction. Stay strong and stay focused because nobody really cares if you do this or not. This is all on you and *you're on your own, you know*. Today you step up and take a look inside your soul, to get a glimpse of who you are and what you're going to accomplish with all of this effort. Kicking meth was always going to be hard, and this is exactly what you expected at this point. You knew there would be difficult days, which is why you skipped this part of your life for so long. Today, you look inside yourself as you have never looked before, because today is when you realize what you are made of, and if you are really cut out to be a strong, rational human being. This is the day you stay as strong as you can and win the fight over your demons. You do this, and you do it now…today. What one man can do, another man can do.

Now is the time that you've picked to go through this misery, so there'll be no second guessing and no looking back. You'll do whatever it takes to keep the meth away from you, so that you can finish this detox period and never have to go through this agony again. This is the one-day-at-a-time portion of the program and success is your decision and your goal. You will not be tricked back into meth addiction anymore, because today you'll experience the pain of someone who wants so badly to get out of the drug life style, that you're actually doing something about it. The strength you feel inside you is real, and the destiny you see is destiny realized because you found this inner strength and chose to use it to your advantage. Today you prove to yourself that you are a winner, that you are winning, and that you have won. The drug is out of your system now, and you are willing to do everything in your power to finish this mess…feel the pain and remember it all…stick it into your ball of bad memories, forever. Use it as the tool that keeps you clean from now on. Because you remember the pain and the agony of quitting…and that was not enough to get you back on that shit. You are winning now, because you are a winner. You always knew you had this person inside of you, now man-up and move forward. Today you will see how strong you really are. Feel the burn!

Today you'll have to focus hard on your motivations for kicking and use the ball-of-bad-memories to counter any urge you may feel to relapse. This simple mind exercise will be your key to a successful journey out of the meth life style, and back into the life you walked away from when you started using the drug. Your death-wish is gone now, and you're fighting for your life. The 'ball-of-bad-memories' is the key that will unlock the door you are standing in front of, as you finally kick this wicked addiction. I know it's metaphorical but in the end, you will take this key and open the door to your future…and that is real, my friend.

Remember that relapsing is for losers that don't possess the powers you have inside you. Your decision to kick your meth addiction for life has given you power over your addiction, and soon you will believe in yourself as you walk away from this terrible mess for good. Nobody said it would be easy and today, you will feel the pain that comes with victory. I have all of the faith in the world in you and this program…and you also have faith in this program and yourself. The proof is in the pudding and getting though today will teach you how you can do anything once you put your mind to it, literally.

Tomorrow, we will add a few more items to your daily ritual but for today, the only addition to the daily plan already in place is the decision to take any prescription pain relievers you may have been prescribed, if you feel it may help relieve some of the pains of withdrawal. Search the internet for any information on anything you put into your bloodstream, and weigh the pros and cons of each decision you make. Remember that this is your program by design, and any decision you make you'll have to live with. It's not that hard. The rules are simple: never take anything that isn't prescribed to you personally by your doctor. Read the labels and always know the cautions and warnings about drug interactions. This program only uses legal over-the-counter remedies because I am not a doctor and I am not qualified to recommend better ways to alleviate pain, but if you do decide to use any pain medicines prescribed to you, then please consider this as a replacement for some of the pain reliever already in the program. Many prescribed medicines are mixed with some of the very same ingredients as some of the recommended over-the-counter remedies used in this program. Always know what is in your bloodstream at any given time, and monitor your over the counter drug intake and adjust accordingly.

This is another big part of the program that is put into your hands. If you do decide to include prescribed medicines in your personal detox program, please do not mix them with any other prescribed medicines for sleep, anxiety, or any other mental condition which may have adverse effects with the pain pills or the Excedrin PM's you're already using to help you sleep. Remember that people who were not trying to kick a drug addiction have died by mixing too many prescribed pain relievers with other prescribed medicines that combat anxiety, sleep disorders, mental illness, and depression. Do not put your life in jeopardy at the very moment that you are finally taking it into you own hands.

It would be a great idea if you could monitor your intake of all other forms of prescribed medicines during this crucial time in your life, while you detox. Your body and mind will be suffering enough, and thinking that the medicine cabinet holds a cure for the pains of detox is something to think long and hard about.

It is common that you would feel a bit depressed while you are kicking meth. It comes with the territory. Not only is your mind trying to talk you into using meth again by playing on your senses, but you have to know that you are going through some tough times right now and of course you're depressed, you're not getting your medicine. That's what being tough enough is all about. It's getting through these hard times when your feelings are put aside as you concentrate on your goals, and know that there is a rainbow on the horizon. Get through these next few days of pain, mood swings, and waiting on the other side is a world where everything is possible. Of course you can do this; you're already in the middle of the worst part, readjusting without the chemical meth in your system.

Remember that I firmly believe that almost all cases of depression, anxiety, psychosis, schizophrenia, or any other form of mental illness, are caused by your drug addiction and not separate from it. Most people aren't addicted to meth, and most people don't have these mental illnesses. Remember that these types of conditions are common among drug addicts and will most likely fade away once the meth is out of the picture. Again, most of the psychological industry has failed the drug addict by treating the symptoms of the drug addiction without finding a cure. It's similar to the AIDS epidemic where the pharmaceutical companies make billions of dollars providing remedies that prolong the life of the patient, while missing the essential elements to eliminate the need for their goods altogether; the cure.

Remember to drink plenty of fluids today and to eat like a king. Food and liquids are essential elements to the recovering addict and at this point in the game, you need to keep fully hydrated and eat every time you feel hungry. Food is your friend and *fat is good*. You're trying to replenish your body's need for vitamins and nutrients to be stored in your empty fat cells, and the constant hunger you're feeling needs to be satisfied, as food begins to play a pivotal role in your new life. Feeding a persistent hunger will help you appear to be healthier, as you regain some of the lost bulk of a drug addiction. *Fat is good* and healthy at this point in your recovery and losing weight in the future can be a priority once you realize that you have the power in you to achieve great things. Once you kick a meth addiction, you can do anything. Everything is easier than what you are going through right now, and you are doing this as we speak. Stay tough and focused and the world is yours. *Think big, be big!*

If you're a functioning drug addict, these are the recommendations for the day. If you're a non-functioning drug addict, just try to sleep as much as you possibly can. Remember, Excedrin PM is your friend. If you could sleep through this whole fourteen-day program you'd be set for life but you can't. Functioning addicts will have a schedule today as follows;

- Wake up with a cup of coffee and feel free to enjoy coffee throughout the day.
- Take your migraine pills as soon as possible. Split the pair by taking one at a time, if you think the caffeine will be too much at once.

- Have a nice breakfast and remember to take your multivitamin with food if you can.
- Take the St. John's wort pill today as part of your regimen.
- Keep the 3 pain medications handy and take them as needed. Remember that ibuprofen is for pain in the muscles and aspirin and acetaminophen (Tylenol) are for headache pain and body pain in general. Use as needed.
- Prescribed pain relievers are much more powerful than the over-the-counter medicines used in this program. If you are prescribed pain medicine from your doctor, read the labels and the warnings and take them at your discretion. I am not a doctor and I am not advising you in any way, as that would be illegal. Please do not mix prescribed pain medicine with anything else that may be prescribed to you for sleep, anxiety, or any other mental condition you may have pills for. People die when they mix these medicines and this detox period is rough enough without the fatal mistakes that can be caused by mixing such items. This is a serious reminder that you must know what you are taking, what you can handle and that you are in charge of this part of the program. Don't mess with prescribed medicines unless you know exactly what you are doing. It's on you!
- If you decided to purchase the Pepto-Bismol keep it close in case feelings of an upset stomach or nausea start to make you feel sick. It's also used to relieve common diarrhea as some addicts will experience this from time to time.
- As the day draws on, count your caffeine intake and if you need the caffeine pills for extra energy, take them with caution to help stimulate your nerve endings. If you can, use a pill-splitter to cut them in half so that you can regulate the caffeine 100mg's at a time.

- If you use energy drinks, be cautious and know the caffeine content.
- Drink plenty of liquids and eat well, all through the day.
- Get home where you belong as soon as you can and avoid people, so you can focus on your needs.
- Excedrin PM's after dinner as soon as possible to induce sleep.
- Relax and enjoy the rest that you need so badly.
- Remember the marijuana speech. It's not a recommendation for everyone, it's a tool…for you to use if and when and how you decide it will help you.
- Remember to schedule enough time in the morning so that you can wake up and read the next chapter before you leave the house.

Now it's up to you. Follow the instructions as you are told and you will be successful in this program. These next 11 days are the most important in your life so please, take this as serious as it is intended. Be strong and make it happen! I will talk to you tomorrow morning. Have a nice day!

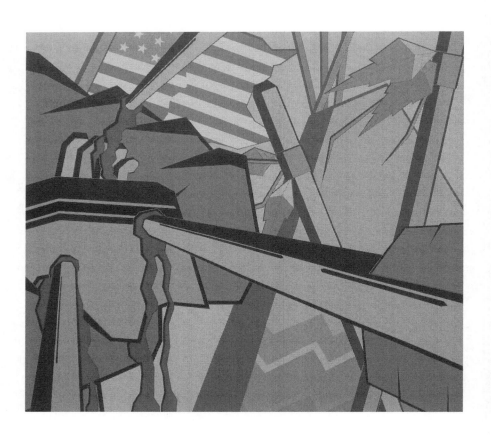

Chapter 16

Day 5

Hi, I'm Robbie Long and welcome to day 5 of your detox. Today may very well be the hardest day in the program, both physically and mentally. You'll be pushed to extreme levels of pain and discomfort, and your brain will exercise all of its energy to try to convince you to relapse. Your body will be so out-of-whack that you'll face the true depths of your motivations and desires to kick this evil addiction once and for all. Today, all of the stars will be aligned against you, and your own 'free-will' will be tested against the severity of your addiction.

    To beat this addiction, you'll have to make it through today with the power and motivation to press on into tomorrow. Again, you will probably be very sick today, and the only thing you can't do to relieve these horrible feelings is methamphetamine. These incredible withdrawal symptoms are the major components in your addiction, which have kept you addicted for all of this time. Kicking is a horrible experience that has an easy solution; don't quit. But that is not how you have reprogramed yourself this time. This is the last time you'll put yourself through this torture. Today is the day that will test your resolve the most, and you will not let that horrible drug back into the picture. Just a few more days and it'll all be over, and that is a fact. Grip it hard and concentrate on your motivations for quitting, and use your ball of bad memories to remind you of why you are putting yourself through all of this torture, and to let your mind know that it no longer controls 'who' you are. You are in total control now, as you fight the good fight on your way out of this nightmare. That should be your 'theme song' by now as the drug has cleared your bloodstream and the only hurdles left to jump over are the pains and confusion of withdrawal. Knowing there would be tough days like today should make the whole process easier for you, as you knew this was going to happen, so the element of surprise has been taken off the table.

Though the detox period is a full 14 days, the 5th day should help you grip the fact that you have now detoxed the chemical meth completely out of your system, and the rest of the detox period is an adjustment phase for learning how to function in a normal state once again. As your body twitches and aches, and your mind begins to moan in agony, you'll feel the harsh realities of the readjustment phase. You'll feel the changes taking place inside of you as you change the chemical make-up of the fuel that runs…all that is you. The damages caused by your drug addiction are being reversed and everything you feel today is a natural occurrence to the adaptation of a life without meth. Just remember that the time period for this brutal assault on your body and mind is almost over, and compared with the amount of time that meth has ruined you as a person, it's a small price to pay to be normal once again. You knew this day was coming, and you prepared for it in advance.

Meth is one-hell of a drug to remove from your personal chemical formula, and the changes that come with its removal contain most of the reasons why you haven't kicked this addiction up to this point. Right now, both the physical and mental addictions are fighting to convince you to kill the pain by getting back on the drug. Your mind will try to convince you that you can do this whole process later in your life, when you can handle it better. This is just a series of triggers being produced in your mind to try to win the fight to get you back on the meth-candy it loves so much. Identify these triggers and you are half-way to eliminating them altogether. Stick them into your ball of bad memories, so you will never forget the pain and suffering you are going through right now. The horrible feelings you will experience today hold within them the power to keep you off of meth for the rest of your life. Keep these memories of today, and use them as power to help you to stay clean forever.

Take the time now, as you are approached by new techniques from inside your mind which are being thrown at you to try to get you to change your mind about quitting. These are the triggers that you can now put pictures and words to, as you identify the techniques that involve memories and emotions that have caused you to relapse in the past, whenever you thought about quitting. If you can identify these triggers, you can recognize them as mere mind-tricks and not actual feelings that you're having.

Remember what you've learned about your brain and your mind, and counter the triggers with a firm notion that you are well aware of the fact that this is mind control, working against you. Put these triggers into your ball-of-bad memories as you identify them. Give them names like "the-nobody-likes-me trick" or the "I will always be a drug addict" trigger. Give them pictures to help you recall them and names to identify them and then, place them into your ball-of-bad-memories as a file called *triggers* which you can pull up in a moment's notice, as individual and collective timestamps that will help to identify and eliminate the triggers altogether.

Once you have a standard for identifying these simple triggers, you can recognize them easily as being false mind-tricks, used to try to convince you to relapse. Now that you can recognize that you're being fooled by your own mind, you can put a stop to these games, and win the fight over your addiction to meth. It's that easy, to regain the use of your own mind, and progress positively in your life. This is a huge step in the treatment of your addiction which most drug treatment programs skip altogether because they just don't understand how the triggers in your mind effect your daily decisions through impulse. Now you know how it works and you can understand how mind-control and meth-addiction can go hand-in-hand to ruin you…and in this case, to save you. The goal for today is to take back your mind through hard work and pain, with the understanding that this is your fight alone and nothing can stop you from winning this war against yourself. *You're on your own, you know?*

Remember to stay focused on the fact that **the truth is a lie.** You're kicking this right now for the last time, and since you've already made it to the 5th day of detox, you would be crazy to step back into the mess that brought you to this program. Fight on through the pain and temptation and remember to include this new statement into your ball-of-bad-memories; **the truth is a lie!** Say it over and over again as you fight your subconscious with a conscious image…that the truth your mind is feeding you…is a lie. Flip the switch on your mind's attempts to play games with your feelings and bad memories. The truth…is a lie. Now find that switch, locate it in your mind, and turn it off! When your mind feeds you the lie, turn off the switch, don't listen to the fake news, and turn it off…let it go.

That should help you stay focused on the fact that your mind is trying to trick you right now into believing the best move for you is back into the meth lifestyle you left behind. The best thing for you is to start running away on the same path which you've been walking on. The truth is a lie…so run from the lies and beat this thing once and for all.

The repetition I'm using here to press these points is deliberate. This is an attempt to use every angle of this lesson to sink the ideas deep into your brain. Your mind uses these same techniques of repetition to convince you that what I am teaching you here is nonsense, so the counter attack has to contain the same types of repetition. I think you're getting this now, but I'm still intent on doing this job right, so that quitting here is for the last time. The goal is to learn how to kick this addiction forever…as I have said so many times before. You have switches in your mind like a simple light switch. When your mind turns on an idea to get you to relapse back onto the drug, you find the switch, and you turn it off. Turn the light off. It's that simple once you figure it out. Idea comes on, you turn it off. You're in control now. Like, for reals man. Can you feel it? (Yes, you can).

Today is a true test of the strength of your body and mind over the influence and pressure of your entire past, against the will you now have of a future without meth use. Today you kick through the hard times and gain strength in knowing that nothing can break you, since you've already made it to this point. The object of the day is to get back to where you started, and to get the sleep you need to make it to tomorrow. You've already learned the techniques required here so use those techniques now to convince your mind to let you take control of your life now. *The power is within you because the power is you.* You are exactly where you belong today. Say it "I'm

Robbie Long…I am where I belong"…as you realize that you are running the show now, in its entirety.

Again, I hope you're reading this while drinking your first cup of coffee in the morning. The program requires that you follow the basic recommendations while molding the more vague procedures to fit your personal needs. It was highly recommended that if at all possible, today would be a day where you would be able to stay out of the public's eye and get the rest required to make the hardest days of detox as easy as possible.

Today is about eating and sleeping and resting, while listening to your new music and watching as many of the movies and programs suggested as you possibly can. Today is about the lessons of others, as they apply to you personally. Today is about art and sleep, to distract you from the serious effects of a major chemical withdrawal. Today is a very important day as you prove to yourself that this can be done, and that you're right on track to being drug free for the rest of your life, and that you can accomplish your goals.

Today there will be two new items that you can add to your daily ritual. Both have been left out of the program so far since they have a tendency to make you sick to your stomach in the early days of kicking a chemical dependency, and because their effective qualities are more beneficial from this point on. Both of these remedies work as a team to replace mood changes with feelings of contentment. Both, in my opinion, are major players in the overall effectiveness of this program. Remember, if you can take away your cravings for meth, you wouldn't be addicted in the first place, right? Both of these items will help take away the cravings by allowing you to feel better now without the use of the drug.

First, I want you to work the ginseng into the mix. It may be better to wait until later in the day so that you don't mix it with the migraine pills and the vitamins that you're already taking regularly. If you can take this item 3 or 4 hours after you wake, it won't upset your stomach and you should feel the benefits it offers within 30-45 minutes of consumption. Ginseng is a unique herb that can help reduce some of the stress involved after the meth is out of your bloodstream. It can help your body and mind during the reorganization phase of your recovery, by calming your nerves and giving you the feeling that everything is going to be alright. This valuable herb will help to negate and reverse some of the effects of withdrawal that are standard in any recovery, while also improving concentration at the times when you will need it most. The calming effects of ginseng are an asset to your program, and I want you to use this item every day until your supply runs out. That should be plenty of time for you to get used to the new life you've created for yourself.

Second for today is the ginkgo biloba pill. This works in conjunction with the ginseng to increase all of the effects I've already mentioned, along with its ability to increase mental alertness while minimizing depression often associated with the detoxification of any chemical dependency. Also, the ginkgo biloba herbs have been proven to help with nerve cell function and blood flow to the brain and nervous system. This combination of ginseng and the ginkgo biloba creates a super herbal remedy that will address the major withdrawal symptoms by attacking the vital signs that most addicts feel while detoxing, with calm and easy feelings, where normally there would be stressful and crazy thoughts trying to re-adjust without the meth. This combination of herbs may very well be the magic pill which helps you through this phase, the most important part of your recovery.

Again, I want you to take this item every day until your supply runs out. This should get you to the end of this detox period, while keeping your mind and body physically and mentally prepared for the future. At this point, starting today, you'll be using every item in your arsenal to combat the ill effects of withdrawal from your chemical dependency. Today, all of the tools are on the table and all of the symptoms of withdrawal are addressed and approached with honest solutions. The rest is up to you, and how you handle the cards you've been dealt.

Making it through today is the goal, and getting on to tomorrow. This is a day-by-day program now and being that this is the toughest day, you will 'find yourself' as the hours wear on, and you'll know what you're made of at the end of the day. Remember to focus on your motivations, and to use the ball-of-bad-memories, which you're continually growing as a weapon to combat the cravings for meth. That, along with these new herbal supplements should make the day go by easier and get you back home where you belong. Stay off the grid today if at all possible and remember that you have no business being out in public as you detox. There is no need for outside influence when you're learning about what's inside of you. Get to your happy place, eat well and get that Excedrin PM sleep you need so bad. Remember that *fat is good* and feed that new aggressive hunger with anything that makes you happy, food wise.

Remember to keep yourself hydrated throughout the day, so you'll need to keep plenty of fluids around. Gatorade is the drink of choice but any of the cheaper knockoffs will do just fine. You'll drink a lot of fluids today, more than usual, and keeping them around will make this part of your program easier. Lots of food and plenty of liquids, right?

Practice every move in the book to make the day pass, as you enjoy some of the new arts in your life. Remember that the movies from the list and the new music are there to help shape your mind into creating that new and different drug-free person you are becoming.

If you're a functioning drug addict, these are the recommendations for the day. If you're a non-functioning drug addict, just try to sleep as much as you possibly can. Remember, Excedrin PM is your friend. If you could sleep through this whole fourteen-day program you'd be set for life but you can't. Functioning addicts will have a schedule today as follows;

- Wake up with a cup of coffee, and feel free to enjoy coffee throughout the day.

- Take your migraine pills as soon as possible. Split the pair by taking one at a time, if you think the caffeine will be too much at once.

- Have a nice breakfast and remember to take your multivitamin with food if you can.

- Take the St. John's wort pill today as part of your regimen.

- Keep the 3 pain medications handy and take them as needed. Remember that ibuprofen is for pain in the muscles, and aspirin and acetaminophen (Tylenol) are for headache pain and body pain in general. Use as needed.

- Take the ginseng herb later in the day so that it can mimic some of the missing elements of meth in your system, and fool your body and mind into being calm, and reduce the cravings for your drug. Remember to take this herb each day until your supply runs out.

- Take the ginkgo biloba pill with the ginseng so that the herbs can work together to soften the minds attempts at relapse, while calming the nerves and minimizing depression associated with a chemical withdrawal. Together these herbs will improve concentration, enhance memory, and improve blood flow to the central nervous system and brain. Together, they will help you feel better and keep you thinking positive thoughts. You'll feel the changes in your thought patterns soon after taking them …This is all good stuff for you. Again, take this herb every day until your supply runs out.

- Prescribed pain relievers are much more powerful than the over-the-counter medicines used in this program. If you are prescribed pain medicine from your doctor, read the labels and the warnings and take them at your discretion. I am not a doctor and I am not advising you in any way, as that would be illegal. Please do not mix prescribed pain medicine with anything else which may be prescribed to you for sleep, anxiety, or any other mental condition for which you may be prescribed pills. People die when they mix these medicines and this detox period is rough enough without the fatal mistakes that can be caused by mixing such items. This is a serious reminder that you must know what you are taking, what you can handle, and that you are in charge of this part of the program. Don't mess with prescribed medicines unless you know exactly what you are doing. It's on you!

- If you decided to purchase the Pepto-Bismol keep it close in case feelings of an upset stomach or nausea start to make you feel sick. It's also used to relieve common diarrhea as some addicts will experience this from time to time.

- As the day draws on, count your caffeine intake and if you need the caffeine pills for extra energy, take them with caution to help stimulate your nerve endings. If you can, use a pill-splitter to cut them in half so that you can regulate the caffeine 100mg's at a time.

- If you use energy drinks, be cautious and know the caffeine content.

- Drink plenty of liquids and eat well, all through the day.

- Get home where you belong as soon as you can and avoid people, so you can focus on your needs.

- Excedrin PM's after dinner as soon as possible to induce sleep.

- Relax and enjoy the rest that you need so badly.

- Remember the marijuana speech. It's not a recommendation for everyone, it's a tool…for you to use if and when and how you decide it will help you.

- Remember to schedule enough time in the morning so that you can wake up and read the next chapter before you leave the house.

Now it's up to you. Follow the instructions as you are told and you will be successful in this program. These next 10 days are the most important in your life so please, take this as serious as it is intended. Be strong and make it happen! I will talk to you tomorrow morning. Have a nice day!

Chapter 17

Day 6

Hi, I'm Robbie Long and welcome to day 6. Say it; *I am where I belong now. I'm exactly where I belong, I'm Robbie Long.* Amazing how this holds true. You are where you belong, free of your chemical dependency (at last) and learning how to continue your life without the drug that's been holding you down for so long now. Today will be a tricky day because you will absolutely feel a sense of accomplishment for making it past 5 days without meth, but you'll still have to fight to maintain your drug-free lifestyle. You've already proven to yourself that you can be clean, and now you have to realize that the goal is to stay clean forever, not just to prove you can do it for a while. This is where a lot of addicts get confused back into meth use. The trip is a long one, and it takes a lifetime.

One of the first and easiest triggers to identify is when your mind knows that you think you have the power to quit (because you actually did). So it tries to talk you into harnessing your new-found power for the future, by falling back onto meth so that you can kick another day. What your mind doesn't tell you is that if you give in, your mind will know how it suckered you in again, and it will use that information to keep you ahead of the 'supply chain' in the future. It's easy to remember that if you go back on drugs, you're throwing in the towel before you've even completed the task. You know this already, and you also know that people who relapse at this point, in traditional treatment programs, will lose at least a year, and most likely their life. Do not fall to this simple trigger that has been used on you already, so many times in the past. Identify the trigger, recognize it for what it is, and use your powers to squash it every time it pops up in your head. This is quitting for life, no more head tricks!

You can beat this addiction now, but you have to stay focused on the main fact, that you can do anything in your life from this point on…except meth. Remember that you will be sent back into slavery for just a 'little taste' of meth. You are a meth addict and your mind knows that just a 'little taste' will bring back everything you walked away from. Everything will be gone, for a small taste. This is a real phenomenon, no meth means zero meth. Trust me when I tell you, that you can't risk your life for just one small taste. That thought which will cross your mind, is just another mind-trick to get you back into the game. Your mind knows that if it can get you to believe you can handle just one small taste, you'll be hooked from that very moment on, and the entire process of becoming a pathetic meth addict begins all over again. You just can't do one thing for the rest of your life…you just can't do meth anymore, not once. Not a little taste, none…because you are addicted to that one thing…and you will absolutely lose everything, if you just take one little taste. The process is clear. Your mind will try its best to trick you back into the long, slow road, which leads to a full-on addiction. You know you just can't touch the stuff ever again. You can do anything in the world…except meth. You can do everything else. The world is yours, in exchange for meth, straight up. Convince yourself of this and you will beat your drug addiction for life. Game over! *(I can do anything I want now, except for one thing I don't even want; meth).*

Most drug treatment programs just don't make that clear. The problem with 'just a small taste' is that *any* amount of meth will open all of your doors and windows in a flash, and you'll be flooded with all of the memories of the great highlights of using the drug. Forget about your ball-of-bad-memories, because your mind has now built a ball of its own, which contains a 'ball-of-great-memories' and it's waiting for you to slip just a little, to have all of those emotions and good times put back onto the top stacks of the top pallets of your memory. Your mind has now figured out that you are using your ball of bad memories and it is ready to counter with a flood of good things (if you think they were few, just wait for the good ball). This will be just one more trigger that you'll have to identify, and yes, hitting it back with the ball of bad memories will work every time. Just picture your ball as being much bigger than the trigger ball. When your mind tries to remind you of any 'good times' you had on meth, you just remember why you kicked…and how later on, down the road, it ruined your life in every way possible. We always concentrate on the worst aspects of meth use, as our mind tries to point out the highlights. The fact remains that it ended up so bad, and it put you on your knees, and it brought you here. There's nothing good about meth use for you anymore, it's all bad. No weak trigger can change your mind anymore so, bring it on, right?

These are the triggers that set you up to lose. It's all a part of the never ending cycle which you're attempting to put behind you now, with this last attempt to quit forever. I'm giving you this heads-up so that the mission you're on stays true and clear. There is no meth in your future and all signals that you receive, which attempt to change your mind will result in doom, if you give into the temptations. You know that already as it was in every single chapter of this lesson.

This is a program that gets you off of meth forever, and the course of action to win this game is to resist and fight, and to learn what's really happening in your head so there'll never be a step taken in the wrong direction. If you learn where you went wrong so many times before, then the chances of a relapse in this course are not happening. You have learned now that mind-control works both ways and you choose to run your own life now, without the influence of the part of your mind that works against your better judgment. *If you free your mind, you will free yourself.*

Remember that you're no longer chemically dependent on meth anymore. The meth is gone now and your bloodstream is clean. It doesn't take the usual amount of meth to get you high anymore because you no longer have a tolerance built up in your bloodstream. The smallest dose of meth will now get you as high as it did the first time you ever used the drug, and it may even kill you. This is where a lot of your friends went wrong. Overdose means that they went over-the-dose that would have kept them alive. Think about that. The word overdose means that the person who overdosed went 'over-the-dose' that would have kept them alive. This happens all of the time. This is a very scary scenario so do not be fooled into believing that you can take it or leave it, because you have learned so much about how to kick your addiction now. You are becoming an expert on your own addiction and how all of this applies to you. Again, these thoughts are simple mind tricks…just like the ones that got you here in the first place.

Though it may take longer, your mind is now attempting to 'feel you out' and work at a new slower pace to convince you that you have a hold on it now. I guarantee you that "one little taste" will get you back to a full-on loser addiction that ruins your life, in whatever timeframe your mind feels it'll need to slowly get back in the mind-candy business it likes so much. The only way to beat this addiction for the rest of your life is to never touch the stuff, ever again. Control your mind, control your destiny!

The rest is just a lie to convince you that it was your idea to experiment just one more time, just one more taste…because your mind knows how strong you have now become. Believe me as I have told you the truth so many times in this program; *the truth is a lie* and you cannot ever do any amount of meth again in any quantity without eventually getting full-on addicted again, and ruining your future. Just say 'no' every time. It may take another month or even two, but you'll be there for a second 'little taste' and the time period before the third 'taste' will be shorter, then the forth is right around the corner, and then the whole process speeds up and your back in the saddle again. And that process comes with a clear death-wish, which eventually will cost you your life. Take control of your mind, stay on the path, and just say 'no more'.

That's just how a meth addiction works. You've most likely been clean for a period of time in the past, when you thought you had it licked for good, and then somehow walked backwards into the same mess again. It's not who you are that makes this happen, it's how the mind slowly tricks you back into the addiction, which you have to be aware of. It's a trigger for the strong-willed believer, who knows that he'll never let himself fall into the trap again…and it's a trick if you believe you're stronger then the drug that has already ruined your life in the past. Remember as I say it over and over…you can do anything you want in your life at this point, except for meth, because you're addicted to the drug, and addiction comes with too much baggage. You opted out for life and accepted the golden rule; anything but meth, from now on.

Day 6 has its advantages since tomorrow it'll all be downhill in many respects. So today may be the last day of extreme torture, as things will gradually improve at the end of the day today, and for the rest of the detox period. Concentrate on the fact that after today, the worst is behind you, and walking you through the program in the morning won't contain so many words like 'pain' and 'agony' and such. Today is a critical changing-of-the-guard where you slowly feel the torment of kicking meth, change into a reality that you've actually been able to do just that.

Although you're not over the hump yet, you have a great program to follow and your daily itinerary is now set in stone. Making it through today will include no new methods that you aren't already familiar with, because you did the same regimen yesterday. Keep in mind that making it to day-6 without meth in your system proves that you're not above kicking this addiction for the rest of your life. It's that easy, my friend. Today, you concentrate as you have, on making it back to your safe and happy place without any outside distractions that put you out in the world, where you don't belong. If you can stay home for the entire day, more power to you. Remember that people do get sick and calling in sick from work today wouldn't be a bad idea, as I personally believe that tomorrow will be a day in which you can appear to function normally, as you clear through this mess once and for all.

Today you'll feel emotions which you are very familiar with, as you have felt them throughout this journey. They should be less intense and the pains of withdrawal will come and go throughout the day, as opposed to the continuing agony which you've been feeling for the last few days. You'll get some relief today, but you'll have mood swings that bounce you from painfully confused to very happy because you know that the end of this program is growing close, and now you know that you have beat this addiction. Focus on the later throughout the day and let the pain and agony take its course on you.

Use the same over-the-counter remedies that you've been taught to use for countering any and all of the withdrawal symptoms. You've come so far on this plan, and keeping to the script should be second nature to you by now.

If today is a day where you have to function in society, keep up your guard and know that temptation is just a mind game within you, and concentrate on the things that motivated you to quit in the first place. When you're feeling those mixed-up emotions, remember to congratulate yourself on the huge accomplishment of kicking the chemical dependency, and remind yourself that feeling this way is just part of the normal action which takes place in a body and mind that are fresh out of the reliance of any chemical dependency. It may be tough today but focus on the fact that it's all downhill from here. You make it through today and the bulk of the fight is over. Yes, it does get easier tomorrow so, get this done today and put yourself to rest.

Remember the staples of the program and practice all of the techniques you've learned as your personal needs will suggest. Stay focused on your motivations, and keep food and liquids close as you are now a major consumer of food products. *Fat is good* and healthy at this point, and you should be able to see improvement in your looks and personality by looking in the mirror. The 'new you' that is forming should soon resemble the person you used to be, before you threw it all away for meth. *You are where you belong* now, on the road to recovery. Say it out loud...I'm where I belong now...*I'm Robbie Long. Fat is good.* And always remember that *you're on your own, you know.* And concentrate on the fact that *'what one man can do, another man can do'.* Think big, be big!

Remember that the worse is behind you now, as long as you can get through today without a hitch. Though the fight may seem long and dragged out, it was all done for good reason. Since the end is near, it should be easier to make it through today with positive thoughts that the outcome from all of your work will be that the program you used had the results that were promised, and that the guarantee will hold true. When you get to the end of this book, you will be clean and you will know how to stay clean for the rest of your life. The future is bright once again so, get this done.

If you're a functioning drug addict, these are the recommendations for the day. If you're a non-functioning drug addict, just try to sleep as much as you possibly can. Remember, Excedrin PM is your friend. If you could sleep through this whole fourteen-day program you'd be set for life but you can't. Functioning addicts will have a schedule today as follows;

- Wake up with a cup of coffee and feel free to enjoy coffee throughout the day.

- Take your migraine pills as soon as possible. Split the pair by taking one at a time, if you think the caffeine will be too much at once.

- Have a nice breakfast and remember to take your multivitamin with food if you can.

- Take the St. John's wort pill today as part of your regimen.

- Keep the 3 pain medications handy and take them as needed. Remember that ibuprofen is for pain in the muscles, while aspirin and acetaminophen (Tylenol) are for headache pain and body pain in general. Use as needed.

- Take the ginseng herb later in the day so that it can mimic some of the missing elements of meth, and fool your body and mind into being calm and reduce the cravings for drugs. Remember to take this herb each day until your supply runs out.

- Take the ginkgo biloba pill with the ginseng, so that the herbs can work together to soften the minds attempts at relapse while calming the nerves and minimizing depression associated with a chemical withdrawal. Together these herbs will improve concentration, enhance memory, and improve blood flow to the central nervous system and brain.

- Prescribed pain relievers are much more powerful than the over-the-counter medicines used in this program. If you are prescribed pain medicine from your doctor, read the labels and the warnings and take them at your discretion. I am not a doctor and I am not advising you in any way, as that would be illegal. Please do not mix prescribed pain medicine with anything else that may be prescribed to you for sleep, anxiety, or any other mental condition you may have pills for. People die when they mix these medicines and this detox period is rough enough without the fatal mistakes which can be caused by mixing such items. This is a serious reminder that you must know what you are taking, what you can handle, and that you are in charge of this part of the program. Don't mess with prescribed medicines unless you know exactly what you are doing. It's on you!

- If you decided to purchase the Pepto-Bismol keep it close in case feelings of an upset stomach or nausea start to make you feel sick.

- As the day draws on, count your caffeine intake and if you need the caffeine pills for extra energy, take them with caution to help stimulate your nerve endings. If you can, use a pill-splitter to cut them in half so that you can regulate the caffeine 100mg's at a time.

- If you use energy drinks, be cautious and know the caffeine content.

- Drink plenty of liquids and eat well, all through the day.

- Get home where you belong as soon as you can and avoid people, so you can focus on your needs.

- Excedrin PM's after dinner as soon as possible to induce sleep.

- Relax and enjoy the rest that you need so badly.

- Remember the marijuana speech. It's not a recommendation for everyone, it's a tool…for you to use if and when and how you decide it will help you.

- Remember to schedule enough time in the morning so that you can wake up and read the next chapter before you leave the house.

Now it's up to you. Follow the instructions as you are told and you will be successful in this program. These next 9 days are the most important in your life so please, take this as serious as it is intended. Be strong and make it happen! I will talk to you tomorrow morning. Have a nice day!

Chapter 18

Day 7

Hi, I'm Robbie Long and welcome to day 7. You have detoxed methamphetamines completely out of your system now and you are exactly where you belong, on this journey out of never-never land. Today is definitely a turning point in your program. Though you may feel a little burned out and beat up, the hardest parts of the self-detox are behind you now, and if you can make it through the 7th day without any problems, then you can do anything in your life from this point on. The meth which was in your bloodstream for so long is completely out of the picture at this point, and only some of the negative side effects of withdrawal will have an impact today on your physical and mental well-being.

Today is a day of mixed emotions and mood swings, so it's important to keep your head focused on the primary goal of making it through the day without any incident which brings meth back into your life in any way. You have no business being around people who do drugs, so avoid all contact with the people you used to do meth with, and avoid any place where your past may remind you of your drug use. Today has no social theme and hiding at home while fixing your biggest problem wouldn't be a bad idea.

Like I said before, the 7th day is a day to be proud of, but you have to get through the day so you can make it to the half-way point in your detox period. I can tell you this as a fact: the first and second week of your self-detox are in no way related. These are two separate events, and completely different in every way. After you finally get through to the end of day 7, you will have finished the toughest parts of the 14-day detox period, and the second week will have a completely different set of rules to follow. Remember the old saying "it's all downhill from here" because that's where you are at now. Make it through today knowing that you no longer have meth in the chemical make-up of your body, and the rollercoaster ride you're on now changes into a readjustment period. Now your body, mind, and soul are trying to figure out what's so different in your life that everything feels like you're not living in a normal state anymore. The truth of the matter is that you are actually changing back to normalcy, which is a feeling that you haven't experienced in quite some time. You just don't feel normal yet because your body is being pushed, pulled, and shoved around, while your mind is still trying to convince you that the cure for this madness is a quick dose of meth.

This is the trade-off that you always dreaded when you thought about quitting in the past. Nobody wants to go through this mess, so we stay addicted to avoid any physical and mental disruption in our daily process. Only because you made this decision to quit, are you feeling such unrest and confusion. This will pass, trust me on that. Your conviction to kicking this addiction is far greater than your need to be a meth addict for the rest of your life. You are winning now, and your future is indeed in your own hands. This is actually what winning feels like. You did the work, and later on, you will realize the benefits of your accomplishment.

So the focus of the day will be this conviction you have to quitting for good. Though you may feel the obvious withdrawal symptoms urging you back towards addiction, you've already learned that you're done listening to the voices in your head which have been lying to you for so long now. You have learned that the strength to beat this addiction is within you, and you have taken all of the necessary steps to rid yourself of this toxic chemical. You realize what a huge mistake it would be to turn against yourself now, as being clean off of meth has always been the dream. But now you have done something about it, and going back to where you started would be the dumbest thing that anyone could ever do. You have to be strong now, and not give-in to your minds attempts to con you back into your personal nightmare.

You read this book to make yourself wiser, and that's exactly what has happened. You are smarter now, and you're a more effective human being who can be strong when strength is needed, and get things done when things need to be done. Your mind is a powerful tool which used to work against your own freewill, but now you have taken back control and you've decided that you'll be in charge of how your brain functions. You will not be fooled back into the meth life ever again.

Today is a day of inner strength when you'll need it the most. Today you'll focus on overcoming temptations which will try to make you believe that "you can always use one more time", because "getting to the 7th day was easy and you could do it again" anytime. Think hard on the reality of that statement. If getting to the 7th day clean was such an "easy task", how come it took you so long to get here? The fact is that getting to this 7th day was difficult, not easy. You earned this 7th day by being strong and learning techniques that taught you how to beat a meth addiction (the hardest thing anyone can ever do) and you applied these techniques to yourself and made them work. Nobody was there for you when you decided to kick this addiction, and that will always be your proof that you are strong enough to see this through, to the end. *You're all alone, you know.* And you are exactly where you belong today.

Remember to practice your mind control techniques, to help keep your head straight and focus on the prize. The goal is to make it to the end of the 7th day, to get back to where you belong, and to go to sleep so that you can wake up tomorrow, one more day cleaner than today. Keep the garbage out of your life and focus on the new art that is your new life. Though you may have a few ups and downs today, this is normal for anyone as screwed up as you were just a few weeks ago. The future is bright but it's still up to you to make this happen. You are in charge of the change that is taking place in your life right now. Grip the hard parts as something that is getting easier every day, and know that this will soon be behind you. Focus on your motivations for quitting and find within you the strength to make this happen. Get to the end of the day. If you can miss work one more time, this would be the day. After today, everything is possible as the withdrawal symptoms you are suffering will weaken each day now.

The only thing that keeps you thinking about meth is your inner conflict. We all have inner conflict which keeps us fighting with ourselves over who we are and who we want to be. It's much like that scenario where the little devil sits on one shoulder and the little angel sits in the other. You can listen to both sides of the argument, but you have to realize that one is there to lie to you, and the other is there to set you free. In actuality, you control the words of both sides. You are the angel and you are the devil, and the inner conflict only exists because you allow it to. Take away the ability of your mind to argue both sides of a point, and you will have a one-way conversation that always points you in the right direction. That, my friend, is mind control. Once you realize that you control both your good and bad thoughts, it becomes easy to persuade your mind into believing that you have already decided to pick a side, and that you are not interested in being influenced by a view that puts you back in the position which you already ran away from. To the victor go the spoils, right? Winners keep on winning.

So let's get through this day without incident. Remember to eat like a starving pig with an all-day buffet pass. Keep plenty of fluids available and set your program to function as you need it to function. At this point in the game, things can be different for different people. You may need the caffeine pills while another ex-addict may be ready to stop using them. Remember that this is a self-help program and that it is designed by you and for you. If you feel the need to change some of the suggestions at this time, remember that they're only suggestions and make the changes that you see fit, to mold this program around your own actions. Whatever it takes to get you through the day is the right way. It's no longer 'my way or the highway' as the ball now rests in your court.

You can do this because you want to, or you can do this because you have to. The wording is not as clear as the message which you are sending to yourself right now. You've always had the power to change, and now you're exercising that power to the benefit of yourself and all of those around you, who count on you for their own sanity. You're fixing yourself for the last time, so that you can take your life back into your own hands. On to the never, we must go!

If you're a functioning drug addict, these are the recommendations for the day. If you're a non-functioning drug addict, just try to sleep as much as you possibly can. Remember, Excedrin PM is your friend. If you could sleep through this whole fourteen-day program you'd be set for life but you can't. Functioning addicts will have a schedule today as follows;

- Wake up with a cup of coffee and feel free to enjoy coffee throughout the day.

- Take your migraine pills as soon as possible. Split the pair by taking one at a time, if you think the caffeine will be too much at once.

- Have a nice breakfast and remember to take your multivitamin with food if you can.

- Take the St. John's wort pill today as part of your regimen.

- Keep the 3 pain medications handy and take them as needed. Remember that ibuprofen is for pain in the muscles, and aspirin and acetaminophen (Tylenol) are for headache pain and body pain in general. Use as needed.

- Take the ginseng herb later in the day so that it can mimic some of the missing elements of meth and fool your body and mind into being calm and reduce the cravings for drugs. Remember to take this herb each day until your supply runs out.

- Take the ginkgo biloba pill with the ginseng so that the herbs can work together to soften the minds attempts at relapse while calming the nerves and minimizing depression associated with a chemical withdrawal. Together these herbs will improve concentration, enhance memory and improve blood flow to the central nervous system and brain.

- There should be no more need for prescribed pain relievers anymore as the over the counter remedies should be all you will need from this point on. These are big-boy decisions now so… It's on you!

- If you decided to purchase the Pepto-Bismol keep it close in case feelings of an upset stomach or nausea start to make you feel sick.

- As the day draws on, count your caffeine intake and if you need the caffeine pills for extra energy, take them with caution to help stimulate your nerve endings. If you can, use a pill-splitter to cut them in half so that you can regulate the caffeine 100mg's at a time.

- If you use energy drinks, be cautious and know the caffeine content.

- Drink plenty of liquids and eat well, all through the day.

- Get home where you belong as soon as you can and avoid people so you can focus on your needs.

- Excedrin PM's after dinner as soon as possible to induce sleep.

- Relax and enjoy the rest that you need so badly.

- Remember the marijuana speech. It's not a recommendation for everyone, it's a tool…for you to use if and when and how you decide it will help you.

- Remember to schedule enough time in the morning so that you can wake up and read the next chapter before you leave the house.

Now it's up to you. Follow the instructions as you are told and you will be successful in this program. These next 8 days are the most important in your life so please, take this as serious as it is intended. Be strong and make it happen! I will talk to you tomorrow morning. Have a nice day!

Chapter 19

Day 8

Welcome to day 8 of your recovery program. You are exactly where you belong now, on the trip of a lifetime, back to the front. Though you may seem disoriented at times, you're now one step closer to being a functioning non-drug addict. You are no longer chemically dependent on meth, and your body is now adapting to the normal chemicals that run through the bodies of regular, healthy people, who are not addicted to any drug at all. Your body is now assimilating to the normal lifestyle you used to live before you tangled drugs into your daily ritual, and started the long downward spiral which led you to this book in the first place. You should consider any mood swings or unexpected changes in the way you think, as welcome relief that may seem to confuse you, but is a positive change that has to take place, as you travel down this new road. You should open your mind to the belief that this is all good stuff, no matter how horrible it may seem at times, and that this is expected and accepted, so you can move forward from this point on. These are not setbacks at all; these are changes for the better. And this is just how it works.

Today is not going to be as hard on your body physically as yesterday seemed, since you're now over-the-hump and headed downhill, as promised. There will be moments, don't get me wrong, but you are now fully prepared for anything that rears its ugly head towards you. You have won the battle and the war is almost over. The feelings you've had for so long of being a loser are almost completely erased. Losers usually don't take the time, or put out the effort, to address the problems that make them feel hopeless. The fight is within you because the fight is about you. You're now creating the person you are worthy of being, and the choices you've made to kick this addiction are real, and you've now taken the steps to correct any of your past mistakes. Today, you have to focus on how you'll get through the day without incident, and make it back home so you can rest and stay out of the society that got you in this mess in the first place. Your life belongs to you now, and the strength that you now hold over the drug will be the strength which guides you, as you develop new wants and needs, and start to develop a plan to fulfill your dreams. Today you get a grip on the fact that meth addiction is in your past, and you have moved-on to a much better place now. As the fog in your mind is lifted away, you can see clearly now that the world is yours once again.

After all of the work you've put into this program, you'll not be thinking about returning to the meth life ever again. The power to carry on is easier now that the chemical has been removed from the equation. If you catch your mind trying to sway you back, you'll use your ball of bad memories and the other mind techniques to put that horrible existence back in its place. You have the tools and now you have developed the talents. Never let it rest that you have fixed your own problems, and that the only thing that can trick you back into meth use is a moment of weakness that you cannot afford to have. Be strong forever, and be clear on your mission. Focus on your motivations for quitting whenever you feel the need to remind yourself what the pain was all about. You can do anything you want in your life now…except for meth, because you're addicted to that drug. Being strong is to convince yourself that nobody on any given day can change your mind under any circumstances. The worst case scenario, whatever that may be, is not enough to drag you down into the gutter you just pulled yourself out of. To be strong is to remember the horrible past you created for yourself, and to be strong enough to stick to these cold hard facts. You are building a wall in your mind that blocks out your own ability to make the decision that lets you fall back into your drug life. The wall you are building is just too high for that one thing. Meth use is out of the question and has a wall around it that you cannot go around, and that you cannot climb over. Make it happen and you save your own life, and the lives of those you touch.

The plan for today is just like the rest of them. You have an absolute ritual now that is different from those you have known in the past, and the goal will always be to get back home where you belong so that you can have a nice meal and get to bed, so that you can put this day behind you and move on to the next. The tragic life you've been living on meth is further behind you every day you wake up clean, and your world is now molded around a dream you had of becoming drug-free, and the steps that you took to get to this place in your life. There is no turning back now, and the light is no longer at the end of the tunnel, it's right there in front of you. You are strong now, and confident, and nothing will stand in your way of completing this program, as it gets easier by the day.

Know that there will be plenty of attempts by your mind to trick you back into using meth, but none of them will be so strong as to trick you back into doing this drug even one more time. Remember that one little hit in any form will take you all of the way back in a single moment. Never forget that fact. Your mind will play tricks with you that you would never guess could happen, until they actually do. You will smell meth while you drive or walk down the street. You will taste meth on your tongue and in your throat, but it won't be anywhere around. The temptations will be strong and come from every direction, and just when you think you've been through the whole list, new techniques of your super-brain will pop up as if to test your own freewill. All of this is normal as meth addiction is the king of mind games, and the only way to beat it is to know these games are coming, and to laugh at how funny and odd the attempts are, as they try to disguise themselves as completely separate from the fact that the goal is to get you to relapse. They will play on your emotions, your sexuality, your common sense, and even your needs, wants and desires. Prepare for the worse, and be ready to win the war.

You are in control of your own destiny now, and you have put an end to all that is bad in your world. Everything which presents itself to you as negative from this point on will be a drop in the bucket compared to the things that you have already lived through. You make it through this adjustment period with your head held high, because the only fight you have now is against time itself. You will see improvements in your life every day, week, month, and year...and you will dream and succeed in ways which you won't even let yourself think of today. Trust me on that, I'm a living example of someone who wouldn't allow himself to dream. There just comes a point where real life success starts to pass up your expectations anyway. Anyone who kicks a drug addiction on their own is a hero to themselves. And with this achievement comes a snowball effect that just keeps growing and growing…and you will find these words to be true someday, trust me on that. So, for right now, focus on the prize. Remember when you defined your motivations? Add these simple facts to your list and know that there is no stopping you after the full effects of a meth addiction are totally removed from who and what you are. *Rome was not built in a day*, so take this one step at a time, and the world will be yours.

Get through this day 8 of your 14 day self-detox, and watch the time go by with a smile on your face. The end is truly near, and the power is in you because the power is you. Never again be at the mercy of a thing, or a person, or a theory, which misguides you through your life. Life is too short, and there is no more floating from one day to the next, without even being aware as the days go by. Life is a gift and the gift is good, and you need to take the steps to get through each day knowing that tomorrow will always give you another chance. The world…will give you another chance. You made it through this day by soul-searching, to examine yourself and your inner being, to see if this life was real or just a trap that you fell into. Today, your mind is much more clear to the fact that you've been tricked, and though you are still living in shades of unanswered questions and fog, this is real life which is beginning to open your eyes…and with time, you'll like what you see for a change. There is no way to put a price on the lessons you've learned while kicking this addiction, as they are the most valuable lessons you've acquired in your life so far. Now, stay the course and finish the job. The light is on you, and everyone is watching and waiting…to welcome you back.

The world is a different place for you now, and you only have one rule to follow. That's not a bad place to be, right? You make it through today and you wake up on day 9 of your 14-day detox program. You know exactly how to do that, as you have learned the techniques which have cleared your body of meth, and all you have to do now is to keep the faith that your life is in your own hands, and remember that you saved yourself. The world was not there for you when you needed help, but you will beat this addiction and take on the world on your own terms. To make it through this program one day at a time, you have learned to function as an individual who decided that a new daily ritual was an easy trade-off for the life of misery which you were once forced into living. Now that you have worked in this new ritualistic set of instructions, you've proven to yourself that people can indeed change, even from their very core beliefs. A drug addiction can be reversed, and you will be proof of that, in a few more days. You can feel the life coming back into your body, and it's a good feeling to know that you have already put the worst behind you now.

Stick to the program and remember that your morning breakfast is as important as every meal you eat throughout the day. Make sure you drink plenty of liquids and follow the program to the best of your abilities. Wrap it up with a healthy dinner, and get the sleep that you need to make it through the night. You may find that by now, it isn't so easy to fall asleep, since you have caught up with all of the sleep deprivation caused by your drug use. Whatever you wish to believe, trust me when I tell you that sleep is still the number one need for the recovering addict. Despite the fact that you feel better now, and don't feel the need for so much sleep, take the sleeping pill that has helped you make it to this point in the program. If you feel the need to increase the dose, just remember to check with the manufacturer's instructions as they know more about their own product than anyone else. The cure lies within the sleep, and you are so close to the end that you have to take these recommendations seriously. You don't leave the program just because you think you have it down now. This is the program that got you here so follow the path, all of the way through to the end. There is still a lot of information you need in the chapters ahead, so push on through.

If you're a functioning drug addict, these are the recommendations for the day. If you're a non-functioning drug addict, just try to sleep as much as you possibly can. Remember, Excedrin PM is your friend. If you could sleep through this whole fourteen-day program you'd be set for life but you can't. Functioning addicts will have a schedule today as follows;

- Wake up with a cup of coffee and feel free to enjoy coffee throughout the day.

- Take your migraine pills as soon as possible. Split the pair by taking one at a time, if you think the caffeine will be too much at once.

- Have a nice breakfast and remember to take your multivitamin with food if you can.

- Take the St. John's wort pill today as part of your regimen.

- Keep the 3 pain medications handy and take them as needed. Remember that ibuprofen is for pain in the muscles, and aspirin and acetaminophen (Tylenol) are for headache pain and body pain in general. Use as needed.

- Take the ginseng herb later in the day so that it can mimic some of the missing elements of your drug and fool your body and mind into being calm and reduce the cravings for drugs.

- Take the ginkgo biloba pill with the ginseng so that the herbs can work together to soften the minds attempts at relapse while calming the nerves and minimizing depression associated with a chemical withdrawal. Together these herbs will improve concentration, enhance memory, and improve blood flow to the central nervous system and brain. Together, they will help you feel better and keep you thinking positive thoughts. You'll feel the changes in your thought patterns and the other benefits of these herbs soon after taking them…This is all good stuff for you. Again, take this herb every day until your supply runs out.

- If you decided to purchase the Pepto-Bismol keep it close in case feelings of an upset stomach or nausea start to make you feel sick. You still may need this from time to time.

- As the day draws on, count your caffeine intake and if you need the caffeine pills for extra energy, take them with caution to help stimulate your nerve endings. If you can, use a pill-splitter to cut them in half so that you can regulate the caffeine 100mg's at a time.

- If you use energy drinks, be cautious and know the caffeine content.

- Drink plenty of liquids and eat well, all throughout the day.

- Get home where you belong as soon as you can and avoid people so you can focus on your needs.

- Excedrin PM's after dinner as soon as possible to induce sleep.

- Relax and enjoy the rest that you need so badly.

- Remember the marijuana speech. It's not a recommendation for everyone, it's a tool…for you to use if and when and how you decide it will help you.

- Remember to schedule enough time in the morning so that you can wake up and read the next chapter before you leave the house.

Now it's up to you. Follow the instructions as you are told, and you will be successful in this program. These next 7 days are the most important in your life so please, take this as serious as it is intended. Be strong and make it happen! I will talk to you tomorrow morning. Have a nice day!

Chapter 20

Day 9

Welcome to day 9 of your 14-day detox period. You are right where you belong now, exactly. After you make it through today, you'll have just 5 days left before you can claim a victory over your drug addiction. Remember to focus on the prize, and the success that comes with winning your battle over this addiction that's been holding you down for so long. You've stepped up to the plate and addressed the single biggest problem in your life, and now you're only a few days away from realizing that kicking this addiction was something you had the power to accomplish, on your own. The secret now is to continue your drive to complete the step-by-step daily rituals involved in finishing this book. You need to get through this ninth day of your program without incident, so that you can wake up in the morning one day cleaner, and on the 10th day of recovery. The instructions at this point are simple; you just have to use the tools which you have learned already and press-on, making decisions throughout the day which will preserve the work you've already done to save your own life. These moves should be natural for you now, as the steps you've taken to get to this point will be virtually the same as those which will get you to your end-game. This doesn't give you permission to set down the book, as there is still a lot more to learn before you can walk away from the topic altogether, which is the goal.

Continue on, and use the lessons as a study in human nature and resilience, to which you are the test subject. Kicking this drug addiction, once and for all, is proof that you can do anything you want, once you put your mind to it. This was your decision to quit, and it was your decision to follow this program so please, don't cut it short by thinking you can skip any of the content that follows. This is a process which must be completed cover to cover. Remember the guarantee that promises you'll be drug-free involves reading and understanding every word, and following all of these instructions. So, it's very important that you ride this rollercoaster to the end. The devil comes out in the details. Today's goal is again, just a goal for today. It instructs you on how to get through the day so that you wake up tomorrow, one day closer to the end.

Today, you take full responsibility for the actions which will get you through the day and back home, so that you can end your day the way that most people do, with a hot meal and an early trip to bed. Your goal is to get back home as soon as possible, and to take the necessary steps to sleep through the night. Any and all actions today will be to complete this goal without putting yourself in a place that reminds you of the attributes of meth. If you feel tempted in any way, go straight to your *ball of bad memories* and then focus on your list of motivations, which are there to remind you what this effort is all about. You'll take full charge of the work which has to be done, and you will remember all that you have been through to get you to this point. All of the suffering you went through during the initial detox should be on the top of your memories, and your commitment to never go back should be based on those actions. It's just not worth it to be high anymore. It sucks the life out of you, and you're finished and done with living the life of a fool. Meth will fool you no more. It will not run your life for you. You are stronger than this drug now. *The power is in you because the power is you.*

Sometimes in your past, this seemed like a phase in your life which you may never have been able to achieve, but now you find yourself dead center in the middle of breaking this habit. This is because of all of the times that meth fooled you into believing you'd be able to quit when you were ready, and that quitting was indeed in the works, eventually. Though your mind never really intended to actually allow you to quit, you have now taken the steps to correct the mistakes of the past. You always envisioned yourself quitting one day, and now you're in the middle of this event. Be strong, and be able to complete this event in a way which leaves the past behind, and never allow yourself to be tempted enough to actually think you can handle drugs in the future. This is just a mind game you're now well aware of. Temptation is going to happen, but you'll be waiting for any attempt of your mind, to trick you back into your addiction, because you are just not interested in going down this road ever again. This is quitting, for the last time, ever.

Today will be easier than yesterday, as promised, but there will still be moments in the day which will seem tougher than others. This is just your mind trying to figure out how to get past the red flags you're now displaying, to block the normal attempts to influence your train of thought. These are just normal bumps in the road to recovery, and you should be able to spot them, identify them, and let them dissolve without having any real effect. You are in full charge of the mind-games now, and using your ball of bad memories as a mind-tool will again, soften future attempts. Food and liquids are still a major addition to your diet, so remember to satisfy your hunger with just about anything that pleases you. Keep in mind that as you eat bigger meals, you'll start to feel healthier and people will notice the change and comment on your demeanor. *Fat is good* and thinking that you are gaining weight is not going to help you if this is something you fear. Embrace the gift of a healthier lifestyle by embracing the new look. *Fat is good*…for now, at least. Remember you are doing this for yourself and that on the surface, people may seem to care, but that's just a natural human reaction and probably not a genuine concern. I hate to say it like this but I can't emphasize it enough that you are on your own in every way here. The only person who really cares about what happens to you is you. *You're on your own, you know?*

Today, you should really notice a difference in the way you feel. You'll have highs and lows today, but the highs will be powerful enough to let you know you have done the right thing here. You may find yourself smiling a lot, as it comes with great comfort to know that the power to kick this addiction was always in you and now, you may feel the power within, as you understand how strong you really are. Just remember to stay on track and to get back where you belong as soon as possible. Until you beat this addiction all the way, you are still on a probation period which requires you to get back home, where you belong, and to hide there from the distractions of the world outside. You have no business interacting with those who are still addicted to drugs unless you simply can't avoid them entirely. Whatever strength you found inside yourself is the same strength that you'll need to convince yourself, and others, that drugs are no longer a part of your life. The power is within you because the power is you, remember that. Quit making excuses for your errors of the past and correct the mistakes you've made, so that your future is not so horrible.

Remember to continue viewing the video and movie suggestions as they are the lights which will open your mind to a new way of thinking. They were picked for you to use through this process, to inspire you to think in a way which will help you see the answers to questions you've had yourself while you were addicted. You're only a few days removed from your chemical dependency and the rest you will need should include a little down time in front of your television. The movie suggestions are a valuable asset to your recovery program and should be considered an important element. This goes for all of the changes in art that were suggested earlier. Don't forget that your daily ritual should include all forms of art. You need to take the time to view the world in a different way, by seeing the new art in your life. Sample the art in this book, if you like, and see if you can figure out why each piece was placed in front of each chapter, or just enjoy them for what they are; new art in your life.

Make sure that the music you listen to, and the things which you do throughout the day involve a new set of rules. Remember that if you really want to change, than change has to include all aspects of your life. Learn to walk away from your drug friends and situations which seem inappropriate for a recovering drug addict. You're not walking away so much as you are running.

Today will be an eye opening experience for you. Your new adjustments to the world you walked away from will be a slight strain on your senses. You've been living in a world that was not real, and the psychological withdrawal symptoms you will be going through, are the pains associated with your mind assimilating back into a normal way of thinking. The withdrawal from your drug life includes a total reassessment of the things you see, hear, smell, touch, and feel, and of course, the way that you think in general. This part of the process can put an uncomfortable strain on your brain, as you work past the need to spend every moment worrying about meth and your need to acquire, use, and hide the fact that you're an addict, along with the physical and mental tortures involved with the chemical dependency itself. This change is not easy but the fact that you're going through this process at this time in your life, will make the world a better place for you in the future.

Now, you know the drill. Get back on the horse and ride through the day, get home, take your Excedrin PM's and get the rest you'll need to make it clean into day 10, a milestone. Follow the same instructions which got you to this place in the program. They can't be wrong if they're working, right? Keep the faith and believe in yourself. You are the driving force of this action to change your life for the better. Press on, be strong, and keep your eyes on the prize. The end is near and the freedom is absolute. This is what winning feels like.

If you're a functioning drug addict, these are the recommendations for the day. If you're a non-functioning drug addict, just try to sleep as much as you possibly can. Remember, Excedrin PM is your friend. If you could sleep through this whole fourteen-day program you'd be set for life but you can't. Functioning addicts will have a schedule today as follows;

- Wake up with a cup of coffee and feel free to enjoy coffee throughout the day.

- Take your migraine pills as soon as possible. Split the pair by taking one at a time, if you think the caffeine will be too much at once.

- Have a nice breakfast and remember to take your multivitamin with food if you can.

- Take the St. John's wort pill today as part of your regimen.

- Keep the 3 pain medications handy and take them as needed. Remember that ibuprofen is for pain in the muscles, and aspirin and acetaminophen (Tylenol) are for headache pain and body pain in general. Use as needed.

- Take the ginseng herb later in the day so that it can mimic some of the missing elements of meth, and fool your body and mind into being calm and reduce the cravings for all drugs.

- Take the ginkgo biloba pill with the ginseng so that the herbs can work together to soften the minds attempts at relapse while calming the nerves and minimizing depression associated with a chemical withdrawal. Together these herbs will improve concentration, enhance memory, and improve blood flow to the central nervous system and brain. Together, they will help you feel better and keep you thinking positive thoughts.

- If you decided to purchase the Pepto-Bismol keep it close in case feelings of an upset stomach or nausea start to make you feel sick.

- As the day draws on, count your caffeine intake and if you need the caffeine pills for extra energy, take them with caution to help stimulate your nerve endings. If you can, use a pill-splitter to cut them in half so that you can regulate the caffeine 100mg's at a time.

- If you use energy drinks, be cautious and know the caffeine content.

- Drink plenty of liquids and eat well, all through the day.

- Get home where you belong as soon as you can and avoid people so you can focus on your needs.

- Excedrin PM's after dinner as soon as possible to induce sleep.

- Relax and enjoy the rest that you need so badly.

- Remember the marijuana speech. It's not a recommendation for everyone, it's a tool…for you to use if and when and how you decide it will help you.

- Remember to schedule enough time in the morning so that you can wake up and read the next chapter before you leave the house.

Now it's up to you. Follow the instructions as you are told and you will be successful in this program. These next 6 days are the most important in your life so please, take this as serious as it is intended. Be strong and make it happen! I will talk to you tomorrow morning. Have a nice day!

Chapter 21

Day 10

Welcome to day 10 of your drug recovery program. This is indeed a milestone because there's a good chance you've not been 10 days clean in a very long time. Getting through today will put this whole 10-day feat in the rearview mirror, so it's important you stay focused on the prize; a life of freedom to do whatever you want, without the fear of being a failure. When you start at the bottom you can only move up, and you have to believe that wherever you were at, in the social scheme (functioning or non-functioning addict), you were indeed at the bottom, in the gutter of life. This journey has been an uphill climb and you're now on your feet, both mentally and physically. All of the moves you're making are for the better now, and in a few more days, you can honestly claim that you are an incredible human being. In a few more days, you can say that you've personally kicked the toughest addiction known to mankind. This is winning, and you know it because you've been losing for so long now. *These times; they are-a-changing.* Think big, be big, my friend.

Today will again be easier than the last 9 days, as promised. The further you walk away from your addiction, the easier it is to see that quitting was not as hard as you thought it would be. Don't get me wrong, we both understand the difficult paths you've walked on, and we know it was indeed hard times, but the human mind has a way of forgetting pain down the road. Just as a woman who gives birth will say the pain was excruciating at the time, but when she talks about it a year later she'll usually say it wasn't all that bad. This will be the same type of experience for you once you've completed the program, but I want you to take the time right now to remember how painful this decision really was, and how difficult the first phase of the detox period was to accomplish. It's very important you save the worst parts of detox into your *ball of bad memories,* so that you never forget the actual torture you went through to complete this project. This will add to your motivations to never end up in this situation ever again.

Remember that relapse is not an option. You are kicking for the last time in your life ever, and 'slipping' is a bullshit trigger set aside by losers who don't have the strength to stay the course. If you've learned anything from this monumental event, it's that you have the power within you to fight and win, and that this mind game of a meth addiction is a part of your past. You know now that the strength you have over meth is all the power you'll need to stay clean for the rest of your life. Today is a day of reflection on who and what you were, and who it is that you intend to be. The path is clear now and in a few days, you'll walk away from this book and the QuitMeth program knowing that you're in charge of your own destiny.

Though your body is already cleansed from the chemical meth, your mind is still adjusting to the new outside world, and any confusion you experience today is just an adjustment that is expected in any drug recovery. You should greet these odd feelings with a smile or laugh, just to know they are part of the deal, as your twisted mind is now trying to figure out how to live in the real world. This should make you happy, correct? Because it is real proof that you have walked-on-over to the other side.

Expect to feel uneasy and satisfied at the same time. Expect to feel dazed and confused, because these are indications that you are indeed changing now, and this is a good thing. You're right on track to be in a better place in less than a week. You are where you belong now (say it) and this is because you've taken the steps to fix the mess which you made of your life. You are now stepping out of the shadows and walking back into the real world. You can't help but feel a natural adrenalin rush when you know in your heart that you're accomplishing your goals as the days go by. Your natural feelings are beginning to come back to you, without the need for mind-altering stimulants. But as you've probably already guessed, some damage has been done to your brain and central nervous system which will take a lot longer to heal than the 14 days of being meth-free.

As you've been using a drug that stimulates your senses for so long, the natural abilities of your body to produce these types of chemicals has been diminished by the drugs. At the same time, you were causing your body's natural production to slow to the point where there was no need to produce them. The removal of the drug meth from your blood stream will eventually force your body to start producing these elements once again, but there'll be different grace periods for each of your body's needs. The reason I refer to this as a 'grace period' is because of the fact that your mind is not fully convinced yet that this cut-off supply of meth is a permanent decision, which you're going to stick with. Remember that you've always come back to meth in the past, and your mind is still convinced it can get you to relapse this time as well. It's pulled off this feat so many times in the past and it'll hold on to the belief that it can trigger you back into addiction at some time in the near future. So, why would your mind want your body to produce chemicals naturally when it believes that might hinder its long term goal of keeping you addicted? It would not. It wants to wait until the last...*tear drop falls.*

Your mind is still instructing your body to stand down; to wait for the pending inclusion of meth, which it believes is probably coming soon. This is a huge phase of addiction and the triggering process, which you have to get a grip on. The triggers that your mind will be using will come out of left field. They'll be both strong and weak, and they will often conflict with each other. They'll be subliminal and they will be clear as day, and you'll be in charge of sorting through your emotions to remove the triggers one at a time. As you address and remove these triggers, the mind will finally get the message that there is a long dry spell and that the need for your body to produce the chemicals needed to function will have to, once again, be produced by the body itself. This is a process which takes time. This is what you've done to yourself, and this is the path you must take to get back to the promise land.

I don't want you to worry long and hard on these facts. As long as you can see the triggers coming, you can defeat them with the mind techniques you've already learned. Take them each as a personal challenge and kick-em to the curb. The quicker you can convince your body and mind that you are indeed finished for good, the quicker your body, mind, and soul will heal and get back to producing chemicals and nutrients the natural way. I guarantee you have not lost anything which you cannot get back, including your sanity.

Many studies have shown that there is permanent damage done by a meth addiction that cannot ever be reversed. Don't buy into that type of negative information for even a minute. That's just more garbage provided by the same people who didn't help you when you needed it the most. The same people who should have provided you with a drug treatment program like this one, which guarantees a full recovery. The same people that failed you, have taken the time to let you know that you'll never be the same again, while they get paid to put out studies which prove post-addiction that their theories are indeed correct. They spend millions of dollars on tests which provide questionable results that did nothing to help you kick your addiction. These irrelevant studies have done nothing but provide false conclusions which give the addict more fuel to believe that quitting is a hopeless venture that'll keep them in a vegetative state forever. Do you feel like a vegetable today? Like I always say, do we really need any more excuses to be a drug addict? These counterproductive studies are wrong and I can't say that any louder. There will be no permanent damage. Everything you've been through is reversible. Every-thing.

The truth is you'll be fine, just as I am, in due time. But there is a gauge on exactly what 'due time' involves, and the time can be severely shortened by your personal conviction to this cause. The sooner you can convince yourself that this is a permanent and final step in your life, the sooner you'll return to complete normalcy. Some changes in your senses and thought patterns (small things, not extremes) can take 6 months to a year to return to a completely normal state, but you'll be just fine, as your body and mind transition back to complete normalcy. This is nothing you can't handle, considering all you've had on your plate while being addicted. You'll be feeling normal soon, and these steps you're taking are the steps that'll get you to where you were when you jumped on this crazy train.

Do not be fooled by any case study with negative results as you'll be your own case study and you'll prove to yourself that all of your senses will return to normal and that over time, there'll be no lasting effects from your meth use that will hinder your future. The authors of these negative case studies are idiots (you can quote me), who have no personal experience with drug addiction and have no real means of comparing any person, before and after. There'll be no permanent damage done to your body, mind, or central nervous system which will not repair itself in time. In fact, I personally believe you'll be stronger and smarter because of this. You'll find inside of yourself a person who you've never met before, and that'll be a fresh, new, and wiser version of your old self. Word-up.

The goal for getting through today will be one which you are very familiar with. As with all of the days in this program, you'll focus on getting back to where you started without incident. You stick to the program and use all of the mind techniques you've learned up to this point, and you focus on getting back home, where you belong, to have a nice meal, watch a little TV, relax and get to sleep so that you can wake up on day 11 of your recovery. The closer you get to the end of this program, the more of a true believer you'll become. Keep your chin up and be proud of all you've accomplished up to this point. Never let down your guard to the fact that you are a meth addict, who is still in recovery, and that meth is a demon to you. Stay out of the social scene that introduced you to this way of life, and concentrate on the future and your own personal needs. Eat well today and keep lots of liquids around, as always. Remember that you are exactly where you belong now, and that fat is good. And always remember that you are all alone in this battle against the world. You decide your own fate and kicking this addiction was your idea. You're the only one who cared enough to do the work to get you out of the mess you got yourself into. You cannot count on other people to help you or even to understand what it is that you're going through. If you are lucky enough to have powerful people around you who support your every move, be sure to thank them when you are far enough away to know that meth will never enter your life again.

Go out there in the world today and quit making excuses for where you've been, and start making plans on where you're headed now that drug addiction is a thing of the past. You're not finished yet, but the end is near and your life is now headed in the right direction. Focus on the light at the end of the tunnel, and do what you have to do to make it back home safe and sound and ready to rest, like it or not.

If you're a functioning drug addict, these are the recommendations for the day. If you're a non-functioning drug addict, just try to sleep as much as you possibly can. Remember, Excedrin PM is your friend. If you could sleep through this whole fourteen-day program you'd be set for life but you can't. Functioning addicts will have a schedule today as follows;

- Wake up with a cup of coffee and feel free to enjoy coffee throughout the day.

- Take your migraine pills as soon as possible. Split the pair by taking one at a time, if you think the caffeine will be too much at once.

- Have a nice breakfast and remember to take your multivitamin with food if you can.

- Take the St. John's wort pill today as part of your regimen.

- Keep the 3 pain medications handy and take them as needed. Remember that ibuprofen is for pain in the muscles, and aspirin and acetaminophen (Tylenol) are for headache pain and body pain in general. Use as needed.

- Take the ginseng herb later in the day so that it can mimic some of the missing elements of meth and fool your body and mind into being calm and reduce the cravings for your drug.

- Take the ginkgo biloba pill with the ginseng so that the herbs can work together to soften the minds attempts at relapse while calming the nerves and minimizing depression associated with a chemical withdrawal.

- You will probably not have to worry about needing the Pepto-Bismol anymore because the worst parts of withdrawal are behind you.

- As the day draws on, count your caffeine intake and if you need the caffeine pills for extra energy, take them with caution to help stimulate your nerve endings. If you can, use a pill-splitter to cut them in half so that you can regulate the caffeine 100mg's at a time.

- If you use energy drinks, be cautious and know the caffeine content.

- Drink plenty of liquids and eat well, all through the day.

- Get home where you belong as soon as you can and avoid people so you can focus on your needs.

- Excedrin PM's after dinner as soon as possible to induce sleep.

- Relax and enjoy the rest that you need so badly.

- Remember the marijuana speech. It's not a recommendation for everyone, it's a tool…for you to use if and when and how you decide it will help you.

- Remember to schedule enough time in the morning so that you can wake up and read the next chapter before you leave the house.

Now it's up to you. Follow the instructions as you are told and you will be successful in this program. These next 5 days are the most important in your life so please, take this as serious as it is intended. Be strong and make it happen! I will talk to you tomorrow morning. Have a nice day!

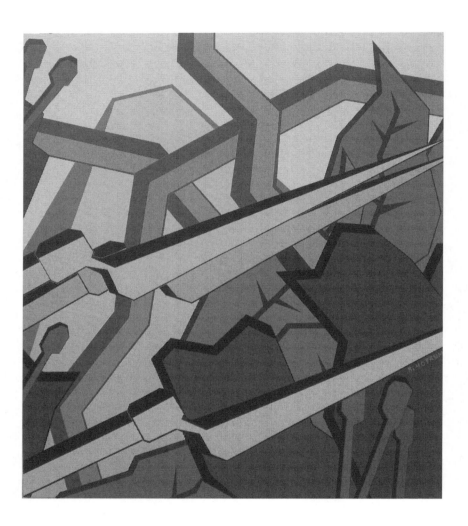

Chapter 22

Day 11

Welcome to day 11 of your meth recovery program. You are where you belong now, exactly. You have now completed all of the steps necessary to quit using meth. You've detoxed your body from the chemical, and now you've woken up 11 days later, ready to finish this detox period. The way you feel right now is exactly how you're supposed to feel, as you've positioned yourself right to this day, this minute, and this very second. You're exactly where you belong, for all of the efforts involved in getting you back to this spot, right here. This is absolutely destiny realized; the kind of destiny that you made happen and the destiny that happened to you. You did everything it took to have all of the stars aligned in your favor now. You're on track to a better life, free of the meth addiction that's been holding you back.

As always, the focus now is to get you through the rest of this program, and the goal for today is to get you through the day without incident, so you can wake up tomorrow morning on day number 12. The techniques used to accomplish this goal should be second nature to you by now, as you are nearing the end of your program and the only withdrawal symptoms at this time is the psychological factors involved with adjusting to this new chemical balance of normalcy. Getting you back to where you started has to involve just as much change as when you first introduced meth into your bloodstream. You're just reversing the process now. This is now a chemical imbalance being corrected as your body fights to adjust to this new normalcy, which is to actually feel normal once again.

Today should be easier than the last 10 days, as promised, but everyone is different and the way in which you approach these changes is directly linked to how bad this withdrawal affects you, and your personal assimilation to your life without drugs. This can be easy if you look back at the steps that you've taken so far, and give yourself credit for putting the worse parts of addiction behind you already. Finishing this program should be easy now and your personal outlook can affect the ways in which you perceive pain and agony. If you refuse to be dragged down by the psychological needs involved with the addiction that you're leaving behind, you can take charge of today, and the rest of your life. The power is within you because the power is you. Stay the course and focus on the main prize. Get through today exactly how you got through yesterday, and this will just be another notch under your belt.

Although it seems like the worse is behind you, you cannot drop the ball and move on without knowing that the ridiculous relapse rates of other drug treatment programs are real. This should always be in your train of thought, even if this program has convinced you, as it should have, that you have finally kicked this addiction for life. The reason I say this is because I don't teach these traditional methods of drug recovery, so I have no way of knowing why they fail so often. I can only imagine it's because of all of the points I have mentioned earlier in this book, about how they conduct their lessons, and how little they actually know about meth addiction and the correct ways to treat the addict. Whatever the true reasons, they're failure rates should be held up as a tool to keep you on your toes in the future. For the sake of those who have not bought into the totality of this program, keep in mind that we will do this, *if for no other reason but to spite those who say that we cannot.* Focus on the fact that traditional methods have failed many addicts, and don't let yourself become another negative statistic. You picked the right program, now it's all about the follow-through.

As you have rejected the belief that meth is a forever drug, so should you let go of the terminologies like the saying *"meth for life"* that have been an integral part of your core beliefs. Meth has ruined your life and the belief that it lasts a lifetime was just a trigger which you've already proven wrong. As you get out of the drug life style, you need to also do away with the drug terminology.

The lesson for the day is about trust. If there's anything I've learned in my years of living on this earth, it's that people can't be trusted. You can put your mind, body, and soul into believing that you can trust someone wholeheartedly, but the truth of the matter is that you cannot. You can only trust in yourself, so using the term "I can't be trusted" or "I don't trust myself" will not help you get someone else to do the dirty work for you. If you can't be trusted and the person you trust can't be trusted as well, then who is really in charge of your decision making process? You are, just you. *You're all alone, you know.*

You cannot count on anybody except yourself because people will let you down, over and over again, if you let them. What is in your heart is who you are, and if you go with your best instincts, you'll be just fine. The only one in your life who truly wants you off of meth is you. You're in this alone and you had better understand that people, family, and friends…are just fluff in your life. The power to kick this addiction and to convince yourself that you can do this forever is only within you. If you start believing in others, they will fail you every time. Do I sound like a man scorned? You betcha. You're on your own, you know…and so am I. When we become addicted to drugs, we had our drug friends and when we kick, we're all alone in a club with only one member. It's all on you today (and from now on), to keep this promise to yourself, that you'll never do meth again. It's on you and you alone and you really can't trust a single other person on this planet, to monitor the way that you feel, and the things that go through your mind.

As with the last few days, the goal for today will be to get through to the end without incident. You do what you have to do out there in the world and then you get back home and, despite the fact that you believe you don't need the sleep anymore, I still want you to follow the instructions and take the sleeping pills that knock you out early, to get a good night's rest so that you wake up on day-12 of this program. Remember that food and liquids are the biggest factors in making it clean through the day. You have a good meal or two and you drink the suggested liquids and you get back home where you belong. You avoid those in your life that would try to influence you back to drug use, and you realize that you don't belong out in the society that got you into this mess in the first place. Anyone who would offer you any drug at this point in your recovery is not your friend. Recognize that fact. The best thing that you can do is stay out of sight, at home in your happy place. If you feel that this move is a form of hiding out, good then, feel free to consider hiding out at home until you have a strong and full grip over all aspects of the chemical addiction which you just walked away from.

Continue to change your art and to add new art into your life. Remember that the things you see and touch and feel, should be different from the things you are used to being around. Take away the things in your life which remind you of your drug days past, and replace them with new things which remind you that you're in a new world now, where all things are different. Listen to the new music you were instructed to acquire and keep on watching movies from the movie list, even if you've seen any of the movies in the past. This is a new you and watching the same movie you watched while high on meth is completely different from viewing them once you are clean, with a new outlook on life. The films are there for a purpose, and even if you think you're not getting the messages, you are...they're in there and being planted into your new way of thinking. It's all good stuff, trust me on that.

Today is a good day to be alive. You can say this out loud or you can feel it from deep inside yourself. It's clear that today is a new day, as you have completely kicked your drug addiction and the only barriers which are holding you now are time, and the understanding that the abilities for you to be tricked back into another addiction rely solely on your efforts to retain the information you've learned up to this point, and to use the tools you've acquired to insure that your life will never take a turn for the worse. Time is the factor which keeps you in this program until the 14th day. Because we put a 14-day time limit on the detox period, you'll learn valuable additional information which will guarantee your success in the future. That's what is meant by a 'full-service' program. We walk together until we walk away from each other forever. I will not let you go unprepared, back out into the world. Remember that the rules of the game involve you taking back your minds ability to trick you back into addiction. The triggers that pop-up, allow you to get a first glance at what will transpire now and in the future, and the mind tricks which seemed so lame to you as they were introduced, have now become a valuable asset to you and your future. You're now so much stronger than the grip that meth had on you just 10 days ago.

Now, let's get this to day-12 by following your instincts to hide until this is all over. Out there in the world you do stand a chance to succeed now, but why mess with fate and destiny? You're in charge of your life now, so you'll do what it takes to make this happen. The power is within you, because the power is you. You are where you belong now, and the future is so clear. Fat is good, and you're all alone, you know. Quit making excuses for the past and start concentrating on where you'll be in the future. The time to start making new plans is now, as your head starts to clear from the fog.

If you're a functioning drug addict, these are the recommendations for the day. If you're a non-functioning drug addict, just try to sleep as much as you possibly can. Remember, Excedrin PM is your friend. If you could sleep through this whole fourteen-day program you'd be set for life but you can't. Functioning addicts will have a schedule today as follows;

- Wake up with a cup of coffee and feel free to enjoy coffee throughout the day.

- Take your migraine pills as soon as possible. Split the pair by taking one at a time, if you think the caffeine will be too much at once.

- Have a nice breakfast and remember to take your multivitamin with food if you can.

- Take the St. John's wort pill today as part of your regimen.

- Keep the 3 pain medications handy and take them as needed. Remember that ibuprofen is for pain in the muscles, and aspirin and acetaminophen (Tylenol) are for headache pain and body pain in general. Use as needed.

- Take the ginseng herb later in the day so that it can mimic some of the missing elements of meth and fool your body and mind into being calm and reduce the cravings for drugs.

- Take the ginkgo biloba pill with the ginseng so that the herbs can work together to soften the minds attempts at relapse while calming the nerves and minimizing depression associated with a chemical withdrawal. Again, take this herb every day until your supply runs out.

- As the day draws on, count your caffeine intake and if you need the caffeine pills for extra energy, take them with caution to help stimulate your nerve endings. If you can, use a pill-splitter to cut them in half so that you can regulate the caffeine 100mg's at a time.

- If you use energy drinks, be cautious and know the caffeine content.

- Drink plenty of liquids and eat well, all through the day.

- Get home where you belong as soon as you can and avoid people so you can focus on your needs.

- Excedrin PM's after dinner as soon as possible to induce sleep.

- Relax and enjoy the rest that you need so badly.

- Remember the marijuana speech. It's not a recommendation for everyone, it's a tool…for you to use if and when and how you decide it will help you.

- Remember to schedule enough time in the morning so that you can wake up and read the next chapter before you leave the house.

Now it's up to you. Follow the instructions as you are told and you will be successful in this program. These next 4 days are the most important in your life so please, take this as serious as it is intended. Be strong and make it happen! I will talk to you tomorrow morning. Have a nice day!

Chapter 23

Day 12

Welcome to day-12 of your drug treatment program. You should feel pretty good today and exceptionally strong compared to some of the other days in your detox, where you woke up feeling dazed and confused with constant pain and discomfort. Today is going to have a certain "vibe" to it, that'll make you feel both happy and successful. But remember that you're not out of the woods yet, and your main strategy will still involve getting you back where you belong at the end of the day.

With this addiction cleared off of your plate, you will be granted a new set of rules, that will be determined by you, on what your future game-plan will be. This of course, starts as soon as you complete day 14 from your schedule of 'things to do'. To get there, you've got to get through today without any incident, so you can wake up on the morning of day-13 feeling even better than you do today. I'm not saying that today is going to be all easy, but the agony and confusion will be minimal compared to what you've endured in the past few weeks. Today is going to be a good day, I promise you that. So, eyes on the prize, right? Remember to use your ball of bad memories and to focus on your motivations. The world is yours now.

When you started this program, you were heavy into believing that your drug addiction was some kind of mind game or psychological addiction which you had real problems understanding. Though this is absolutely true, you've now learned some important lessons on how to reverse these powers and use them to your advantage. Though these tricks were a little hard to understand at first, the techniques you've been counting on are now second nature to you, and now you use them with ease. It's these mind altering methods which have been the pivotal point in keeping these psychological triggers at bay. Your *ball of bad memories* is the best example of how you'll approach the cravings for meth that come up in the future. If you've mastered this technique now, don't forget to use this as a weapon in the future, should your mind wait months or even years to bring this battle to the forefront once again. Your motivations will steer you in the right directions for now, but that *ball of bad memories* will cement itself into your brain, and be there for your use in the future as needed.

Today is a day to prove to yourself that you can enter this end phase of addiction much stronger than the way you began. Today you exert confidence in finishing the program with style. Go out into the world knowing that you are done with meth, now and forever. Though there will always be temptations out there, they're not as strong as your ability to minimize the attempts, and to let them go forever. Temptations to relapse will be weak at times, and very strong at other times. This is just your mind trying different techniques to trick you back. You're so aware of this now, that there is little you've not already seen and conquered. You should find these mind tricks to be humorous now, as they fail in comparison to the way they used to get you back into the downward spiral. You should be proud that they have little or no strength over you, since they used to run your life.

This is post-addiction talk now. That's because I believe wholeheartedly that you've already beat this addiction, and we are just waiting for the time to pass where you can proclaim without a doubt that you are victorious. You've already cleansed your body of the chemical meth, as you know, and the days go by now with less of a commitment to stay focused on being strong and countering the cravings. At this point in the program, you are no longer "chemically dependent" on meth, and it is only the psychological addiction that you are fighting with now. There's a part of you that is so used to the daily rituals, so you just need to find new rituals, daily. It wasn't that long ago that the cravings were the main reason you believed you were addicted in the first place, right? Now that you're clean and you know how to counter the cravings, it does seem easier to believe that you can handle pushing away meth for the rest of your life. But, don't be fooled by the strong belief in your mind that you have total control just yet. Remember that your mind is counting on you relaxing your control soon, so that it can trick you into believing you could handle just one little dose. That's another trigger that'll hit you over and over, the more you believe that nothing could send you back. Watch and wait for the signs that your mind is shifting to a new kind of temptation, the kind that appears to not be temptation at all, but a natural choice that you're making as a grown adult to partake in the drug just one more time.

I'll tell you now and again, that *the truth is a lie*. You cannot use one more time ever. It always gets you back to where you started this program from. It always works its way back in, as soon as it finds a method that finally breaks though the walls you have built up. I cannot stress this enough. You're a meth addict and when you're clean, you can do anything you want in this world, except meth. You have one rule to live by: you can't do meth, you are an addict. You can do anything else, except for the drug you are addicted to. You have to say no to meth every time the question comes up. If you do not, you're not really in control. Meth is still the monster that it always was. And that's what we're fixing in these 14 days. We are taking back the power over meth, and your own minds control over you. We're taking away its influence over our lives and we're walking away clean, forever.

Today will be just like the last few days. You'll make it through by having full meals and keeping liquids around so that you can hydrate regularly. Consumption of food is a major concern of yours now, since you're replenishing all that has left your body through the use of meth. Now you're storing all of these nutrients into your fat cells, as your mind is still stuck on believing that there'll come a day soon, where you'll go back to your drug, and it'll need these stored nutrients as you starve your body, like you've done in the past. Little does it know, you're done with meth for life, and the fat that is being stored now will just make you appear healthier than you have in the past. Remember that *fat is good* and that you are on your own in this quest, and that the fight which is in you has finally showed itself, and you've proven to yourself that you have total control over what goes on in your life from now on.

Approach today as if you're finishing the program in style and use the techniques that you've learned as methods to improve the way you respond to pressures from the addictive personality which got you into this mess in the first place. Try to scale back on the over-the-counter recommendations now, if you believe that some of them are not as important as others. Remember that this is your program, designed by you, and that following any or all of these rules are choices which you made, and the choice to change is now in your hands as well. With today comes the reminder that as you finish the day, there will be only 2 days left in the program. That means that you'll do all that it takes to get back home and get the rest that you need to wake up fresh tomorrow, one day closer to the end. This one is on you now.

If you're a functioning drug addict, these are the recommendations for the day. If you're a non-functioning drug addict, just try to sleep as much as you possibly can. Remember, Excedrin PM is your friend. If you could sleep through this whole fourteen-day program you'd be set for life but you can't. Functioning addicts will have a schedule today as follows;

- Wake up with a cup of coffee and feel free to enjoy coffee throughout the day.

- Take your migraine pills as soon as possible. Split the pair by taking one at a time, if you think the caffeine will be too much at once.

- Have a nice breakfast and remember to take your multivitamin with food if you can.

- Take the St. John's wort pill today as part of your regimen.

- Keep the 3 pain medications handy and take them as needed. Remember that ibuprofen is for pain in the muscles, and aspirin and acetaminophen (Tylenol) are for headache pain and body pain in general. Use as needed.

- Take the ginseng herb later in the day so that it can mimic some of the missing elements of meth and fool your body and mind into being calm and reduce the cravings for drugs. Remember to take this herb each day until your supply runs out.

- Take the ginkgo biloba pill with the ginseng so that the herbs can work together to soften the minds attempts at relapse while calming the nerves and minimizing depression associated with a chemical withdrawal. Again, take this herb every day until your supply runs out.

- As the day draws on, count your caffeine intake and if you need the caffeine pills for extra energy, take them with caution to help stimulate your nerve endings. If you can, use a pill-splitter to cut them in half so that you can regulate the caffeine 100mg's at a time.

- If you use energy drinks, be cautious and know the caffeine content.

- Drink plenty of liquids and eat well, all through the day.

- Get home where you belong as soon as you can and avoid people so you can focus on your needs.

- Excedrin PM's after dinner as soon as possible to induce sleep.

- Relax and enjoy the rest that you need so badly.

- Remember the marijuana speech. It's not a recommendation for everyone, it's a tool…for you to use if and when and how you decide it will help you.

- Remember to schedule enough time in the morning so that you can wake up and read the next chapter before you leave the house.

Now it's up to you. Follow the instructions as you are told and you will be successful in this program. These next 3 days are the most important in your life so please, take this as serious as it is intended. Be strong and make it happen! I will talk to you tomorrow morning. Have a nice day!

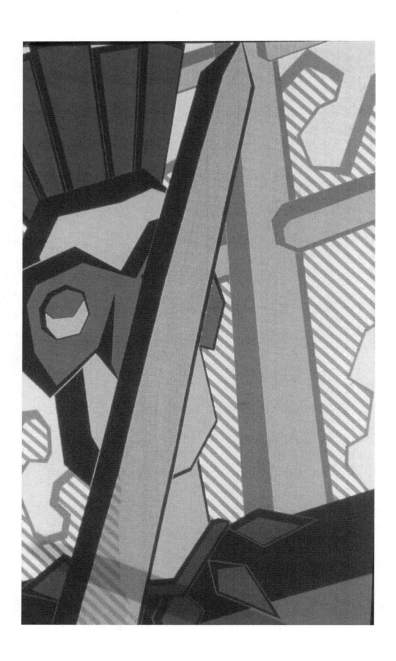

Chapter 24

Day 13

Welcome to day 13 of your drug treatment program. It seems as though the days are going by faster now, so let's get past today quickly, so you can concentrate on finishing the 14-day detox period tomorrow. The only thing left after tomorrow will be a quick explanation about phase-3 (payback) and a simple lesson on duty and ethics, and how you should live your life by doing positive things from here on out. Remember that the 14 day detox period is not the end of the program, but it's pretty darn close. The future is yours, my friend, and the end of this mess is very near. You should be able to make it through today by skating through it, since the program is second nature to you now, and the knowledge that the end is near should give you a natural high which you haven't felt in a long time. If you can make it through today, you'll wake up in the morning on the very last day of the 14-day detox period, and you'll be finishing this program in style. You have proven to yourself, day after day, that you're tougher than you thought you were, and that kicking a drug addiction was just a process that you'd have to work on someday. Now, that day has come and gone and your life is back in your hands. You're no longer suffering from a chemical dependency which makes you appear to be less of a person than you really are. The strength to kick this addiction was inside of you the entire time, and now the final stages of your whole history of meth use is about to come to an end.

These are good times indeed, so we need to wrap this up with a bow and call it a done-deal. But first, you have to continue on with the mind building exercises that got you through this program. Today should include using your ball of bad memories any time that you feel the cravings for meth, or if you smell it in the air or taste it on your tongue. These are natural occurrences that all recovering addicts experience from time to time. You will dream about it as well, for a long time to come. These phenomenon may even go on for a few years, as your mind has the ability to recreate the events of the past in a moment's notice, depending on what you're thinking consciously or subconsciously at any given time. Meth will be in your future, whether you like it or not, so you have to be as ready for the urges as you are today. Your *ball of bad memories,* combined with your motivations for quitting, should be on record for easy access, should you ever find yourself craving the drug you just walked away from. You are now an expert on these simple mind techniques, and using them in the future will be as easy as using them today.

Remember to keep on reviewing the movies that were suggested to you, as you are now walking away from the hardest parts of the program. You will need to keep in mind that this long list of films will still play a particular part in your full-recovery, as they are packed with intentions which are there to help you think in a different way, and to figure out how and why things happen in life that can throw us into situations which can take years to recover from. Don't stop watching the movies just because you've made it through the detox period, watch until you believe that you no longer need any more lessons because you are so solid to the fact that you have fully recovered.

Also remember that the art in your life has a substantial effect on how you perceive the world around you. Stay tight with the belief that changing the art in your life is your decision about seeing things differently now. This part of the program is paramount to your continued success. This is the art which you see with your eyes, that enters into your brain and gets sorted, judged, and placed. This art theme includes music as well, which enters your ears and goes into your brain to get sorted, judged, and placed. If you are rearranging your old art by placing new art on top of it, then your mind is convinced that change is across-the-board, and that's what's you're going for here. When you open your eyes in the morning, you see new things now, things that don't remind you of your past meth addiction. When you hear music or even while watching TV shows, it's important that they don't remind you of things that happened while you were using meth. Those days are over now. Change all of your art, change your life. *Think big, be big.*

Today is about getting through the day without incident, so you can once again, make it back home and have a nice meal, take those sleeping meds and get to bed, where you belong. Like I said so many times in the beginning of this program; sleep is the recovering addict's best friend. It still is and always will be. You think more clearly and without delusion when you are well rested, like normal people. Today and tomorrow will finish the main parts of the program, so make sure you plan on sleeping early for the next two days. Eat well and remember that *fat is good* and that's why you look so much healthier now than you did before you started this program. Remember to keep liquids close and hydrate all day long. Focus on the fact that you are almost out of the woods, and that the power to kick this addiction was always inside you. All you have to do now is just concentrate on your goals for today, and to get back where you belong so you can wake up on the last day of the program.

This program is winding down now because you are no longer chemically dependent on meth to make it through the day. You are where you belong now, exactly, and nothing could get you to walk backwards and reverse the work you have done to this point, where you have always dreamed of being. You will not make excuses which allow you to convince yourself that relapsing is even a possibility. You 'say no' to meth every single minute of every single day. *You're all alone, you know?* And there will be nobody to remind you of that fact anymore. But look at what you did when you finally put your mind to it, when you were all alone. You became somebody who is valid, who can make a difference in this world now. That, my friend, is a huge accomplishment for anyone, let alone someone who was hooked on drugs just a few short weeks ago. The future is bright indeed.

Now, it's time for you to start thinking about what you would like to do with your life once you come out of this mess. With two days left, it's a good time to start thinking about and setting goals for what you would like to do in the future. Think about doing things now which you've excluded yourself from doing in the past, because you were so heavy into your addiction. Start thinking about how you want this to end. You don't need any more help from me today. Just get through today and get back home where you belong, and wake up fresh in the morning. I will see you then, on the last day of your 14 day detox. This is going to be epic!

If you're a functioning drug addict, these are the recommendations for the day. If you're a non-functioning drug addict, just try to sleep as much as you possibly can. Remember, Excedrin PM is your friend. If you could sleep through this whole fourteen-day program you'd be set for life but you can't. Functioning addicts will have a schedule today as follows;

- Wake up with a cup of coffee and feel free to enjoy coffee throughout the day.

- Take your migraine pills as soon as possible. Split the pair by taking one at a time, if you think the caffeine will be too much at once.

- Have a nice breakfast and remember to take your multivitamin with food if you can.

- Take the St. John's wort pill today as part of your regimen.

- Keep the 3 pain medications handy and take them as needed. Remember that ibuprofen is for pain in the muscles, and aspirin and acetaminophen (Tylenol) are for headache pain and body pain in general. Use as needed.

- Take the ginseng herb later in the day so that it can mimic some of the missing elements of meth and fool your body and mind into being calm and reduce the cravings for drugs. Remember to take this herb each day until your supply runs out.

- Take the ginkgo biloba pill with the ginseng so that the herbs can work together to soften the minds attempts at relapse while calming the nerves and minimizing depression associated with a chemical withdrawal. Together these herbs will improve concentration, enhance memory and improve blood flow to the central nervous system and brain.

- As the day draws on, count your caffeine intake and if you need the caffeine pills for extra energy, take them with caution to help stimulate your nerve endings. If you can, use a pill-splitter to cut them in half so that you can regulate the caffeine 100mg's at a time.

- If you use energy drinks, be cautious and know the caffeine content.

- Drink plenty of liquids and eat well, all through the day.

- Get home where you belong as soon as you can and avoid people so you can focus on your needs.

- Excedrin PM's after dinner as soon as possible to induce sleep.

- Relax and enjoy the rest that you need so badly.

- Remember the marijuana speech. It's not a recommendation for everyone, it's a tool…for you to use if and when and how you decide it will help you.

- Remember to schedule enough time in the morning so that you can wake up and read the next chapter before you leave the house.

Now it's up to you. Follow the instructions as you are told and you will be successful in this program. These next 2 days are the most important in your life so please, take this as serious as it is intended. Be strong and make it happen! I will talk to you tomorrow morning. Have a nice day!

Chapter 25

Day 14- The final day of detox

Welcome to day 14, the final day of your 14 day self-detox. As you know, this is the very last day that you'll be detoxing your body and mind from your addiction to methamphetamines. You know it doesn't end here, but the 14-day detox which you committed yourself to in the beginning of this program, ends tonight, after you fall asleep. You'll wake up tomorrow morning, free of the chemical dependency that's been holding you down for so long and only the psychological aspects of your addiction will remain. This is the final day of self-detox and only a few more chapters remain in this book that'll help to guide you in the right direction as you walk away from meth, once and for all. This has got to be an incredible relief for you, and you should feel the excitement running up and down your spine. The thrill should overwhelm you as you look forward to finishing this day, and walking away from the pain and agony which has ruined your life for such a long time. Tomorrow morning, you can officially proclaim to have kicked your drug addiction for good. The only task at hand now, is making it through today.

Today comes with a unique vibe of being the beginning of the end. You should look at the world in a different way now, as you have found within yourself the power to make and execute critical decisions which affect who and what you are. Your future is now in your hands, and whatever the cards have in store for you, it will not be clouded by the fact that you have a chemical dependency which guides your every move. You have won every battle and the war is now officially over. Today is indeed a milestone in your life and the time to celebrate can start now, as you finish your commitment to go through the motions of day-14, where it all ends. The theme of the day is both excitement and relief. You're happy to get this over with and relieved that the program actually worked and you were able to self-detox as promised. So, how do we move on after today?

Tomorrow gives you the rare opportunity to discover what it's like to be clean after being addicted to meth for such a long time. There are a few more chapters in this book which you must read before you can close the book and live under the full guarantee I gave you, that you'd be drug free for the rest of your life. You're now living proof that these words were accurate, as you cruse through this last day of your self-detox. You are completing a feat that major drug treatment programs provide in a hospital setting, with tubes running through your body and constant supervision, and you did this on your own, while supervising yourself.

Do you see how the responsibility has been shifted from counting on other people to counting on yourself? This is what the QuitMeth program has taught you. The ability to kick this addiction was taken out of the hands of caregivers and put in your lap, because the only real way to kick a meth addiction for life is to take control of all of the steps and to do them on your own, without counting on other people to fix you. That is a major flaw in the game-plan of other ineffective drug treatment programs, and the reason why so many people relapse. Addicts believe that they can always go back and get the help they need from people who helped them in the past. In this case, you helped yourself and the ability to stay clean is on you, just as kicking the addiction was a move which you made to fix yourself.

The moral of this story is to not get back to where the problems started. Just knowing what you went through to kick this addiction should supply you with all of the incentives to stay clean for life. Your new motivation is designed by you, to remind yourself that you're in charge of your own destiny and that all of the cravings are just mind tricks to get you back on drugs again. You understand the inner workings of the human brain now, and you fully grasp what has happened to you as a result of giving in to a mind that is consumed by its own needs to keep its doors and windows fully functioning. The lessons you've learned in this book will stay with you the rest of your life, and you'll be capable of teaching these techniques to others as you'll be living proof that the program is as effective as you thought it would be. As promised, you are real close to becoming one of the world's top drug treatment experts because you know how to kick a meth addiction, and you know how to teach someone else to do the same, if you chose that path. After today, you'll have kicked meth, the most addictive drug on the planet...and you did so all on your own. The advice you followed was nothing more than a guide for you to make your own decisions with and the process was one that you followed by your own advice.

So, here we go, back to the front of your life. As with the last few days of this program, today will be a mockery which asks you to stay the course, in the same fashions that got you to this point in the first place. The techniques and steps which have led you here are the same that'll take you to the promise land. You are where you belong today, exactly, wrapping up the program in style by getting through the day without incident and getting yourself back home for one final night that requires you to have a good meal, watch a little TV, and take the sleeping pills that'll get you one last full night's sleep. You'll wake up fresh in the morning, ready to start your first day as a person who used to be addicted to meth, but kicked the addiction on your own, once and for all. If for no other reason than to spite those who thought you could not do it.

You are now a perfect example of someone taking their own destiny into their own hands. After today, you'll be a role model for people who act on their own beliefs, should you choose this path.

It's important that you know who you are now, as this is no small deal. You are a clean, ex-drug addict who took it upon himself to beat a chemical dependency, by yourself. This puts you in the elite category of being a rare human being who fixes his own problems and doesn't ask for charity when it comes to self-enlightenment. You're in control now and you'll never let your minds influence step into the way of how you think or run your life. You have taken the power back from your mind, and taken steps to ensure that this doesn't happen again in the future. You fully understand that you are all alone in this and that stepping back into that horrible life of addiction is something that you and you alone, have to take charge of. Getting through today does not automatically get you through to the end of your life. That's a slow journey with many forks in the road, and the decisions you make at each fork, are the choices you have to live with for the rest of your life. It'll be up to you to quit making excuses which put you back in a place where you do not belong, both socially and theoretically. The choices you make from this point on are made to improve who you are personally and how you want others to perceive you.

Remember that we are not hypocrites now. You cannot be a drug addict for so long and then condemn those that have not found the need or the means to kick their own habits. Be very careful how you approach people you used to know, as most addicts are turned off by someone who rubs being clean in their faces. Nobody likes a hypocrite, so don't become one. If you just dropped off a copy of this book at a drug house, you know they would all take turns reading it, even if they had no interest in cleaning up. That's what drug addicts do with information on drugs, they eat it up and they'll want to read every page. They like knowing more about the drug they're hooked on, no matter what the lesson is. After you're clean, you can visit these people once again if you like, but you'll go in with the understanding that there is nothing that will transpire inside which could ever get you to even look at the drug, let alone consider touching it. You're strong now and no first attempt to persuade you will have any real effect on the firm belief you live by, that won't ever see you back in the saddle again. All that you'll notice is that these people, who were your friends, didn't even notice that you were gone. They're living on the same day, over and over, like the movie *Groundhog Day and* that, you will see as pathetic. But do not be a hypocrite and try to put yourself above them. They are you, just a few weeks ago, right? You walked in their shoes. You will eventually pity these people and hate the drug which used to put them in your daily life.

I would like to say here that I am proud of you for making it to the end of this program. If you're reading these words, you've succeeded in kicking your addiction. You're just going through the motions of the last day. I say I am proud of you because I don't want you to hear these words from others and take them to heart. They don't know what I mean when I say I am proud of you, and their words mean something else completely. You should take lightly anyone who tells you they're proud of you, because they don't even really know what they're proud of. They're proud that you are presenting yourself in a different demeanor than you have in the past, but they reserve the right to consider this a part time clean-up, like you've done so many times, over the years. They don't know that you're intending to quit forever, even if you tell them it's so. They won't trust you still, as they have burned the bridge of trust with you so many times in the past. This is for life now, and it'll take years for others to realize that you have truly changed now.

Believe me when I tell you that the day will come that you will refer to those who will not quit as "losers" even though you walked the same path as they walk. This is a natural occurrence as time and distance begin to separate you from your old friends anyway. It's the realization that they're always on the same day that'll help you to realize you have walked away from something that you never should have been a part of in the first place. You'll eventually find yourself hating meth and any reference to the drug, and eventually hating the thought of anybody who is still using it. You'll see people and know that they're on meth and you'll look at them with a bitter taste in your mouth, as they become a constant reminder of where you used to be, and who you were. This is a healthy feeling that you'll soon recognize as a byproduct of kicking meth and moving on. Until this revelation takes place, you'll stay true to your old drug friends because you can relate to them, but you will stay away, for the sake of temptation and staying clean for life. This is the single most important factor in the lifelong goal of staying clean forever.

So on with the show, right? The goal today, as you know, is to eat great meals and to keep liquids close so you can hydrate your body and mind while filling those fat cells with the needed nutrients to carry you through the days when you're working hard. Today you float through the day with pride and a new understanding of both who you are and what you are. There'll be no major obstacles to jump today as most of the realignment in both your body and mind have been adapting well to your new life styles. You'll always have the items that you purchased for this detox period to use at your discretion after the program ends. You'll know what is missing and you can use these great items as you see fit. We are all different in that way and some will see no need to use any of the items after the detox period, while others may carry on with some of the items for the rest of their lives. I still use several of these items on a daily basis, especially the sleeping pills that insure that I get the sleep I need to make intelligent decisions every day. This is just about how you manage your own program, your own life, and your own self.

So, today is the go-to day where dreams come from. Focus on the prize and get back home where you belong at the end of the day. Stay away from places where you don't belong, and stay away from the social circles that helped you get in this mess in the first place. Like I always say, you don't belong there anymore. Your place in life is somewhere else now. I wish you all the best.

`   Remember to continue reading through the rest of this book at your convenience. You're not finished with this program until you've read every word in this book. While I congratulate you on your last day of the self-detox period, I also remind you that your work is not all finished yet. If you trust that this program has led you down the right path, then you must trust me when I tell you to seal the deal, by finishing the book that taught you how to kick your chemical dependency for good. I will see you on the other side.

If you're a functioning drug addict, these are the recommendations for the day. If you're a non-functioning drug addict, just try to sleep as much as you possibly can. Remember, Excedrin PM is your friend. If you could sleep through this whole fourteen-day program you'd be set for life but you can't. Functioning addicts will have a schedule today as follows;

- Wake up with a cup of coffee and feel free to enjoy coffee throughout the day.

- Take your migraine pills as soon as possible. Split the pair by taking one at a time, if you think the caffeine will be too much at once.

- Have a nice breakfast and remember to take your multivitamin with food if you can.

- Take the St. John's wort pill today as part of your regimen.

- Keep the 3 pain medications handy and take them as needed. Remember that ibuprofen is for pain in the muscles, and aspirin and acetaminophen (Tylenol) are for headache pain and body pain in general. Use as needed.

- Take the ginseng herb later in the day so that it can mimic some of the missing elements of meth and fool your body and mind into being calm and reduce the cravings for drugs.

- Take the ginkgo biloba pill with the ginseng so that the herbs can work together to soften the minds attempts at relapse while calming the nerves and minimizing depression associated with a chemical withdrawal. Together these herbs will improve concentration, enhance memory and improve blood flow to the central nervous system and brain. Together, they will help you feel better and keep you thinking positive thoughts.

- As the day draws on, count your caffeine intake and if you need the caffeine pills for extra energy, take them with caution to help stimulate your nerve endings. If you can, use a pill-splitter to cut them in half so that you can regulate the caffeine 100mg's at a time.

- If you use energy drinks, be cautious and know the caffeine content.

- Drink plenty of liquids and eat well, all through the day.

- Get home where you belong as soon as you can and avoid people so you can focus on your needs.

- Excedrin PM's after dinner as soon as possible to induce sleep.

- Relax and enjoy the rest that you need so badly.

- Remember the marijuana speech. It's not a recommendation for everyone, it's a tool…for you to use if and when and how you decide it will help you.

- Remember to schedule enough time in the morning so that you can wake up and read the next chapter before you leave the house.

Now it's up to you. Follow the instructions as you are told and you will be successful in this program. This last day is the most important in your life so please, take this as serious as it is intended. Be strong and make it happen! I will talk to you tomorrow morning. Have a nice day!

Chapter 26

Success and Failure

Said and done but never completely finished. As far as I'm concerned, you've just completed the hardest task known to mankind; you've kicked a meth addiction. That absolutely makes you a human success story, and as long as you live your new drug-free life style, you'll continue to thrive from this success. I've always taught that kicking a meth addiction involves coming from the gutter-up. There's no more falling, and no more failure than when you started in the bottom of the gutter, right? Whatever you do to succeed from this point on is a step-up and out of the gutter and nobody can ever be jealous of what you achieve from this point on because there was nobody offering you a hand-up when you fell to the bottom. You did this on your own, for yourself, by yourself. It's game over and you won, straight up.

In every human success story, there's always a perceived view that at some point, someone intervened and helped with money or ideas to catapult the individual into a life of riches undeserved. That's not how your life story went, so any new feelings of accomplishment will be internal in every way. You'll be the cause of everything you become, acquire, and accomplish, from this day forward. From the gutter up, my friend…the sky is the limit. Though it may take some time to function in a normal state once again, you have the advantage of a mind that's packed full of new ideas and thoughts, which would never cross the mind of a person who wasn't once addicted to meth. Yes, I am saying there are advantages you may never fully understand, advantages entirely different from other people, because you understand what it is to be a drug addict, and what it takes to pull through that and to get yourself completely free of the addiction. You are different from normal people now, because you have a clear understanding of society's flaws, and you are in fact a better human being than most who walk in your same shoes. Consider yourself to be a super-human now, because in reality, that's what you have become. Tread wisely, grasshopper.

I personally believe that using meth has changed the ways in which the doors and windows of your mind open and close. Even though they won't work in the same ways they've worked in the past, your doors and windows have been exercised, and now their hinges are well oiled. The way your mind works after you've kicked may show you a clear train of thought, which stimulates your imagination in ways which would never have occurred to you before you became addicted. These are big words that no other treatment specialist of any kind would ever use or even support, but trust me when I tell you, this will all make sense to you after the fog clears.

Even though it may take 6 months to a year for you to fully recover from this mess, please don't be discouraged, as the time does go by and day by day, week by week, month by month...you'll feel the difference. The walk away from meth provides strength and understanding at every fork in the road. Relief comes with self-respect, pride, and dignity.

The main goal in accomplishing your continued success in this program will be to avoid failure at all costs. Now that you've experienced the thrill of kicking a drug addiction, always keep in mind that failure is an option which takes meth to produce. Just because you've proven to yourself that you can kick a drug addiction, do not be sucked into the belief that you can avoid becoming an addict again, or that you have that option because you know you can quit again if that ever happens. This is just a trigger in your mind which is set to go off from time to time, to check on your moods and vulnerability. Watch for these types of mind tricks (triggers) trying hard to send you back to being a drug addict once again. That's their only goal. Your mind will always want its candy. It will always remember that it likes meth. Do not fail this course by allowing these easy to identify triggers back into a persuasive part of your ability to think. You can never do meth again because you are addicted to the drug. Remember the horrible days of quitting and plant them deep into your memory, so that nothing you do can influence you back into the mess of a life you just left behind.

Success and failure are brothers in crime, just like love and hate. You can do anything you want in life now, you just can't do meth. There are no gray areas here, just straight-up black and white. There is success, and there is failure.

With success will come much work on designing that new person which you are now transitioning into. You went from loser to winner in just a few weeks, and now you have to define how this change is going to affect you the most. You have the option of moving slow and easy, or you can jump right into your new life with both feet, guns a-blazing. It's completely up to you, and how you feel about the adjustment period into your new life. Different people move at different paces, and there's no shame about taking your time here. A horrible existence has just been removed from who you are, and the time you take to adjust to all of the changes is time well spent. As I kept saying throughout the program, the world is yours now. Do with it what you see fit, without the confusion of a chemical dependency. To continue successful post-drug treatment, there are new skills which you must learn which have to do with hiding and avoiding people and places where drug use takes place. Be forever on your guard that the society which got you into this mess is still out there running wild, as if you never left. It is your duty to stay away from these people to avoid all temptations that could get you to think about relapsing. This is your enemy number-one now, and you just don't belong around these people anymore. Today and from now on, you are where you belong.

I also want to teach you a few small points which should help with your recovery in the future. For one, I don't like it when other drug treatment programs try to use the term "drug of choice" when they get people to admit drug use. I know when you first started using, meth was a choice that you were making, but referring to meth as a drug of your choice is a contradiction in terms of the word 'addiction'. Addiction means that you had no choice. You needed the drug to supply your blood stream with the chemical it was dependent on. There is no choice once you become addicted. So, I don't want you to ever answer when someone asks the question "what was your drug of choice?" Because the answer should be that you didn't have one. That drug chose you and ruled your life. In fact, I want you to lose the word 'meth' from your vocabulary altogether. As you walk away from meth and the drug lifestyle, you should get to the point where you stop talking about the drug altogether. If the goal is to distance yourself from the drug, then you should be distancing yourself from all of the terminology as well. There is no need to continue on with any part of the game, once the game is over. Walk away clean and true.

You should also consider taking a few unusual steps which can help to sway you away from other triggers that you may not be aware of yet. I warned you that triggers will pop up from time to time, and they'll appear in many different forms as your mind flips through your entire history looking for ways to trick you back to using meth just one more time. I like to tell people to stay away from 'like drugs' which remind them of the drug they just kicked. I know I used a lot of caffeine in the detox period of this program, but the caffeine pills will have to be avoided in the future. You'll have to get used to drinking a lot of coffee in the morning, but the need for these straight caffeine pills is no more. Get rid of them and never bring them back into your life. I would also strongly urge you against using any product that contains ephedrine, which is one of the key components in methamphetamines.

Ephedrine is monitored just about anywhere in the world now, so getting a product which contains the chemical has to be hidden behind the locked doors of a pharmacy anyway, so there is no need to worry that you may be buying it on accident. Ephedrine is the main ingredient in the most effective nasal decongestant products, but consumption of this drug will always bring you flashbacks of your drug days (believe it or not). You just don't need that kind of stuff in your life anymore.

Another problem I have with any program is keeping track of your quit-date. I believe that there will come a time when you should stop trying to remember how long it's been since you quit. Once you're positive that you'll never return to meth again for the rest of your life, let it go - let it go - and quit counting the days, weeks and years. When someone asks you, just tell them it was a long time ago, in another world.

Always remember that what got you into this mess in the first place is you have what is termed an 'addictive personality'. Though it is basically a trigger which allows you to see yourself as different from other people, you should know that we all have some sort of addictive personality flaws. That means you're not different for having these personality traits, you're the same as most people, but your mind has convinced you that you are different. It was not the reason you got yourself addicted to meth (because you had some sort of unique addictive personality). You don't, we're all unique and we all have addictive personalities. So, let that trigger go as it was never real in the first place.

The program is ending now and you've learned so many clever techniques to fight your own mind control and win this battle with drugs, but you have to still press on and identify any and all of the triggers that'll rear their ugly heads in the future. They're easy to spot as they'll always try to remind you of the best parts of your drug use. The sex, the friends, the fun, the all night parties and everything else that made the drug so attractive to you from the start. You should have no problems spotting these attempts and your *ball of bad memories* along with your new list of motivations to stay clean, should do the trick every time. You have won all of the battles and now you have won the war. The future holds success for you in everything you do, and failure for your mind, every single time it attempts to trick you into getting back on meth again. You're done with the meth-for-life program and now you can move on and live happily ever after, as promised.

The next step is to move on to the phase-3 of this program and learn how to pay-back to the world what you have taken away (you). I think it is a valuable part of the program so take every word to heart. This is your program, designed with your needs in mind.

Chapter 27

Phase-3 Payback

Welcome to phase-3 of the QuitMeth program. If you're reading this now, it means you have successfully kicked your drug addiction and you're making your way through the end of this book. As you may or may not remember, this was a 3-phase program which included quitting, a 14-day detox period, and a phase-3, Payback. Payback is your way of creating a means to forgive yourself for the choices you've made in the past. Now, you have the rare opportunity to reflect on your life, by viewing your past from the eyes of a clean addict, and deciding what it is you think should be done to remedy the situation. It is my findings that when a person kicks a meth addiction, they are overwhelmed with a guilt-based happiness, which needs to be addressed by looking deep inside and figuring what should be done to make this right. I call this **restitution for the soul.**

Restitution for the soul is a means to walk away from this chapter in your life, with the ability to not use it as a crutch for the rest of your life. A 'full-bodied' recovery program must include information which allows the addict a way to forgive themselves for the burden they've been on the people around them, including their family members and society as a whole. Any person who has not been contributing to society, has been taking away from it. A drug addict is a burden in so many ways. Not only does the nonfunctioning addict avoid taxes altogether, but he also uses government programs to his advantage to facilitate his own needs, since he cannot provide basic needs for himself. Although the functioning addict may believe they are fully covered in these events, there is usually something missing in their life which would have been different had they not spent so much time tracking down and using illegal narcotics. Either way, the theory is that there is an unspoken debt to society which has been diverted but is 'still owed'. It's your job to see that this type of debt gets paid by you, so that one day you can walk away from this addiction entirely, without thinking you took away something you can never give back. That debt is still owed, and it's up to you to figure out what you need to do to get this out from under your belt. As of now, that debt is still owed (I can't say that enough).

As I mentioned before, drug addicts who find themselves clean are a rare breed, and usually they are filled with both happiness and an overwhelming desire to get on with life, and to payback somehow, for the void that has been in their life for so long. So, how do you find this *restitution for the soul* and how do you solve this puzzle and pay the debt?

Like it or not, this is something you're going to have to figure out for yourself. What will it take for you to feel satisfied that you've done all that's needed to completely walk away from this episode of your life with zero feelings of guilt or self-disgust? This is something that I want you to think about for some time. Whether you decide to help out with local charities, or try to reach other addicts by pursuing a drug counseling career, or whether you decide you need some time to feel like giving back, take all of the time you need. This third phase is one that can take years to work itself out, and when you get to the point where it finally comes to you, you'll know that it was the answer you were looking for. *Restitution for the soul* has broad implications, which require a tight fit between who you are and what it'll take for you personally to walk away clean and guilt free, from this entire experience.

I often wonder if this whole QuitMeth idea was to convince myself that I had to stay clean so I could remain some sort of unknown representative of the program, who had the ability to kick and stay clean. I talked myself into believing that if I ever relapsed, the entire program would be garbage. How could I become an unknown spokesman for a product which I knew for a fact was a fraud? Since I couldn't do that, I would have to stay clean. So, your motivation to stay clean for the rest of your life should hinge on your need to prove to the world that this is not a fluke, this is real, and that you are living proof. Like I always say, if for no other reason than to spite those who said that you could not, right?

I also wonder sometimes if this entire program was my way of paying-back like the phase 3 which I mandated for the program. I must have personally been overwhelmed by the need to pay back in some way for the gifts that I denied society, while I was gone-away on my drug-addiction trip. But I also know that my motivation for putting this program together was not so much that I wanted to help other people (in fact I really didn't want to), it was the fact that I had figured out how to kick a drug addiction, and felt that it was my duty to my fellow drug addicts, society as a whole, and the entire world, which seemed to lack a concerted program with the guidelines that would successfully cure the addict. I felt like Spider-Man in that having such knowledge was my gift, and at the same time, my curse. Because I was in a position where I had the knowledge which so many people needed, but I didn't want to personally put in the time to get the message out there. This was not an easy task at all, and it consumes me.

I also have a strong, intense feeling, that by waiting to ensure that this program was absolutely effective, I let down thousands of people, perhaps a million, who could have used parts of the program to help them clean up, when I personally did not believe that I should release any information until it was all there. In this way, I have the burden of knowing that so many people suffered because of the years and years of research that I put into this, before I even started writing this book. This book then becomes my failure to society as much as it becomes my gift to the very same people. This was not supposed to be my job or my burden in the first place. I only did this because nobody had ever done it before, and that meant I had a duty to provide this for the world. I have never thought of this as a money-making venture. This was always a curse that has kept me in a box, working for nothing, to complete my goal of disseminating my work to the public, for your consideration.

I have gained and lost so much in this effort. I like to call it the *Jesus syndrome* because it makes me feel special, because I believe I have suffered for my work, and that I've been denied the right to enjoy certain aspects of my life, as I set aside so much of my time to complete this project. Like as if I'm doing God's work here on earth. Not because I worked for God, but because he has failed us all by not providing this valuable information to this point, and I have suffered where others rejoiced because of my need to do this work, which should have been done years ago, by someone else. I was not a writer when I started out to write this book. I was not qualified to teach a course on drug addiction and treatment. But I do feel like I'm being used as his tool to complete this project, because I was one of the very few that would actually see it through, even if it took well over 10 years to accomplish. Am I then a servant of God?...or do I just like calling it *Jesus syndrome* because I feel like I have suffered so that you can be saved? Or again, is this just the belief that I had to keep in my head to make sure that I stayed focused on the prize, so that I could stay clean and payback to society without the need for riches, as a motivation for finishing the task? Since money was never the motivation and the fact that I don't even know if I'll ever make a dime on the deal, you'll have to believe that I did this for you, for all of the right reasons, so that you could learn what I already know. This is true, unadulterated duty (like when Jesus died on the cross).

As you pick through my crazy words, as I have laid out my true thoughts, you can see, revealed before your eyes, that I haven't yet figured out what it'll take to find my own restitution. It seems that I'm counting on the completion of this program as a way of paying back, and walking away altogether from the subject. I only hope that there is truth to that. I'm even hoping that some who pass this course with flying colors, will take it upon themselves to pick up where I left off. Feel free to correct any mistakes which I made and to expand on this course to make it even more successful as time goes by. There could always be better mind games and better tricks which could help someone who hasn't mastered the ball of bad memories. There could always be a better version of how to detect, identify, and squash, the triggers which cause one to relapse, and there can always be a better set of rules to follow which expand on this program as time goes on. Feel free to share this information with the world, should you ever feel compelled to do so.

Duty is not the need or desire to right the wrongs of this life which we are gifted. Duty is your God given ability to feel compassion for your fellow man, and to respect the society in which you live, and to give back to that society, what you have taken out. To succeed in life, you should always find a way to leave something behind that benefits society long after you're gone. You have a duty as a member of your society to accomplish this mission, as if it was your sole purpose for being here in the first place. Take the time to examine yourself and determine what it is that you have to contribute to society, that they have a need for, and answer that need with effort to convince yourself that your work is valid and acceptable, and that you will fulfill your promises to yourself and your fellow man. It's your duty to do the right thing, where before you were doing things wrong. I hope all of this makes sense to you. Duty is the ultimate sacrifice you can offer, when there is no reward for your actions. If you do things for reward, you're not acting from duty, you're acting from necessity, and those are two different things altogether. Make yourself proud and do the right thing. This will be your gift to the world.

Remember there is no time limit on phase-3 of this program. This becomes an exercise in self-discovery and vulnerability. You find out where you fit in, after you figure out where you want to be and how you want to get there. The world is yours now.

CHANGE THE ADDICT, SAVE THE WORLD.
GlobalAddictionSolutions.org

As a side note for the end of this chapter, any help with spreading the word about this book or the websites would be greatly appreciated. If you possess skills at any level to review this book online, on Amazon, or to spread the word that this information is available to those who need it, you may end up saving the lives of other people who are caught up in the same game, suffering the same horrible experiences that you know so well. Yes, you can be a hero now. You are an expert on drug addiction and treatment. And now you can make a difference in someone else's life.

SAVE THE ADDICT, CHANGE THE WORLD.
GlobalAddictionSolutions.org

CHANGE THE ADDICT, SAVE THE WORLD.
GlobalAddictionSolutions.org

CD Cover for the music of Kill Era, designed by Jay Hotrum, Copyright 2012

Chapter 28

Find your God

I call this chapter *find your God* because I want to bring up spirituality completely separate from the rest of the course. I will try to tread lightly here, because there are so many different lessons in spirituality on this planet that it would be ridiculous for anyone to claim they were an expert on all of them, let alone a few. I put this chapter at the end here, because you may be feeling a connection with some sort of spiritual world now, but you may not be sure exactly what it is. I know I did, and it was hard to put a finger on it. All I know for sure is that those who believe that people in this world have no spiritual connection are dead wrong. There are no two ways about it. Some people try as hard as they can to deny spirituality, but most people embrace the fact, and that's where the soul-searching comes into play.

QuitMeth was never a program that used God or religion to help you to kick your addiction, and I'm a firm believer that God is not in charge of the drug addict, or where was he when you needed his help? The fact remains that there are so many atheists, agnostics, and other forms of non-believers who are true to the point that not everybody believes in God, or even a higher power of any sort. But spirituality is not about a God, really, it's about what's inside of you, and how you go about to connect with it. The path to "finding yourself" has always been about getting in touch with your inner self, to be one with your mind, your heart, and your soul. You are most likely learning this now as you have used these human qualities to take back control of your life. And now you feel the power that was always inside you, and that is very spiritual, man. And I have nothing to do with any of those feelings because this chapter was an after-thought, something I came up with when I thought the book was already finished. It just hit me one day that this program would not be complete if I didn't talk about spirituality, and how it affects the recovered addict.

Although the figures about the percentages of believers vs. non-believers is a study in irrelevant book-keeping, the fact remains that in the United States alone, it is believed that about 95% of people do believe there is a God and that he hears them when they pray. I found those figures to be staggering when I first heard them. I really believed that there were as many people out there who didn't believe in God as those who did. So, what are we to make of these numbers? Are we to say that we don't believe in a God and that 95% of the rest of this country is full of stupid people who are gullible and believe in a God that doesn't even exist? Or are we part of the 95% who do believe in God and we wonder why the 5% who don't have missed the boat entirely?

Of course, I have an opinion on the topic but I'm not really here to try to convert anybody from one side to the other. I just want to point out a few things that I found interesting on the topic. First of all, there is the belief that God was either there with you or not there at all, as you kicked your own drug addiction. I like to believe that he was not there, but those who believe are allowed to stake the claim that they beat this addiction with the help of God, because he led them to this book and gave them the power over meth to complete the course.

This is a valid argument and I support it wholeheartedly. But what about the addict who cleaned up for himself? What about the lessons where you were taught to count on nobody and find the power within yourself to kick this addiction? You must believe that there was no God helping you, and that all of the pain and suffering was felt by you as you kicked, with no help from the outside because the whole time you were looking on the inside. Is this a valid argument as well? You betcha!

Kicking your addiction can be seen from both sides of the spectrum, but the intense feeling you have of success leaves open a feeling that you're now part of the real world. Does this mean that all of a sudden you should consider that there is a God? I don't know, maybe.

If 95% of the people living in the United States believe that there is a God, playing the odds would make it so that you would have to consider there is a good chance that they may be right. How could such a high percentage of people be wrong? I should add that these are not necessarily the same people you hang out with. Always remember that the world is huge, and in the United States alone, there are millions of homes spread through every city in the nation. Some of these homes are huge and show prosperity, while some are small and old, but livable. The fact of the matter is that every house in the United States is occupied by someone who was either able to rent the place or to buy the place flat out. In each house there are people who live there, rich or poor and 95% of them…believe in a God. I'm not a preacher by any standards and in fact, I have not stepped foot inside a church for decades. So, this is not a trick at the end of a book to preach the lord onto you. I'm just saying that if 95% of the people in the United States believe there is a God, who am I to call them fools for the mistake they are obviously making? What if they are right and I am just a stubborn man who thinks he knows everything?

There are many factors which come into play that are making me write this chapter. First, the numbers are shocking to me. It seems to me that maybe the 5% are the fools but who knows? When you're on drugs, it really seems like there is no God or why would he put you through such misery? Then when you kick your addiction, it seems like there may be a God after all, since you feel an intense feeling of being content with who you are and what you've become.

Like it or not, this book ended up being a book on 'applied philosophy', where philosophical ideas where actually applied to real life needs, producing real life results. This whole program was surrounded by my philosophy that a broken man must fix himself. The systems and methods used were all philosophic in nature, because they were my beliefs, and I told them as facts, because I believed them to be so. Now, stay with me here.

The 'great philosophers' of our time always refer to and rely-on the teachings of the original philosophers known as the 'early

Greeks'. The early Greek philosophers (part of the Roman Empire) were intent on studying the world in a 'non-religious' way, to answer life's basic questions such as "why are we here" and "what is our purpose", along with several other topics including my favorite; political psychology. To this day, the early Greeks created the belief system where modern day Western philosophy has its roots. Names which you may recognize like Plato, Aristotle, and Socrates, and most others from the era of critical thinking, were praised because of how intelligent they were, in solving societal problems and such. The 'early Greeks', who developed incredible theories portrayed in multiple writings which still hold true to this day, all shared in the belief that there had to be either a God or Gods, or some form of creator who made us who we are. Most of them believed that the teachings where we evolved over millions of years into our current humanistic form, could not explain the perfections of each working part of the human model, some using the human eye as the best example. If this early teaching was correct, then the belief in God has not only risen from the ashes of our past, but it seems to have snowballed into a much bigger belief than when it was originally put on paper. But it is a fact that most of the smartest people who were ever on our planet, believed they were created by a God, or Gods. So...is there really a God or not?

This question, I leave up to you. This really should be a part of your 'quest' post-addiction, to search for the truth and see where it takes you. Take the time to look inside yourself and get in touch with your inner spirituality. Somewhere in there, you will find peace, and peace of mind. And those will be the tools you need to get through the rest of your life with an awakened sense of who you are, and perhaps what your purpose will be.

I should tell you, at this time, I was a non-believer for much of my life. I went through the motions of attending church when I was a kid, because my parents had a policy of 'church on Sunday' and I really had no choice. I just wasn't sure, and I wasn't buying all of the religious mess that goes on between the different religions. One religion tells you one thing and another religion will teach completely different ideologies (same God though). It just comes out different in each culture, or lifestyle. Religion as a whole is a turn-off when they all point fingers at each other, and swear that those who don't believe as they believe are going to hell. It's a bit hard to believe that a God would let this kind of hypocrisy take place. But I was afforded a first-hand view at something I later found out was called mysticism. I didn't read about this until 15 years after it happened to me, and I should also point out that this may have been a turning point for me which helped me to eventually write this book. Mysticism is a bit scary on its own, especially when I read about it and it described exactly what I went through, almost word for word. It's a real phenomenon, as I experienced it myself first hand, with some of my best friends watching. Feel free to look it up some day when you get the chance. It changed my life and pointed me to the fact that there absolutely is a spiritual world which is not in plain sight, but is real.

Nevertheless, I leave you with this; if there really is a God and the 95% who believe are correct, perhaps you should consider finding out for yourself. Start anywhere and follow a path of your own design. But if you feel the need to find out why 95% of the people in the United States believe that there is a God, you owe it to yourself to find out if it's true or not. Pick a few churches and go inside and see if you 'feel the magic' or not. Search the internet for different forms of spirituality and remember that they all talk to a God, one way or another. The only religions I would warn you against, would be those which teach hate and holy wars. If "God is love", then there will be no hate involved in real spirituality.

In this world I find three things which fascinate me. I believe in fate, and faith, and destiny. Fate is a power that predetermines an outcome in your life, and faith is the belief that something is there, whether you can see it or not, and destiny is the trip you take when you are trying to determine the difference between fate and faith. Please go out into the world, and 'find your God' and have some faith in yourself and the world around you, and learn where your fate and destiny collide with your future. The world is yours now. Go live your life, happily ever after.

CHANGE THE ADDICT, SAVE THE WORLD.
GlobalAddictionSolutions.org

SAVE THE ADDICT, CHANGE THE WORLD.
GlobalAddictionSolutions.org

Author Jay Hotrum in Egypt, April 2019

I believe that one man can change the world, but he can't do it alone... He will need help.

— Jay P. Hotrum

CHANGE THE ADDICT, SAVE THE WORLD.
GlobalAddictionSolutions.org

SAVE THE ADDICT, CHANGE THE WORLD.
GlobalAddictionSolutions.org

Made in the USA
Columbia, SC
17 August 2023

21678718R00183